Contemporary Cases in Heritage

Volume 1

Also available online

All the cases within *Contemporary Cases in Heritage Volume 1* are available for individual download from the Contemporary Cases Online website at:

www.goodfellowpublishers.com

Ideal for student and seminar use, the online cases are packed with hyperlinks to original sources, further readings and websites. Readers can immediately follow these links to obtain further information about the specific concepts, terms, issues and organisations identified in each case.

Cases can also be purchased in a 'pick-and-mix' fashion to suit course content or research requirements.

Also in this series

Contemporary Cases in Tourism: Vol 1

Hardback: £65.00

ISBN: 9781906884536

Contemporary Cases in Sport: Vol 1

Hardback: £65.00

ISBN: 9781908999214

All of thier cases are also available for individual download from the Contemporary Cases Online website at:

www.goodfellowpublishers.com

Contemporary Cases in
Tourism Heritage Hospitality Leisure Retail Events Sport

Series editors: Brian Garrod (Aberystwyth University) and Alan Fyall (University of Central Florida)

Contemporary Cases in Heritage

Volume 1

Edited by
Brian Garrod
Alan Fyall

 Goodfellow Publishers Ltd

 Published by Goodfellow Publishers Limited,
Woodeaton, Oxford, OX3 9TJ
http://www.goodfellowpublishers.com

British Library Cataloguing in Publication Data: a catalogue record for
this title is available from the British Library.

Library of Congress Catalog Card Number: on file.

ISBN: 978-1-908999-54-2

Design and typesetting by P.K. McBride, www.macbride.org.uk

Printed by Marston Book Services, www.marston.co.uk/

Cover design by Cylinder, www.cylindermedia.com

Contents

Contributors

Stephen Boyd, University of Ulster, UK

Krzysztof Chuchra, Edinburgh World Heritage, UK

Mary Beth Gouthro, Bournemouth University, UK

Kevin Hannam, Leeds Metropolitan University, UK

Joan Henderson, Nanyang Technological University, Singapore

David Hicks, Edinburgh World Heritage, UK

I-Ling Kuo, London Metropolitan University, UK

Anna Leask, Edinburgh Napier University, UK

Peter Mason, University of Bedfordshire, UK

Alison J. McIntosh, University of Waikato, New Zealand

Daniel H. Olsen, Brandon University, Canada

Ashley R. Puriri, University of Waikato, New Zealand

Amos S. Ron, Ashkelon Academic College, Israel

Robert Shepherd, George Washington University, USA

About the Editors

Dr Brian Garrod is Reader in Tourism Management at Aberystwyth University. His interests span all aspects of tourism and recreation but his particular areas of specialism are in sustainable tourism, ecotourism and heritage tourism. He is also fascinated by the role of photography in tourism. He has published widely, including several text books with Alan Fyall. He has worked as a consultant to the United Nations World Tourism Organization (UNWTO), the Organisation for Economic Cooperation and Development (OECD) and the Welsh Assembly Government (WAG). He is Co-Editor of Elsevier's *Journal of Destination Marketing & Management*, Book Reviews Editor of the *Journal of Heritage Tourism* and a member of the editorial boards of the *Journal of Ecotourism*, the *International Journal of Tourism Research* and *Tourism in Marine Environments*. He lives deep in the Welsh countryside with his wife and three children, and in his spare time he enjoys rocking out on his bass guitar.

Dr Alan Fyall is Professor at the Rosen College of Hospitality Management, University of Central Florida. Prior to arriving in the USA, Alan was Professor of Tourism and Deputy Dean, Research & Enterprise in the School of Tourism, Bournemouth University, UK. He has published widely in his fields of expertise and is the author of over 100 articles, book chapters and conference papers, as well as 14 books including *Tourism Principles & Practice*, one of the leading international textbooks on the subject published by Pearson. Alan has organised a number of international conferences and workshops for academic, professional and governmental audiences and is frequently invited to deliver key note addresses. He is Co-Editor of Elsevier's *Journal of Destination Marketing & Management*, while he also sits on the editorial boards of *Annals of Tourism Research, Journal of Heritage Tourism, International Journal of Tourism Research, Anatolia* and *Regional Statistics*. Alan is also a visiting professor at the universities of Ulster and Edinburgh Napier in the UK and the Université d'Angers in France. Alan's current research interests lie in destination management and emerging destination management structures, and the impact of generational change on patterns of buying behaviour in the context of attractions and destinations. Alan is a former member of the Bournemouth Tourism Management Board and has conducted numerous consulting and applied research projects for clients across the UK and overseas, including the European Union, Commonwealth Secretariat, Grant Thornton and Malaysian Ministry of Tourism. Alan lives in Florida with his wife and two children and spends as much time outdoors as possible.

1

The Case Study Approach

Academic Pariah or Wrongly Maligned?

Brian Garrod and Alan Fyall

Introduction

The case study approach has often been marked out as an academic pariah, depicted at best as a highly inferior method of advancing human knowledge about a subject (Xiao and Smith, 2006), at worse as a refuge of academic charlatans "whose disciplinary origins do not include the tools necessary to analyze and theorize the complex cultural and social processes" associated with tourism (Franklin and Crang, 2001: 5). Xiao and Smith (2006) further note that case studies have been described as atheoretical, ungeneralisable, fundamentally intuitive, primitive and unmanageable. Much of this denigration of the case study approach has actually come from within the social sciences, with those hailing from disciplines with a quantitative tradition tending to be among its most vociferous critics.

Such arguments, which can probably be attributed as much to academic snobbery as they can to a clear understanding of the principles of research methodology, have tended to suppress the use of the case study approach in tourism research. Many academics have avoided case study research because they fear that it will not be accepted by peers, let alone published in the learned journals. Even so, Xiao and Smith (2006) identified a total of 78 articles based on case studies published between 2000 and 2004 in the *Journal of Travel Research, Annals of Tourism Research, Tourism Analysis* and *Tourism Management*, representing nearly 10% of the total number of articles published in those four journals over that time period. This represents not an insubstantial proportion of the research that tourism academics have been publishing.

Setting aside for the moment arguments concerning the value of the case study approach in the context of research, it will be evident to readers who regularly work in the classroom that students, at all levels of ability and from all backgrounds, appreciate the opportunity to learn through case studies.

When asked why they like case studies, students often reply that they help them to consolidate what they are learning and to apply it to the 'real world' they see around them. Are we then to believe that our students must be misguided in their desire to learn through case studies? Perhaps they have failed to appreciate that case studies really have no intellectual value and hence deserve no place in the classroom? Their craving for case studies must simply be a phase they are going through; all we really need to do is to wait patiently for them to grow out of it?

We believe otherwise. The intention of this series of books is to demonstrate that not only do case studies merit a place in the classroom but that they can be extremely effective pedagogical tools. Indeed, no scheme of work should be without one or more in-depth case studies to help students to appreciate more fully the conceptual and theoretical material we are delivering to them. We believe that students are not fundamentally mistaken in their liking of the case study approach. When students are continually fed a diet of dry theory, it is only natural that they will show cravings for the occasional juicy case study to help them to swallow down their meals. Rather than being something to avoid at all costs, case studies can be a positive asset in our teaching.

The major problem faced by potential users of case studies in the classroom is, however, that case studies can take an inordinate amount of time and effort to write. The purpose of a case study should be to communicate facts, not broad concepts or general principles, so that students can situate their learning in a particular context, thereby developing their understanding of how concepts and theories can be applied to the world outside their classroom window. But the facts specific to a particular case are often hard to track down. Writing an effective case study also requires that the author appreciates not only what the readers are supposed to learn from the case but how they are supposed to learn it. Writers of cases will need to anticipate the learning process in order that by reading the text of the case, examining the accompanying material, discussing issues raised in the case with each other, answering the questions at the end and reflecting on what it all means, readers will be able to develop a deeper understanding of what the case is all about. If writing good case studies was easy, then presumably there would be a lot more of them freely available for educators to introduce directly into their courses.

Sadly this is not the case. Until the publication of this book series, there have been very few sets of ready-made case studies for the educator to call upon that are relevant to the needs of students, instructive and contemporary. Part of the problem is that much material that is labelled as a case study turns out not to be especially useful in the classroom. Many of the so-called case studies included in textbooks simply take the form of extended examples: perhaps a few hundred words to illustrate a particular point the author wishes to emphasise. This kind of case study tends not to be sufficiently extensive or in-depth for students to get a very good grasp of the background to the subject, the forces coming to bear on a particular problem, the actors involved, the potential range of solutions, the constraints presently faced or the implications of any of this. Students therefore tend to struggle to use such case studies to develop their understanding of the subject they relate to. They are, to be blunt, often of strictly limited value as pedagogical tools.

Case studies can also quickly go out of date: economic conditions alter, government policy contexts change, new actors enter while others exit, and existing problems are overcome (or accommodated) while new problems emerge to take their place. Young people do not have long memories; nor do they relate well to case studies set in the context of the world they lived in when they were children, maybe even before they were born. As such, there is always room for new cases to be developed for use in the classroom: contemporary cases that relate to the problems of today in the context of today. It is often possible for existing cases that have become outdated to be modernised. Cases that consider very recent issues and subjects will usually, however, have to be written from scratch. Keeping one's case studies fresh is always going to be a problem for the instructor wishing to use them in his or her schemes of work.

The purpose of the *Contemporary Cases* series is to rehabilitate the case study approach and instate it on the educational map by establishing a ready resource of in-depth, high-quality, up-to-date case studies for instructors to use in their teaching. Each volume will focus on one of the subject areas covered by the series as a whole – events, heritage, hospitality, leisure, tourism, retail and sport – and provide a number of detailed, in-depth case studies that can be inserted, more or less directly, in the scheme of work of a module covering these subjects. At the end of each chapter will be a number of self-test questions for students to consider. These are designed to encourage students to reflect on the case, mentally wrestle with the issues it covers, apply their prior learning to the case and draw appropriate lessons from it. Each case study chapter will also include some suggestions for further reading and websites related to the material presented in the case study.

Each case study will also be made available electronically via the *Contemporary Cases Online* (CCO) website. The benefit of purchasing the case studies in this way is that the electronic version will include a large number of hyperlinks to websites. Readers with a web browser will be able to follow these links to obtain further information about the specific concepts, terms, issues and organisations identified in each case. The CCO website will also include an instructor's pack for each case study for separate purchase. These will include a number of essay questions based on the case, ideas for specific themes that can be developed from the case material, links to further teaching resources and a number of questions that can be used in an examination, along with guideline answers. The instructor's pack will also include a slideshow presentation that can be used in the class to remind students of the themes considered in the case and look at any photographs or diagrams accompanying the case in full colour.

It is the intention of the series editors that, wherever possible, the material published on the web will be regularly updated. This will help to ensure that the cases remain contemporary, relevant, vibrant and easy for students to relate to.

What is a case study?

Stake (1995: xi) provides a basic definition of the case study approach, that being:

> "the study of the complexity and particularity of a single case, coming to understand its activity within important circumstances".

The purpose of a case study, then, is to attempt to develop a nuanced understanding of what is happening at a specific point of time in a specific context, and why it is happening. As such, a case study will attempt to answer questions such as what are the processes of change, what are the external and internal factors that influence those processes, and what the changes might imply for those implicated in them, be it directly or indirectly, actively or passively.

Stake goes on to identify three types of case study: *intrinsic*, *instrumental* and *collective*.

♦   The first type, the intrinsic case study, is intended simply to study a particular case, with no attempt to learn about other cases or draw wider lessons.

♦   Second is the instrumental case study, the purpose of which is to learn wider lessons for the study of the subject, issue, organisation or problem at hand. The intention is that by studying one case in depth we will get a clearer picture of what is going on in the broader context. In view of this aim, it is sometimes better to choose to study an atypical one rather than a typical one. Indeed, an atypical case study may allow us to draw more relevant lessons than a typical one. For example, holiday companies expect, or at least hope, that their holidays will usually be delivered successfully from the holidaymaker's point of view. Sometimes, however, things will go wrong. Arguably there are more valuable lessons to be learned from the minority of cases where the holiday has been unsatisfactory than from the majority of cases where it has proceeded successfully.

♦ The third type of case study, according to Stake, is the collective case study. This is part of a set of case studies related to a particular context or problem, the cases being selected in such a way as to enable comparisons and contrasts to be drawn across them. In this way a broader and more detailed picture can be built up of the subject as a whole.

Perhaps the best-know definition of the case study approach, however, is that of Yin (1994: 13), who defines a case study as the:

> "investigation of a contemporary phenomenon within its real-life context, especially when the boundaries between phenomenon and context are not clearly evident, and that relies on multiple sources of evidence, with data needing to converge in a triangulating fashion".

For Yin, then, the emphasis is on investigating a phenomenon that is so deeply embedded in its context that it is hard to distinguish one from the other. To divorce the problem from its context would be to risk, almost guarantee, that the problem will be misunderstood. In order to learn about the problem, and hopefully develop solutions to it, we need to study it in the specific context in which it is situated. Abstracted study of the problem that is divorced from its context will not yield meaningful or effective answers. The definition suggested by Yin also emphasises the need to draw upon multiple sources of information, bringing them together in the context of the case study through a process of triangulation (Decrop, 1999; Oppermann, 2000). This enables the researcher to examine the issue or problem at hand from a number of different perspectives, yielding insights that they would not be possible to gain by examining the situation from a single viewpoint. In this way, case studies paint a rich picture of the subject, enabling readers to appreciate more fully what is going on and why.

Yin (2003) then goes on to identify six different kinds of case study that fit within his definition. First, any case can be a *single case study* or a *multiple case study*, depending on whether it focuses on just one instance of the phenomenon or on several instances. Either way, the purpose is to draw out wider lessons about the subject. Secondly, any case, whether single or multiple, can be an *exploratory*, *descriptive* or *explanatory case study*. The first of these, exploratory case studies, are intended to help to define questions and hypothesis about the phenomenon being studied. These questions can then be effectively addressed by other kinds of case study (descriptive or explanatory) or through alternative research methods if they are deemed better suited to the task. The purpose of the second type, the descriptive case study, is to describe the phenomenon at hand, perhaps in greater detail than has been achieved before or perhaps focusing on some aspect of the phenomenon that has hitherto been overlooked. The third type, the explanatory case study, attempts to identify cause-and-effect relationships, explaining how and perhaps why things happened in the way that they did.

The purpose of single case studies will often be *deductive*: to see how well a concept or theory can be applied to a real-world situation, or to investigate how a concept or theory might be modified to fit a particular context. The purpose of multiple case studies, meanwhile, will often be *inductive*: to compare, contrast and identify patterns and regularities within and between cases, thereby enabling a broader understanding of the subject to be achieved (Xiao and Smith, 2006).

While single case studies are often criticised on methodological grounds, Yin (2003) provides a number of styles of single case study which he considers to be potentially useful: the *critical case study*, which tries to bring out the pros and cons of a particular case (for example, to consider the critical incidents in a process); the *extreme/unique case study*, which attempts to bring out lessons by considering what happens at the extremes of the phenomenon; the *representative/typical case study*, which attempts to explain what 'normally' happens in a particular context; the *revelatory case study*, which attempts to challenge and reshape the reader's preconceptions; and the *longitudinal case study*, which provides a series of snapshots of the case over a period of time, often encouraging readers to decide what they would do to solve a problem and to discover whether that solution would indeed have worked. This latter kind of case study is actually very similar to a simulation exercise, which may be based around some form of decision tree so that users can go back and explore the implications of alternative decisions they could have made.

The benefits of using case studies in the classroom

While the case study approach is often maligned by academics, it also has a number of fierce proponents. The latter tend to advocate the use of case studies in the classroom for the following reasons:

♦   Case studies can help students to see for themselves how theory links to practice, encourage them to think more deeply about the subject at hand and persuade them to consider more carefully the implications of what they have learned.

♦   The multi-source nature of case studies enables alternative viewpoints of various stakeholders to be illustrated, as well as demonstrating the interaction among and between the different actors and variables concerned.

♦   The open-ended character of case studies helps to show students that there is very often no 'right' or 'wrong' answer to a problem. As such, case studies reflect the true nature of knowledge-building, which is frequently contextual, situated, complex and ambiguous.

♦   Case studies can stimulate students' interest and get them thinking seriously about the issues concerned. This promotes active rather than passive learning. It also emphasises free-thinking and exploration as opposed to prescription or prediction.

♦   It is possible to simulate the passage of time through longitudinal case studies, which allows students to see the consequences of decisions made by actors in the case or by themselves (a form of simulation game).

♦   Working with case studies helps students to develop and apply various transferable skills, including problem-solving, critical thinking, inter-personal communication and team-working.

♦   The 'real-world' nature of case studies helps students to link their learning to their personal goals, helping them to see the relevance of what they are learning and thus harnessing their enthusiasm to learn.

♦   Using case studies can encourage greater, two-way interaction among students, and between the students and the instructor.

The cases in this book embody the various authors' attempts to capture such benefits. The editors sincerely hope that readers will adopt some of these cases for use in their classrooms and would be very interested to receive users' feedback. Whether you have had positive or negative experiences of using these cases, please do let us know.

References

Decrop A. 1999. Triangulation in qualitative tourism research. *Tourism Management* **20** (1): 157-161.

Franklin A, Crang M. 2001. The trouble with tourism and travel theory. *Tourist Studies* **1** (1): 5-22.

Oppermann M. 2000. Triangulation: A methodological discussion. *International Journal of Tourism Research* **2** (2): 141-145.

Stake RE. 1995. *The Art of Case Study Research*. Thousand Oaks, London and New Delhi: Sage.

Xiao H, Smith S L J. 2006. Case studies in tourism research: A state-of-the-art analysis, *Tourism Management* **27** (5): 738-749.

Yin R K. 1994. *Case Study Research: Design and Methods*, 2nd Edition. Thousand Oaks: Sage.

Yin R K. 2003. *Case Study Research: Design and Methods*, 3rd Edition. Thousand Oaks: Sage.

2

Writing Case Studies

Reaction and Reflection, Rigour and Relevance

Alan Fyall and Brian Garrod

Introduction: Reaction and reflections on case authorship

One of the catalysts for the creation of the *Contemporary Cases* series was the sense of frustration the editors had with the paucity of high-quality case study materials in the tourism, heritage, hospitality, leisure, retail, events and sport subject areas. This frustration was only heightened by the recognition that the student learning experience could be improved so much through the use of carefully designed, well-written, in-depth case studies. Most of the case studies in existence seemed to be too short, too shallow, too bland or too out-of-date to be of real use in university teaching. What was needed was a series of cases with more ambition, that educators could adopt and use in their classes almost straight away, and which students would find relevant, instructive and – perhaps most importantly of all – stimulating. The scarcity of such case materials raised a number of questions in the editors' minds, including why there seemed to be so few fully developed case studies in publication, why academics are not more widely engaged in writing such cases for their own use and, more fundamentally, what constitutes a 'successful' case study?

Students at all levels seem to appreciate and benefit from learning through the use of case studies and tutors always seem to be on the look-out for contemporary case material to use in their classes. This demand on the part of tutors is in fact one of the key messages communicated by publishers when they negotiate book contracts with aspiring authors: the promise to include copious amounts of 'high-quality case material' is almost a standard prerequisite for winning a book contract. It is therefore a perpetual source of astonishment, as well as disappointment, that there are so few published works that actually deliver on this promise. To put it bluntly, there is a very real and expressed need for high-quality case material, yet the academic community – at least in the fields of tourism, heritage, hospitality, leisure, retail, events and sport – does not seem to be delivering the materials required to meet this need.

The aim of this series of case studies is to help address this paucity of high-quality case material. In doing so, it aspires to 'raise the bar' in terms of the quality of case-study writing. It also seeks to stimulate higher levels of engagement in the use of the case studies, both by students and tutors, by providing a body of materials that are challenging, thought-provoking and instructive. This, in the view of the editors, is best achieved by making the case studies rich in terms of visual materials, numerical data, references, hyperlinks to sources and further reading, and so on. In this way, readers can immerse themselves in the case study and almost feel that they are there, in context, learning from real life rather than out of books.

While it is still undoubtedly too early to judge the success of this approach, the first volume in the series, which is on the subject of tourism, has so far been well received. For example, Sigala (2012: 299) comments that the book does much to highlight case studies as a "valuable educational tool to enrich instruction", through its integration of "theoretical concepts with practical evidence gathered through a wide spectrum of international case studies". While this is clearly only an early vote of confidence in the approach adopted, the editors hope that it marks the beginning of a genuine and continuing effort to raise the overall quality of case studies in the fields of study covered by the series. The intention of the second volume, which comprised cases examining a range of contemporary issues in sport, was to consolidate the start that has been made. This third volume comprises cases in heritage.

Case studies have a number of benefits as a pedagogical vehicle: they can serve to help transfer knowledge, develop critical-thinking skills, explain theory by applying it, provide a route-map for tutors and students to grasp complex issues, and – perhaps more importantly – enable students to engage more fully in the learning experience. This last point is particularly pertinent in view of one of the stated aspirations of this series of case studies, which is to rehabilitate the case study, bringing it back into mainstream education and helping to put students back into "active learning mode" (Lane, 2007). Rather than to articulate the potential benefits of case studies, both for tutors and students, however, or to debate the use of the case-study method of research, the purpose of this chapter is to bring together a number of important lessons for case authorship.

One question that arises is why students cannot simply make use of journal articles. After all, as academics we read these all the time, to keep up to date with the state of knowledge in our subject area and to gain insights into cutting-edge ideas. Given the exponential growth in the number of downloads from scientific journals seen over recent years there is no doubt that students are increasingly accessing such material. This is, in and of itself, surely a good thing. Its effectiveness as a teaching strategy might, however, be questionable. Many students view peer-reviewed journal articles as being inaccessible, turgid, abstract and irrelevant, involving overly complicated methodologies and incomprehensible research paradigms. The increasing significance of research evaluation exercises, such as the Research Excellence Framework in the UK, is arguably driving a particular pattern of authorship behaviour among academics, which is only serving to increase even further the gap between academic research papers and their relevance to the educa tion of our students (Turner, Wuetherick and Healey, 2008). Furthermore, in the age of 'copy and paste', it is all too tempting for students simply to skim-read material they find disengaging and difficult to read, select only those sections or paragraphs of perceived relevance, and copy them straight into their essays. The ability to copy references from the end of journal papers and paste them into their own bibliographies is a particularly worrying fea-ture of the digital age of education.

Journal articles need to be underpinned by sound research and the educa-tional case study is really no different in this respect. The main difference be-tween the way in which case studies and journal papers need to be written is the intended audience. Those attempting to write case studies have to under-stand their students' needs in the process of learning as well as possessing an expert grasp of the research upon which it is based. As such, case-study authors ideally need to be both highly experienced researchers and passion-ate educators. This will enable them to communicate the research they have undertaken for the case in a style that is accessible, stimulating and engag-ing, with a strong narrative running through the entire piece. The process of writing case studies should involve analysis, evaluation and interpretation, along with the synthesis of information and ideas (Lane, 2007). In this way, the case study can (and should) enrich both academic research and teaching.

Interestingly, despite the growth in recent decades in higher education across many parts of the world, the number of academics with a sufficiently strong interest in both research and education would seem to be limited. The problem is perhaps not so much that academics do not like writing case material, more that the rewards do not seem as great or as tangible as those associated with writing academic research articles, which clearly carry more weight in the recruitment, promotion and tenure processes worldwide. Although many academics politely cite 'lack of time' as a reason not to accept invitations to submit case studies to collections such as this one, this is most probably a smokescreen for pedagogical outputs not being as high in the pecking order of departmental strategies, where the reward systems are heavily weighted in favour of the quantity and/or quality of research papers published. This system-wide bias is unfortunate, in that the development of research-informed but education-oriented, student-friendly case study material is of so much value to the educational learning environment. This is a real shame, as writing case studies can be hugely rewarding, especially when the author sees first-hand the positive reaction from students and the enhancement of their learning that a good case study can deliver.

The following section now builds on these reactions and reflections, beginning with an overview of the key criteria involved in successful case-study writing.

Rigour and relevance: The essentials of successful case writing

The potential benefits of using a good case study in class are clear, as is evident in the previous chapter (see also Garrod and Fyall, 2011a). What is less clear however, is what makes a good case study. Based on the reaction to and reflections on the first volume (Garrod and Fyall, 2011b), this section presents the criteria for a successful case study. A good case study should be:

♦ **Introduced by a clearly articulated set of learning outcomes** – where each learning outcome is introduced and discussed through the case narrative. Irrespective of what type of case is being written, it is imperative that learners are clear about what it is they are expected to understand and learn, their role in examining and using the case, and how they are expected to learn from it. Writing clear and logical learning outcomes necessitates a thorough knowledge of learners and their learning modes. This is why the earlier point was made that authors really need to be both dedicated researchers and passionate educators, who demonstrate empathy not only with research processes but also with the processes involved in learning. It is also important for learning outcomes to articulate a clear sense of purpose of the case study, the chronological order of the case material and the logic of the narrative flow. Ultimately, all case studies should place the application of knowledge in a real-world setting and encourage learning through a consideration of practice.

♦   **Embedded within their particular case context** – whereby the context, or the individual instance, is the core focus of the case study. While it is usually quite easy to see what this means in practice, case study authors do not always grasp what this means for the subject matter in which they have expertise. As a rule, it is normally easier to select the particular concept or theory, and then to chose a particular context or individual instances as the case. In reality, however, most authors work the other way around. As an example, if one was contemplating writing a case study on visitor management, a case study author would select a suitable case context, such as Skara Brae Prehistoric Village (Leask and Garrod, 2011). This would then be used to help readers to learn about the visitor management theory and practices. Similarly, Knott, Fyall and Jones (2011) used the specific case of the hosting of the 2010 FIFA Soccer World Cup by South Africa to examine the broader relationship between sport, tourism and mega-events, particularly in terms of the issues of legacy and nation branding. What is special about case studies is that there is no need to disentangle the phenomenon from its context, as would normally be necessary using the traditional learning approach. In a good case study, they are one and the same thing.

♦   **A one-stop knowledge shop** – where all the material required for a good understanding of the phenomenon in its specific context is included within the case. It is simply too easy nowadays to direct students to an Internet search engine without fully considering the consequences of students obtaining poor, superficial and descriptive information, which although on the surface may look good illustrative material, lacks the academic rigour necessary for deep learning. Ad hoc research reports, news clippings and glorified gossip are readily accessible. Less so are rich case studies that truly facilitate learning. It is also worth noting that traditional textbooks and journals are primarily paper-based, making them linear and one dimensional. This is in part driven by publication costs and copyright fees. However it is not necessary for case studies to be so limited. In fact, the approach taken with this series of case studies is to encourage imagination, creativity and innovation in case writing. In particular, the case studies in this series all include the use of hyperlinks to make teaching and learning more engaging, allowing readers to dig down beneath the surface of the case and examine the source documents upon which it is based. This means that a wealth of information necessary for understanding the learning outcomes is either contained within or hyperlinked to the case. Both the electronic and hard-copy versions of the cases in this series enable this, the former through live hyperlinks in the actual text and the latter through the use of a QR code at the end of the case.

♦ **Underpinned by multiple sources of evidence** – so that the reader has all the material and evidence necessary to understand the learning outcomes of the case. Triangulation is a key component of case study methodology and, as such, is a critical feature of any case material for it to have academic credibility (Yin, 2009; Woodside, 2010). It also helps underpin the objectivity of the case study, bring theory to life with real examples, real material and real evidence, and encourages readers to build their knowledge based on a variety of different sources of evidence. Readers will thereby have a breadth of material made available to them, which they have been directed to by the author. This helps to ensure that the reader bases their understanding on high-quality materials, as opposed to the often superficial and biased material that can be downloaded from the Web. When beginning to write the case, therefore, it is imperative that the author clarifies what information is necessary for inclusion, so as to ensure that all dimensions and perspectives are covered, including key themes, theories and concepts.

♦ **Visually engaging** – with tables, figures, photographs and boxed material bringing the case to life and making it both visually appealing and contemporary. One under-used approach is the use of spider diagrams (see Figure 1), word bubbles, cartoons or storyboards. These can help bring drier material to life for both tutors and students. In the first volume of this series, the case on sport tourism by Hudson (2011) is a good example, being visually appealing with its integration of boxed press releases, offline and online marketing collateral, a customer satisfaction survey form, maps, secondary research data, and diagrams of conceptual models. While some authors may worry about including 'too much' non-text material, it has to be borne in mind that many readers will learn as much from the non-text material as they do the text, particularly those who have a predominantly visual learning style. As such, it is almost always better to have too much than too little such material, provided of course that all the material relates specifically to the learning outcomes of the case

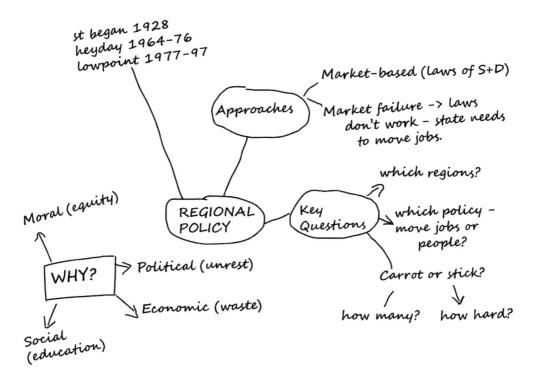

Figure 1: Spider diagram

- **Challenging and controversial** – in order to truly stimulate students' minds and engage them in critical debate with their peers and tutors. Case learning is driven by both intellectual and practical questions. This means that studying the case can help readers to form connections between academic theory and concepts on the one hand and practical ways and means to solve real problems on the other. There is a fine art to this and in this respect the peer review process is of critical importance. Both authors and editors also need to exercise great patience as the case writing passes through numerous iterations until the case study is finally ready to be used with students.

- **Contemporary** – as students of today struggle to grasp out-of-date case material, especially that which pre-dates the digital age. Case study material dates ever more quickly in today's dynamic and fast-changing world, so it is imperative to keep case studies current through regular updates. With each update, the author should seek to revise information on the key players, evidence, data, examples and trends featured in the case. Even though it is increasingly difficult to achieve this aim, especially when the speed of change is ever rising, it is essential if the case is to stay relevant to its intended users. The publication of online versions of the case studies in this series is intended to facilitate regular updating (most notably in respect of the hyperlinks). Meanwhile advances in on-demand printing allow more regular updating of 'hard' copies of the case books.

♦ **Rigorous and relevant** – or otherwise the educational worth of case studies will be questionable. To be sufficiently rigorous, every stone needs to be uncovered and every angle explored in the case. Similarly, if the case study is to be relevant to its readership, the material contained within it needs to be reasonably comprehensive, serviceable and appropriate to the needs of the users, as well as to meet as fully as possible the learning objectives set at the beginning of the case study. The material also needs to be multi-faceted and complex, to connect with the key issues identified in the case and to provide a learning experience that encourages and facilitates critical thinking.

What makes a successful case study?

A number of relatively simple techniques can be used to achieve the above. Figure 2 is intended to serve as a framework for the design of case studies. Eight elements are identified as being core in designing a successful case study.

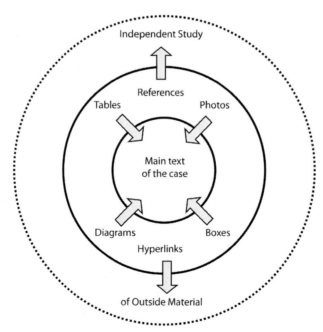

Figure 2: How the elements of a case should fit together

♦ **Main text of the case** – the core narrative is critical to the success of any case study. Although perhaps an obvious point to state, this is easier said than done. To be able to write a good case, authors need to be highly self-critical as well as to have broad shoulders upon which to take constructive criticism from reviewers. From experience, cases will be usually written three or four times, be subject to numerous changes in their structure, including major re-ordering of the material, possibly even being turned upside down, and then be reconfigured yet again to ensure that the learning objectives of the case are met (see Table 1). The case study will require clarity of context, need to offer theoretically informed explanations and engage in a continual interplay between theory and practice. Limited prescription is required with regard to the sense of direction of the case evident on every page. Throughout the writing experience, authors need to put themselves in the shoes of students (rather than their peers) and be prepared to adapt continually in what will be an emergent writing process. Attention to detail is paramount, with a need to grasp, connect and present all the component parts of the case study 'jigsaw'. Ultimately, any case study needs to motivate and engage the reader, contain a high level of description and detail, be problem-based, and bring events and people to life. Although normally chronological in order, this does not necessarily have to be adhered to and a case can be particularly effective when it breaks with expectations. More important is the need to be consistent with the learning objectives established for the case and to ensure that the central idea is clear at all times.

Table 1: Reviewing case studies

1	Will the case produce the intended learning outcomes?
2	Are the problem issue(s) presented in the case related to the learning outcomes?
3	Is the case sufficiently complete, complex and focused?
4	Does the case present a situation, problem, or issue?
5	Dose the case appear to be realistic?
6	Are all the elements of a narrative style used in the case?
7	Are the events and actions in the case sequenced in a logical order?
8	Are the events connected with appropriate transitional signals?
9	Is the content in the case accurate, relevant, and appropriate in terms of subject matter?
10	If there are external resources, are they appropriate?

Source: Lane (2007)

- **References** – accurate and up-to-date referencing is of equal significance to case studies as it is journal articles. However, the volume of references is normally lower, with only key and seminal academic studies referenced, along with a greater proportion of research reports, policy papers, advisory notes and suchlike: source materials that are instrumental in the evidence-based world of case writing. It is particularly important to avoid disrupting the flow of the narrative, otherwise levels of motivation and engagement will impact negatively on the process of case learning. In such cases, footnotes may be a good option.

- **Photos** – the need to be visually appealing and engaging necessitates the inclusion of good-quality images and photographs, with location maps an extremely useful tool in demonstrating setting, proximity to competitors and related infrastructure (e.g. airports, highways, ports and railway stations), and so on.

- **Boxes** – the inclusion of 'boxed' material is particularly welcome in case studies when there is stand-alone material that can add to, but also sit outside of, the core case study. This allows for a more expansive case. For example, the inclusion of newspaper articles that develop a specific theme or aspect of a case study provides perfect ammunition for 'boxes'.

- **Hyperlinks** – one of the principal benefits of electronic publication is the ability of authors to embed hyperlinks within their case studies that take readers directly to 'live' material on the Internet. This feature contributes significantly to bringing the case study to life and helps to ensure that it is kept up to date (insofar as when the website is updated, so is the case study). It also allows case studies to be taken anywhere on portable electronic devices; an approach that is already commonplace in many primary and secondary schools around the world. The hard copy of the case studies that is published in the conventional book, meanwhile, still makes use of the internet through the use of QR coding. Readers who scan the codes with their smart phone or webcam will have the links uploaded to their devices. They can then reach the web material by clicking through.

- **Diagrams** – the need to include high quality, relevant, well-drawn and accurate diagrams is paramount. Diagrams can help learners to structure the material, to explore the case more deeply, to facilitate the creative interpretation of core case material or to serve as a foundation for group discussion.

◆   **Tables and figures** – cases are only as strong as the evidence contained within them, so good quality, up-to-date and relevant statistical and trend data are valuable components of any case.

◆   **Independent study of outside material** – while cases are written as inclusive self-contained vehicles for learning, authors should always offer students opportunities to expand their learning horizons through signposting further reading and additional web-based resources. Independent study can also be encouraged through the provision of self-test material, multiple-choice questions, exam questions and suchlike, as well as providing advice as to how best to learn from the case in question.

Conclusions

With three volumes of case studies published to date, the *Contemporary Cases* series aspires to raise the bar for case writing in the fields of tourism, heritage, hospitality, leisure, retail, events and sport. Developed in response to the surprising paucity of high quality case study material in existence, and a genuine desire to enhance the student learning experience, this volume brings to the reader nine quality case studies that are contemporary and accessible yet challenging, thought provoking and, most importantly, instructive. Each case has been carefully written and edited to avoid the inaccessibility of many scholarly articles, with all authors working hard to make the process of learning more enjoyable and engaging for both tutor and student, and encouraging and facilitating a culture of critical thinking by all. It is hoped that each case study in this volume meets the high standards set for the publishing of quality case material while it is also hoped that both this and the previous volumes serve as a catalyst to entice academics away from a one-dimension world of publishing to include case study writing in their future portfolio of academic activity. For, not only will the writing of case studies enhance their ability to teach, but the combined discipline and creativity necessary for good case study writing will also make them better researchers and academics.

References

Garrod B, Fyall A. 2011a. The case study approach: Wrongly maligned. In Garrod B, Fyall A (eds) *Contemporary Cases in Tourism: Volume 1*. Oxford: Goodfellow Publishers; ix-xvi.

Garrod B, Fyall A. 2011b. *Contemporary Cases in Tourism: Volume 1*, Oxford: Goodfellow Publishers.

Hudson S. 2011. Bumps for Boomers: Marketing sport tourism to the aging tourist. In Garrod B, Fyall A (eds) *Contemporary Cases in Tourism: Volume 1*. Oxford: Goodfellow Publishers; 165-190.

Knott B, Fyall A, Jones I. 2011. South Africa 2010: Leveraging nation brand benefits from the FIFA World Cup. In Garrod B, Fyall A (eds) *Contemporary Cases in Tourism: Volume 1*. Oxford: Goodfellow Publishers; 33-56.

Lane J. 2007. *Case Writing Guide*. Schreyer Institute for Teaching Excellence, Penn State, University Park, PA 16802.

Leask A, Garrod B. 2011. Visitor management at a world heritage site: Skara Brae prehistoric village. In Garrod B, Fyall A (eds) *Contemporary Cases in Tourism: Volume 1*. Oxford: Goodfellow Publishers; 81-98.

Sigala M. 2012. Book review: Contemporary Cases in Tourism, Volume 1. *Anatolia* **23** (2): 298-299.

Turner N, Wuetherick B, Healey M. 2008. International perspectives on student awareness, experiences and perceptions of research: Implications for academic developers in implementing research-based teaching and learning. *International Journal for Academic Development* **13** (3): 199-211.

Woodside AG. 2010. *Case Study Research: Theory, Methods, Practice*. Bradford: Emerald.

Yin RK. 2009. *Case Study Research: Design and Methods (Volume 5)*. Los Angeles: Sage.

3

Learning and Teaching with Case Studies

Alan Fyall and Brian Garrod

Introduction

Cases can take a great deal of time and effort to prepare. Set against this, the benefits of using cases may be considerable. To ensure that the benefits of using cases substantially outweigh the costs, it is important that they are used to their full potential. The purpose of this chapter is to review the potential benefits of employing the case study approach to learning and teaching and to examine the keys to unlocking them.

Benefits of case learning and teaching

Perhaps the most significant strength of the case study approach is that it employs an inductive (or experiential) approach to learning and teaching. This approach encourages students to learn by considering, comparing and contrasting carefully chosen examples relating to a specific context. The general principles of the subject can then be more fully understood be examining the circumstances, incidents and outcomes discussed in the cases. This 'case-first, theory-second' approach involves students examining one or more examples of the theory working in context before they are expected to understand the principles involved. Then, provided the case has been properly designed and written, a sound appreciation of the theory can be drawn out by working with the case material.

Many students seem to prefer this approach to learning and teaching, as opposed to the essentially deductive approach they tend to encounter in class. The deductive approach usually starts by expounding the general theoretical principles. Examples are then often (but by no means always) used to illustrate these principles, reinforcing them in the students' minds. Instructors tend to prefer this 'theory-first, case-second' approach, which is typically based around first giving lectures to deliver the general principles of the subject and then using tutorials (often known as seminars or discussion groups) to illustrate the principles with a range of examples.

The choice of which learning approach the student is expected to adopt is, of course, almost always determined by the teaching approach of the instructor. If the instructor prefers to teach using the deductive approach then that is what the students will get, whether they like it or not. It might be argued, however, that employing the learning approach that students tend to prefer should be the norm in education. For one thing, students are more likely to attend and engage in the class if they believe they are going to enjoy it.

Before proceeding, it is important to stress that the case study approach to learning and teaching will only be truly effective if the instructor has first invested sufficient time and energy thinking through how the case is going to deliver its intended learning outcomes. It can be tempting to think of cases as ad-hoc 'time fillers' that can be slotted into the teaching programme when the instructor has had insufficient time to write a 'proper lecture' or wants to take a 'week off'. In truth, using case studies effectively requires a great deal of careful forethought and pre-planning. Having first determined what the learning outcomes for the class are to be, the instructor needs to think through how engaging with the case will help students attending the class[1] to achieve them. The onus must be on the instructor to ensure that the students fully appreciate what they are supposed to be learning from working with the case and how they are supposed to be learning it. It is imperative that the instructor sets clear expectations, and encourages in the students a sense of ambition to learn and an enthusiasm for the tasks ahead of them.

Planning is therefore essential if the instructor is to capture the benefits of the case study approach as fully as possible, and hence pay off the costs of time and effort required to develop and use it. The principal benefits of the case-study approach can be summarised as follows:

Higher-order thinking skills

Firstly, case studies can assist students to evaluate, analyse and apply the ideas and concepts they have previous encountered. These are the higher-order thinking skills that are strongly valued both by educators and employers (see Table 1). The deductive approach focuses on students simply remembering the information that is presented to them and being able to

---

[1]   In countries such as the UK, the instructor is also expected to ensure that students who are absent from the class are not disadvantaged and are given an equal opportunity to achieve the learning outcomes as those who attended. Simply posting the case on a virtual learning platform unlikely to be sufficient to achieve this, so the instructor will need to think about including additional materials to prepare the student who is 'catching up' with the class to use the case effectively and achieve the specified learning outcomes.

replicate that information accurately. There may also be elements of sum-marising, classifying and explaining involved, but these are all lower-order thinking skills. 'Knowing' the subject using the lower-order thinking skills is based simply on being able to absorb and pass on information, rather than consolidate it as knowledge and use it in practical contexts outside of the classroom. The case study approach, in contrast, requires students to apply their existing knowledge to the case, to analyse and synthesise what is going on – all higher-order thinking skills – and to construct their understanding of the subject accordingly. In this way, students' understanding can not only be more complete but also more flexible, in that it is ready to be applied to any context encountered by the students, both in their further studies and in their eventual employment. The inductive approach used in case study learning and teaching encourages students to grapple with the subject, to immerse themselves in it and to relate the subject to the real world they see around them. Such skills are considered vital in the modern workplace.

Table 1: Bloom's revised typology: higher- and lower-level thinking skills

Creating	Generating new ideas, products, or ways of viewing things. Designing, constructing, planning, producing, inventing
Evaluating	Justifying a decision or course of action Checking, hypothesising, critiquing, experimenting, judging
Analysing	Breaking information into parts to explore understanding and relationships Comparing, organising, deconstructing, interrogating, finding
Applying	Using information in another familiar situation Implementing, carrying out, using, executing
Understanding	Explaining ideas or concepts Interpreting, summarising, paraphrasing, classifying, explaining
Remembering	Recalling information Recognising, listing, describing, retrieving, naming, finding

Source: Romanowski (2013)

Contemporary relevance

Cases also tend to be more effective if they consider issues of contemporary relevance. A good case study will link to issues that the students encounter in their everyday lives, know about from the media, maybe even chat about in the cafeteria (Romanowski, 2013). A class will surely be more engaging for students when it is dealing with issues they already know something about, perhaps even care about. Although case studies can, and often do, go out of date quickly, the onus must be on the case author to maintain the accuracy and relevance of the case. This will help to ensure that it remains topical and useful for achieving inductive learning. One of the benefits of the Contemporary Cases Online series is that the cases are intended to be updated regularly. Every effort will be made to keep the many hyperlinks included in each case up to date, so as to ensure that the case links back to the most up-to-date sources, further readings and study materials.

Flexible solutions

The case study approach can also help encourage students to recognise and accept that there are rarely easy solutions to real-world problems. Typically, each problem requires its own, bespoke solution. Tackling real-world problems requires students to establish their own problem-solving approach and sense of direction in working through the case, albeit within the parameters that have been established by the case author and under the guidance of the instructor. Nothing is more rewarding for an instructor to see students appreciate for themselves how theory can be used to inform practice and to recognise the implications of the decisions they make.

Responsibility and ownership

Finally, using cases in class can help students to take responsibility for their learning and develop a sense of ownership of it. Working on the assumption that most problems are complex and do not have predictable outcomes, cases can develop in students the ability to appreciate the importance of the wider context of the case as a crucial part of the problem-solving process. Students will also become more aware of the need to identify and consider the many variables that can have an impact on the outcomes of the case. Students will also gain confidence as they successfully tackle the depth and complexity of the case material to draw important lessons from it.

Planning the case class

A case class is more likely to achieve its potential if it has been properly planned (Stanford University, 1994). Some of the essentials of good case class planning are discussed in this section.

Case preparation

Preparation is everything if a case study is to be an effective teaching tool. It is critical that the instructor arranges for the student to receive a copy of the case and be given enough time to read it properly. In this way they will gain an overall feel for the depth and complexity of the case before they come along to the class.

The case can only be effective if the students have first read it properly. Doing this will involve the student making several passes through the case, starting with a rough scan to identify the purpose and basic shape of the case. The best way to do this is to look only at the introduction or abstract, the section headings and sub-headings, any tables and figures, and the conclusions. The student should then make a second pass through the paper, reading it more carefully in full. In doing so, the student should identify the main decision makers, timescales and outcomes of the case, particularly in terms of the decisions that have had (or have still) to be made and the resources available with which to implement these decisions. They should use any self-test questions given at the end of the case to check that they have picked up and understood the key points. When reading for the second time, students should be encouraged to identify and think through the key themes, theories and concepts involved in the case. They should then familiarise themselves with the sources of the material and the alternative viewpoints represented. A third pass through the case should then be made to analyse the case in more depth. This should involve identifying the backgrounds and beliefs of the actors involved, investigating how they interact with each other and considering how they respond to internal and external forces.

While the cases included in the Contemporary Cases Online series make extensive use of boxes, photographs, diagrams, tables and hyperlinks to make the case as rich as possible, many are far less comprehensive. As such, the onus must be on the instructor to direct students to additional and possibly more contemporary material that can add to the depth, relevance and currency of the case. In addition, the instructor should also prepare the case, looking at it from a variety of perspectives, so that they can be fully involved in the class discussion. Above all, the instructor needs to set out very clearly the parameters of the class and communicate to students the ways in which the case study will develop their knowledge of the subject, their transferable skills in problem solving and critical thinking, as well as provide an environment conducive to inter-personal communication and teamwork.

The inductive approach encourages students to recognise the relevance of their learning so that it can be linked to their personal goals. As with any good class, it is good practice to provide feedback at the end of the session on what elements went well and what did not go so well, and what students would perhaps do differently next time around to ensure a more meaningful case study learning experience. Depending on how the class is organised, the instructor may wish to involve students at the closure of the class. For example, the task of synthesising the outcomes of the case may be delegated to specific students, giving them added responsibility (Carnegie Mellon, 2013). This can enhance their learning by encouraging them to engage and concentrate more fully on the tasks at hand. Students asked to synthesise the outcomes of the case may, for example, be asked to develop a flow diagram or 'rich picture' of its learning outcomes. This could then be either photocopied and distributed to the other class members, or scanned and posted on the virtual learning platform.

Classroom atmosphere

The benefits of the case study approach will only come about if the classroom atmosphere is conducive. Above all, it is paramount that both instructor and students feel relaxed enough to engage in the free exchange of ideas. Debate and discussion are critical components of an effective case study class, so every effort should be made to bring the class to life. This can be achieved in a variety of ways but simple measures are to reduce group sizes to make them more manageable and to ensure that all students have been allocated an active role to play. Close-ended questions and dyadic questioning should be reduced to a minimum. Positive, constructive and challenging two-way communication should be established and maintained instead. An unstructured, engaging and possibly even 'highly charged' classroom atmosphere is preferable than one that is prescriptive, one-way and overly serious. The latter only encourages students to adopt a passive learning approach, rather than to embrace an active one. More than anything, the instructor must ensure that the class setting is void of the opportunity for ridicule and negativity. Instead, the classroom should be a place of mutual respect and the benefits of case learning constantly reinforced.

Collaboration and group work

One of the most beneficial teaching and learning environments for case studies is that of group work and the opportunity for students to work collaboratively on case-based problems. Not only do many students enjoy interacting with each other in groups but the additional allocation of roles within the group can give them an added sense of responsibility, particularly insofar as they will not wish to 'let the others down'. Group work also helps students to develop their negotiation skills and get used to collective decision making, which is the norm in many workplace contexts. Students can be expected to respond positively to an engaged setting and an environment of energetic debate, which are perfect vehicles to promote self-directed learning. A positive and facilitating group environment will encourage active and animated engagement and interaction, as well as to provide an atmosphere for students to build on each other's curiosity, challenge the status quo, hear and discuss different ideas and opinions, respect each other's opinions and perspectives, and ultimately to contribute to a deep, engaging and productive learning experience.

Instructor's materials

One of the many benefits of the Contemporary Cases Online series is that it provides detailed instructor's materials, comprising teaching notes which highlight the key themes for discussion and ideas for organising the class, detailed further reading, additional websites and audio-visual materials, sample essay questions, sample examination questions with detailed answer guidelines, and a PowerPoint slideshow. The onus is on the instructor to use these materials to their maximum potential and to build them into their case study lesson plans. A variety of other classroom techniques exist that are highly compatible with case study teaching and learning. These include, but are not restricted to, the following:

Pyramid discussions

Identify one or more of the discussion questions and start the class by getting them to discuss the main issues involved in pairs, preferably by working on a piece of paper, e.g. points in favour of a course of action on one side of the piece of paper and points against on the other. After a set period of time for discussion, ask each pair of students to join with another for further discussion as fours, still working on a piece of paper, e.g. comparing their list of points in favour and against the decision, then grouping and synthesising them. Next the groups of four should join into eights. Pyramid discussions come to a close when each group of eight finalises their thoughts on an A2 sheet of paper or on a PowerPoint slide when such technology is available. These can then be used as visuals to which an elected spokesperson for the group of eight and speak to the class as a whole. More engagement and responsibility can be engendered through the allocation of roles such as this within the group: for example, another person can serve as the scribe, another as chair of the discussions, and so on. If students have roles such as these allocated at the beginning of the class, the outcomes tend to be deeper and more focused as a result of the added sense of responsibility they feel.

Role-play debate

An alternative to the above is to use of role play, whereby individual students or small groups are allocated the role of a particular individual or group included in the case (Boston University, 2013). First they should re-read the case through the lens of their role: what are the views of their individual group likely to be toward specific issues covered in the case and what would kinds of argument would they put forward to justify such views? How should they relate to other individuals and groups in the case? On what issues would they agree and disagree? How willing would they be to collaborate to achieve a solution? The instructor should then act as chair of a mock debate in which the students act out their roles. This could be, for example, in the form of a public enquiry or a televised debate. If a Contemporary Cases Online case is being used, the essay questions provided in the instructor's pack could serve as the agenda for the debate for the chair to use. By allocating specific roles, students will often have to challenge their own thoughts and prejudices and read, interpret and analyse the case study from an entirely different perspective to their own. This can be very challenging for students, who are usually not practiced in adopting viewpoints contrary to their own (Carnegie Mellon, 2013). It can also be immensely beneficial as a form of deep learning, especially in that it emphases that there is no one solution to most problems and that all viewpoints have to be considered before a joint consensus can be achieved.

Team debate

While in some ways similar to the above, a team debate is focussed entirely on a 'motion' being allocated on team, which is to be debated with an 'alternative' motion given to a competing team. Each team should be quite small – perhaps comprising three or four members – while the rest of the class become the audience. By setting two contrary motions, teams of students are encouraged to prepare a defence of their respective (and necessarily extreme) motions before competing head-to-head in the class. Each team is then given a period of time (normally about 10 minutes) to present their motion, which should be backed up by evidence from the case study. Once both teams have had the opportunity to clarify their positions, the debating floor is then opened up for questions between the two teams with the instructor serving as the arbitrator of the contrasting viewpoints being put forward. Once the two teams have exhausted each other's standpoints, questions can then to be encouraged from those in the class who have not been members of the participating teams. The two teams are then given the opportunity to close their motions with a 'closing statement' before the entire class is then invited to vote on that motion that was argued, evidenced and presented most effectively. Although commencing with two contrasting, and sometimes even quite extreme motions, the lesson of debates originating from case material is that the 'answer' normally lies somewhere in the middle with consensus of views. While it is not always possible, compromise is an admirable goal for those seeking to solve problems previously considered intractable. Debates of this kind tend to be great fun, to energise students, and to encourage even shy students to enter into the spirit of debating and problem-solving.

Essay discussion

Another alternative is for instructor to ask the students to answer, under examination conditions, an essay or examination question. If a Contemporary Cases Online case is being used, a selection of such questions is available in the instructor's pack. Having completed their individual answers, the students should then be placed into small groups and asked to compare their answers to the question. Who had the best answer to the question and why? Where did their answers agree and where did they disagree? How did they justify their arguments? What would be the ideal answer the question?

A slight variant on this technique, is to ask the students to answer the question from the perspective of an individual person or particular stakeholder group included in the case, e.g. a third of the class should answer the question from the point of view of how tourists would wish to see a tourism destination develop, a third from the perspective of local residents and a third from the local government planning department's viewpoint. The discussion groups would then consist of three members, one representing each stakeholder group. This will again contribute to students' learning development through the need to consider alternative viewpoints when drawing conclusions from case studies.

Research

While the cases in the Contemporary Cases Online series have been written with reference to the best available source materials at the time of their writing, there is always scope for additional research to be conducted. Asking the students to bring the case up to date is a good way for them to appreciate the speed with which real life changes and how such changes may influence the outcomes of the case and the conclusions that can be drawn from it. The contemporary nature of the cases also serves as a catalyst for asking 'what happens next?' and what future research ought to be conducted to plan for the longer-term management of the issue at hand. The instructor could introduce a range of research scenarios and/or methodologies to the class and ask them to weigh up the advantages and disadvantages of each. They could also be asked to identify particular aspects of the case that would benefit from academic inquiry-led research or industrial practical-led research activity.

Full-day assessment

One very useful and potentially highly engaging experience for both students and staff is to hold a whole-day assessment, wherein the students are given the question, or choice of questions, at the beginning of the day and must submit their answer by the end of it. During the day they can use any resources they desire, including the library and the Internet. Students should be free to discuss the question with their peers but not with the instructor. In conducting such an assessment the instructor could incorporate some or all of the above classroom techniques in an attempt to make the entire day as intensive, engaging and interactive as possible. Although often well received by students, one of the warnings of such an approach is for the instructor not to over-occupy the students and submerge them in a sea of 'case context' at the expense of theory and the ability to develop higher-order thinking skills.

Field visit

To take the full-day assessment to the next level, the instructor could organise a field trip to the location of the case study. While field visits tend to be time-consuming to organise and may have considerable financial (or risk assessment) implications for the department (or the student if the cost of field visits is passed on to them), the learning experience is likely to be highly valued, keenly engaged with and much remembered. During the course of the fieldtrip, the students could be invited to interview key decision-makers in the case, to investigate the direction and scale of various impacts, to explore barriers and constraints to sites, maybe even to conduct a questionnaire survey or series of street interviews. If it is not possible to visit the location of the case study itself, an alternative is to visit a competing location. This will add a comparative dynamic to the case in question and enable students to undertake their own analysis, develop their own ideas and ultimately to generate their own knowledge.

Final thoughts

This chapter brings together some thoughts on how best to teach and learn using case studies. Writing, learning and teaching cases can be frustrating and exhausting but seldom is the outcome of such an exercise a negative one. Too often it is too easy for instructors to simply 'run with what we have', rather than to invest the time necessary to create a special learning environment within which case learning and teaching can flourish. Case learning and teaching are not effective if they are a last-minute, ad-hoc classroom exercise. Rather, they require substantial planning and careful consideration as to how the class is to be structured, managed and motivated.

Although there are many reasons in favour of the case study learning and teaching approach, perhaps the most significant is the ability of cases to tap into students' general preference for inductive (experiential) approaches to learning in contrast to the more traditional deductive approaches preferred by many instructors. The case approach can engender a highly stimulating, interactive and enjoyable educational experience, whether delivered through pyramid discussions, role plays, debates, essay discussions, research or field visits (to name but a few of the possibilities). Cases ought to be fun to write, to study and to teach, but as with most good things in life they require effort, commitment and an investment in intellectual energy for the full 'return on investment' to be accrued. The lesson is not to use cases in a naive way. Simply handing the students a hard copy of the case, giving them 10 minutes to read it and then firing some questions at them is unlikely to make best use of the cases in the book.

The remainder of this book brings together a number of case studies in the area of heritage which add to the existing library of cases of the Contemporary Cases Online series. It is hoped that they will contribute to the advocacy for the case method as a highly appropriate, relevant, challenging and contemporary approach to teaching and learning.

References

Boston University. 2013. *Using cases to teach*. http://www.bu.edu/ceit/teaching-resources/in-the-classroom/using-case-studies-to-teach/

Carnegie Mellon. 2013. *Case studies*. http://www.cmu.edu/teaching/designteach/design/instructionalstrategies/casestudies.html

Romanowski, MH. 2013. *Teaching using case studies*. http://www.qu.edu.qa/offices/ofid/presenration_Spring2009/2Teatching_Using_Case_studies_2.pdf

Stanford University. 1994. *Speaking of teaching: Teaching with case studies*. http://www.stanford.edu/dept/CTL/cgi-bin/docs/newsletter/case_studies.pdf

HERITAGE AS TOURISM

4

Singapore's Little India

Ethnic Districts as Tourist Attractions

Joan Henderson

Introduction

Little India is an ethnic enclave closely associated with the population of Indian descent in the city state of Singapore. The Historic District of Little India is a formally designated conservation area and recognised as a tourism precinct by authorities, reflecting its popularity with visitors and potential for further development. In addition, it is a place of residence and employment. The district illuminates features of ethnic urban heritage and the multiple purposes it serves, especially in societies of relatively newly independent nations of mixed ethnicity, and the relationship between tourism and heritage. The case of Little India also affords lessons about managing, marketing and developing ethnic districts as tourist attractions.

In the discussion that follows, the term 'tourist attraction' will be used interchangeably with that of 'visitor attraction'. Furthermore, the terms 'multi-ethnic', 'multi-racial' and 'multi-cultural' are employed synonymously in this case. Ethnic diversity is a defining characteristic of Singapore. Such pluralism can enrich the lives of citizens and visitors in destinations when it is present, yet there may be frictions if power and influence are believed to be unfairly distributed among ethnic groups. Tourism can be a tool in nation-building policies aimed at cultivating unity, and the promotional imagery employed frequently conveys selected versions and visions of populations, perhaps transmitting fictions of socio-cultural harmony which may be distant from reality (Buzinde, Santos and Smith, 2006). Ethnic districts are often a focus of tourist attention in larger cities which have well-established ethnic communities that are historically linked to a particular locale. These are sometimes classed as enclaves and ethnoscapes (Shaw, Bagwell and Karmowska, 2004) or referred to as ghettos (Conforti, 1996), and are exemplified by the various 'Chinatowns' found worldwide. The transformation of such sites into leisure and tourist spaces has generated debate around the anticipated outcomes. Outsider interests may favour protection and conservation, but there is also a potential for excessive commercialisation and conflict among the multiple stakeholders (Caffyn and Lutz, 1999; Erdentug and Columbijn, 2002).

The challenges of making use of ethnic districts as a tourism resource, along with the possible responses to such efforts, are apparent in the context of Little India. These are outlined below after some background information about Singapore and its ethnic quarters is presented in order to set the scene. The author has drawn on a student project (Quek, Quek and Tay, 2012) in the penultimate section and is pleased to acknowledge their help, as well as that of the Singapore Tourism Board (STB) in providing information.

The Singapore context

Singapore is an island of approximately 712km² lying at the southern tip of the Malaysian Peninsula in South East Asia. The city state's modern history is generally agreed to have begun in 1819 with the arrival of Stamford Raffles, who claimed the island as a trading post on behalf of the British East India Company. Subsequently a British colony, it became an independent republic in 1965 and has been ruled by the People's Action Party (PAP) since elections taking place in 1968. The government is well known for its economic success and efficiency alongside the pursuit of order and control, encompassing many different aspects of life and the physical environment. There have been criticisms of a political system which inhibits dissent and has frustrated the emergence of a convincing opposition, but the regime's policies and strategic planning have transformed the island and given the populace one of the highest standards of living in Asia. Nevertheless, the PAP's share of the vote fell to an historic low in the election of 2011 which prompted talk of greater responsiveness and revision of the traditional top-down administrative style (EIU, 2011).

The authorities have been active in nation building, endeavouring to forge a sense of national identity, in which hegemonic motives have played a part. The task is made more urgent because of a disparate population which exceeds 5 million, making it one of the world's most densely populated cities. Inward migration commencing in the nineteenth century led to indigenous Malays being outnumbered by those of Chinese origin who now constitute around 74% of Singaporeans. Malays make up 13% and Indians 9% with a fourth category of 'others' in the formal classification, embracing smaller groupings such as Eurasians (Department of Statistics, 2011). The presence of almost 1 million migrant workers should not be overlooked, a large proportion of whom are semi- or unskilled and hail from developing countries in Asia. Among Singaporeans, Chinese pre-eminence and concerns about the marginalisation of non-Chinese have made race a sensitive issue (Lai, 1995; Rahim, 1998) and political parties based on race are banned in an attempt to avert its politicisation. Self-help organisations are permitted and the Singapore Indian Development Association (SINDA), for example, was founded in the early 1990s with the initial mission of enhancing the educational performance of Indian students. Other measures to manage race relations include the prevention of ghettos in the public housing in which most Singaporeans live by imposing racial quotas and a commitment to meritocracy.

Heritage is considered to be a nation-building tool that is capable of assisting in alleviating racial tensions, a function which partly explains heightened official interest in conservation. Imperatives of economic growth predominated in the early decades of independence when there was little sympathy for conservation in the rush toward urbanisation and industrialisation. Attitudes started to change in the 1980s and the value of heritage economically, socially and politically came to be more widely recognised (Teo and Huang, 1995). There was awareness that the city state was at risk of losing its individuality and that conserving reminders of the past would augment tourist appeal and help anchor Singaporeans to their homeland, nurturing feelings of a shared history and identity that incorporates, yet also transcends, ethnic allegiances (Yuen and Ng, 2001). Conservation has thus acquired a higher priority and is a responsibility of the Urban Redevelopment Authority (URA), which deals with long-term planning. By 2012, the URA had awarded conservation status to 94 areas covering over 7,000 buildings (URA, 2012), requiring adherence to guidelines about structural alterations and building use. In addition, there were 64 National Monuments selected by the Preservation of Monuments Board (PMB, 2012) which reports to the National Heritage Board (NHB). The NHB is charged with fostering "nationhood, national identity and creativity through heritage and cultural development" (NHB, 2008: 3). Economic development, however, still tends to be dominant in decisions about scarce land and adaptive reuse of old buildings is urged so that they can earn revenue where possible.

Little India and other ethnic districts

Government agencies sanction and promote the appreciation of Chinese, Malay and Indian ancestral cultures as core components of Singapore nationhood for domestic and international audiences. This is evident in STB marketing, where focus is on colourful and non-threatening expressions of ethnicity such as dress, food, architecture and festivals (Chang 1997 and

2000a; Henderson, 2003). These manifestations are on show in the historic ethnic quarters, which originated in the early 1820s when Raffles and the Garrison Engineer, Lieutenant Jackson, devised a plan of the town in an attempt to secure its orderly expansion. Land was allocated for different purposes and races, with the Chinese to be settled west of the river and the Muslim Malays in Kampong Glam. Reference was made to the South Indian Muslim traders, known as Chulias, but a zone for Indians was not reserved. One was, however, soon to evolve.

As a burgeoning international port, Singapore enticed people from around the world and substantial numbers came from India. They were employed as servants, teachers, priests, soldiers and businessmen, and several were convicts transported by the colonial power to be manual labourers (Walker, 1994). Some settled on Serangoon Road. This appears on an 1828 map which shows that land was being farmed there. The district now known as Little India grew up along that road. The opening of a racecourse in the vicinity proved a lure for European residents, leaving a legacy of streets which once led to private houses bearing the names of their owners. Cattle rearing and related enterprises were introduced, overtaking agriculture in importance and giving rise to a concentration of Indians because of their control of the trade. Supporting infrastructure was installed and Indians from sectors unconnected to cattle moved in, increasing the demand for goods and services to meet their particular needs: for example, temples and mosques were erected for religious devotions. The construction of residential and business premises intensified at the beginning of the twentieth century, necessitating the draining of swampland and dealing a blow to the cattle trade. The district was eventually given over largely to a mix of commerce and housing inhabited by all races, although Indians were still heavily represented (Ong, 2009).

The Second World War, during which Singapore was occupied by the Japanese following an ignominious British surrender of the island, was a turning point in its history. The post-war years were a period of dramatic changes, one aspect of which was the clearance of slums and relocation of inner-city dwellers to suburban estates of high-rise Housing Development Board apartment blocks. This was as part of a transformative urban development programme which also entailed the disappearance of rural villages or 'kampongs' as the countryside was turned to other uses. Many thus left Little India, which was to act more as a commercial hub, although there was still a community of residents staying in rudimentary worker accommodation and, in the 1980s, new public housing. As a whole, the district had been spared the redevelopment characteristic of much of Singapore and something of its late nineteenth- and early twentieth-century qualities was retained. Nevertheless, some tangible heritage had disappeared, such as the old market (Siddique and Sholam, 1982). Calls for better protection went largely unheeded until the end of the 1980s, at which time the Chinese, Indian and Malay enclaves were all selected for conservation.

Conservation and development in Little India

An area of 13 hectares was designated by the URA as Little India Historic District in 1989 and the accompanying conservation plan argued that a "conscientiously conserved environment can and must be achieved if we are to attract visitors, expand business scope and sophistication and, above all, transmit our heritage to future generations" (URA, 1995: 83). Four objectives were set of "retaining and restoring buildings of historical and architectural significance; improving the general physical environment and introducing appropriate new features to further enhance the identity of the area; retaining and enhancing ethnic-based activities while consolidating the area with new and compatible activities; and involving both the public and private sectors in carrying out conservation projects" (URA, 1995: 83). Key features included conservation, the creation of a bazaar, pedestrianisation, infrastructure upgrading, improvements to street furniture and signage, and adaptive reuse of conservation buildings (URA, 1995).

The URA (1995: 23) describes the "historical value" of Little India as lying "not only in the rich variety of design of individual buildings, but in the urban texture as well as the streetscapes, the grid of main streets, side roads, back lanes and open spaces" which constitute an "eloquent historical statement". The street layout is strikingly skewed because, as previously noted, some streets were formerly lanes to private bungalows, and the architecture is predominantly shophouses of a simple two-storey type (see Figure 1). Shophouses are terraced properties in which the ground floor is intended for business and the upper storey for residence, usually linked by covered pavements knows as five-foot ways. Design can be classified into early (1840-1900), first transitional (early 1900s), late (1900-1940), second transitional (late 1930s) and Art Deco (1930-1960). According to the URA (1995: 27), the shophouse is "one of the most significant building types in Singapore's architectural heritage, reflecting much of the island's history and development. Its predominance owes much to Sir Stamford Raffles' early planning proposals".

Figure 1: Little India shophouses and streets. Photo credits: Quek Joo Yeng, Quek Li Xuan and Tay Hui Jin

Following the award of conservation status to Little India there were a number of initiatives to upgrade the physical environment and maximise commercial opportunities, not least from tourism. Restoration of shophouses was undertaken, new businesses set up, and signage and other interpretative facilities added. The then Thematic Development Unit of the STB organised meetings to discuss future prospects and a Little India Arcade was opened after a tendering exercise by the URA (see Figure 2). The arcade was to be an outlet for ethnic products and managed jointly by the Hindu Endowment Board (HEB), which was the owner, and a property company (Chang, 2000b). An STB-commissioned study sought to uncover stories of interest to visitors, and heritage markers in four languages were erected at sites deemed historically, socially and religiously meaningful. Among other new developments were a modern shopping centre (City Square Mall) and

two mass rapid transport (MRT) light railway stations (Little India and Far-
rer Park) built as part of the rail network extension. Budget hostel operators took advantage of the lifting of regulations on land use to move in and
amendments to URA rules in 2005 suggested an easing of restrictions on
approved businesses in conservation areas as a whole to satisfy the demands
of the market (URA, 2005).

Figure 2: Little India Arcade. Photo credit: Quek Joo Yeng, Quek Li Xuan and Tay Hui Jin

A Little India Task Force of public agencies, headed by the URA, was formed
in late 2006 with the aim of making further improvements, especially with
regard to vehicle and pedestrian movements, which were severely congested. Participating bodies were the Land Transport Authority, STB, Singapore
Police Force, National Environment Agency, Singapore Civil Defence Force,
Public Utilities Board and Singapore Land Authority which collectively li-
aised with the Little India Shopkeepers and Heritage Association (LISHA)
representing business and society. Walkways were widened and surfaced
with non-slip terracotta tiles for better safety in Serangoon Road, described
as both a cultural destination and traditional shopping street, and some minor roads. Multi-functional lamp posts with energy efficient lighting and a
decorative lotus-flower motif were put in place, providing stronger support
for festival street illuminations and banners. The Task Force programme was
fully completed by 2011 and officials spoke about having struck a balance
in meeting the needs of pedestrians, motorists and commerce (Tng, 2010).
Examples of signage and interpretation are shown in Figure 3.

Little India today remains busy and its streets and pavements are regularly crowded. Although certain buildings may appear somewhat shabby and neglected, there is a lively atmosphere of a sort rarely found elsewhere in Singapore (Henderson, 2008). A selection of street scenes is displayed in Figure 4. The district contains an eclectic mix of shops, food and beverage outlets and other enterprises. One famous retailer is the Mustafa Centre, which began as a modest affair and is now a department store complex open 24 hours a day. Many businesses trade in Indian or Indian-related commodities and services, and are owned and operated by those of Indian origin, although non-Indian tradesmen are at work there too. Traditional activities such as spice grinding persist, yet Little India's special characteristics and quirkiness appeal to artists and creative arts businesses as well as media firms. Budget hotels, pubs and internet cafes too have increased in number. As a mark of its 'cool' status, a Singapore entrepreneur chose Little India as the location for his latest luxury boutique hotel, Wanderlust, which is housed in a former school.

Figure 3: Information boards and street signage. Photo credits: Quek Joo Yeng, Quek Li Xuan and Tay Hui Jin

A slightly seedier side also exists, as illustrated by the proliferation of massage parlours in one street, which has been condemned as a 'red light district'. The influx of migrant workers from the Indian subcontinent, particularly on Sunday, is another topic of contention for some inhabitants. An estimated 5,000 to 10,000 gather in the area to socialise, relax, purchase familiar foodstuffs and remit money home. The crowds have been observed to congregate by nationality and linguistic sub-group in a territorialisation of space (Chang, 2000b). Complaints of over-crowding and littering have led to police monitoring, but the spending of these visitors is welcomed by many retailers and it should be remembered that their leisure opportunities are strictly circumscribed by the very long hours they work and their low disposable incomes.

Figure 4: Street scenes. Photo credits: Quek Joo Yeng, Quek Li Xuan and Tay Hui Jin

Managing and marketing Little India as a visitor attraction

Little India was visited by an estimated 25% of the 9.7 million international tourists to Singapore in 2009, rendering it the third most popular 'free-access' attraction after Orchard Road (the premier shopping street) and Chinatown, which drew 49% and 29% respectively (STB, 2010). Total arrivals had fallen by 4.3% that year due to global economic conditions, but reached a record 13.2 million in 2011 (STB, 2012a) and there are expectations of further growth in the forthcoming decade. The majority of tourists are from the Asian region, although Australia, New Zealand and Europe remain important markets. Foreign visitors frequently comment on the colour and liveliness of the street life they encounter in Little India, judging it to be 'less touristy' than Chinatown and Kampong Glam (Ng, Pok and Zhang, 2011). These attributes are highlighted in guidebooks and on the STB website which promises visitors "one of the most vibrant and culturally authentic districts of Singapore", regarded as a "home away from home" by Indians (STB, 2012b: n.p.). Indian culture is presented in terms of temples, festivals, the arts, food and shopping which constitute an "explosion of sights, sounds and smells" (STB, 2012b: n.p.). The Board asserts that Little India has "developed into a trendy area where visitors can enjoy its authentic charms and indulge in the many bars and restaurants that have opened to add new flavour to the visitor experience" (STB, 2011: 47). Singaporeans of all ethnicities, but especially Indians, are also regular visitors to Little India and come to shop, eat, attend events and pray.

The Historic District, along with Chinatown and Orchard Road, are tourism precincts that are the responsibility of an STB unit focusing on providing visitors with a "multitude of memorable experiences", including "exploring and reliving history and heritage" (STB, 2011: 46). However, the STB emphasises that its role is to help local 'place managers' such as the Chinatown Business Association in their task of place management rather than to dictate and direct agendas. Its underlying objective is to ensure that precincts are "positively cultivated" in accordance with "Singapore's appeal as a rich multi-cultural destination' and 'bustling with activity" (STB, 2011: 46). The place management and precinct development models adopted by the STB encompass the four elements of space, software, staff and sustainability in alignment with the Board's underlying strategy. The STB acknowledges LI-SHA as the key player in managing the Little India precinct and the two are cooperating on a "working plan to ramp up its management capabilities" so that the area "continues to be relevant and exciting to visitors" (STB, 2011:

47).

LISHA dates from 2000 and was set up by the Serangoon Merchants' Association, the Little India Restaurant Association and the HEB in response to STB calls for a centralised committee to promote heritage, culture and commerce in the district. While concerned about the health of the business environment, LISHA is also interested in the overall vibrancy of the district and mindful of the social and cultural significance it holds for Singaporeans of Indian descent. One of its main goals is the "betterment of Little India as a multi-cultural and multi-ethnic tourist destination" (LISHA, 2012: n.p.). The 'software' elements and strengthening Indian identity and culture are stressed, although a representative interviewed was not fully cognisant of the management and development frameworks. There are four full-time LISHA staff and an executive committee of 17. Most of the 192 members, comprising about 30% of shop holders, are small retailers.

Much of LISHA's energies are devoted to organising a series of annual events, such as the Hindu festivals of Deepavali and Vesak Day, which is celebrated by Buddhists. Pongal (Harvest) Festival and Indian New Year are also commemorated and there are further events held as part of various Singapore-wide food and art festivals. LISHA is supported in this work by the HEB, SINDA, the Indian Restaurant Association of Singapore and Indian cultural groups. The STB provides part of the funding, supplemented by financial aid from the Ministry of Community Development's Heritage and Integration budget. Telecommunication companies selling phone cards targeted at the foreign labour force are also backers. Attendance ranges from 2,000 and 4,000, almost 60% of whom are Singaporeans with the remainder being equally divided between tourists and migrant workers. LISHA liaises with the Ministry of Education and expatriate organisations to invite children and non-Indians to share in and learn about the festivities. Enticing the younger generation is, however, challenging. LISHA also finds it difficult to secure sponsorship from the private sector, especially from large corporate donors. There is acceptance that available resources inhibit innovation, leading to the repetition of established events. Nevertheless, the regular programme does bring crowds to Little India and customers for several businesses and is thus welcomed by many LISHA members (Quek et al., 2012).

In addition to organising events, LISHA conducts online marketing through a website, Facebook page and Twitter account. It is represented on the Indian Heritage Committee of the NHB and actively advocates greater pedestrianisation of the area to facilitate night markets and more cultural activities. Although the association has little direct control over the physical environment, it does communicate with the appropriate government agencies and offers feedback which has been acted upon in certain instances, such as the Buffalo Road car parks and access routes to the Little India MRT Station. LISHA has also highlighted areas where tourists are concentrated, such as Bukit Timah Road to Lavender Street, between Clive Street and Race Course Road, and between Tekka Market and Mustafa.

LISHA is constrained by limitations of finance and other resources. The four employees deal with administration, finance, public relations and event organising, and a recent staff reshuffle has seen an entirely new team installed. Some shop-holders are reluctant to join the association because they cannot see any direct benefits and prefer to save on the membership fees. At the same time, existing members seem satisfied with the association's efforts, despite commercial anxieties about rising rental rates and labour shortages (Quek et al., 2012).

Recent and future developments

A committee was set up at the beginning of 2009 to steer the commissioning and construction of an Indian Heritage Centre (IHC) in the heart of the Historic District. A Chinatown Heritage Centre and Malay Heritage Centre already exist in Chinatown and Kampong Glam respectively, and the scheme was hailed as timely. The IHC will be overseen by the NHB's Heritage Institutions Division and trace "the history of the Indian and South Asian community in the Southeast Asian region", with "small scale museum facilities as well as programming and educational spaces" (NHB, 2011: 2). The total budget will be around S$25 million. There was a design competition: models of the four shortlisted designs were displayed and public reactions invited. The winner was announced in mid-2011 and comprises a four- or five-storey centre, purporting to blend Indian influences and modern architecture, which will cost about S$12 million. A translucent façade will shimmer during daytime and be a screen for illuminated murals at night (Asiaone, 2011). Feedback was solicited through a Facebook page and focus group sessions were held to raise awareness of the centre and gather views on preferred programmes and exhibits on completion of the building in 2013. In the interim, the IHC and LISHA mounted a three-month outdoor exhibition named 'Our Indian Forebears and their Trades in Singapore'. It consisted of 14 cardboard figures depicting traditional tradesmen positioned appropriately throughout Little India which were also the subject of a brochure and guided tours. The exhibition had a website which included an interactive game in which images had to be matched to professions.

The formal intention of the tourism authorities as articulated by the STB is to constantly rejuvenate all the precincts to keep up with market trends and changing customer profiles while devising unique products and experiences. Development of Chinatown and Kampong Glam in the past has, however, brought criticisms of excessive commercialisation, an absence of authenticity and the creation of tourist spaces which alienate and exclude locals (Henderson, 2000; Ismail, 2006; Leong, 1997; Yeoh and Huang, 1996). With regard to initiatives for Little India, some observers describe a diminution of its distinctive character and ambience, with traditional businesses struggling to survive while others comment on its resilience. Overall, there is a feeling that Little India has resisted becoming a destination primarily for tourists in the fashion of parts of Chinatown (Furland, 2008) and a hope that this will continue to be so in the future (Huang, 2008).

Conclusion

The case of Little India suggests how heritage is valued in Singapore within and outside government as socio-cultural, economic and political capital. Despite the threats to the survival of some of its built heritage due to rapid modernisation and urbanisation, Little India is afforded a degree of protection by its conservation status and function as a representation of Singapore's history and ethnic diversity. It is also a unique visitor attraction and seems to exercise a particular appeal compared to the other ethnic enclaves related to perceived authenticity. The official approach to the management of the tourist precinct is indirect, concentrating on international marketing and encouraging the local business association to take the lead. There are, however, questions about the agency's readiness and ability to do so. There are also concerns about the potential for tensions to mount among the numerous groups with a stake in Little India. Effectively managing and marketing Little India and ensuring its future sustainable development is thus a formidable challenge. The advantages and disadvantages of current methods are matters for debate.

References

Asiaone. 2011. Balaji's heritage dream takes a step forward, 14 July. http://www.asiaone.com

Buzinde CN, Santos CA, Smith SL. 2006. Ethnic representations: Destination imagery. *Annals of Tourism Research* **33** (3): 707-728.

Caffyn A, Lutz J. 1999. Developing the heritage tourism product in multi-ethnic cities. *Tourism Management* **20** (2): 213-221.

Chang TC. 1997. From Instant Asia to multi-faceted jewel: Urban imaging strategies and tourism development in Singapore. *Urban Geography* **18** (6): 542-562.

Chang TC. 2000a. Theming cities, taming places: Insights from Singapore. *Geografiska Annaler* **82B** (1): 35-54.

Chang TC. 2000b. Singapore's Little India: A tourist attraction as a contested landscape. *Urban Studies* **37** (2): 343-366.

Conforti JM. 1996. Ghettos as tourism attractions. *Annals of Tourism Research* **23** (4): 830-842.

Department of Statistics. 2011. *Monthly Digest of Statistics*, December. Ministry of Trade and Industry.

EIU. 2011. *Country Risk Service: Singapore*. London: Economist Intelligence Unit.

Erdentug A, Columbijn F. 2002. *Urban Ethnic Encounters*. London: Routledge.

Furland, EB. 2008. *Singapore, from Third to First World Country: The Effect of Development in Little India and Chinatown*. Unpublished Masters thesis, Norwegian University of Technology and Science, Trondheim.

Henderson JC. 2000. Attracting tourists to Singapore's Chinatown: A case study in conservation and promotion. *Tourism Management* **21**: 525-534.

Henderson JC. 2003. Ethnic heritage as a tourist attraction: The Peranakans of Singapore. *International Journal of Heritage Studies* **9** (1): 27-44.

Henderson JC. 2008. Managing urban ethnic heritage: Little India in Singapore. *International Journal of Heritage Studies* **14** (4): 332-346.

Huang L. 2008. Will it end up like Chinatown? *The Straits Times*, 9 November.

Ismail R. 2006. Ramadan and Bussorah Street: The spirit of place. *Geojournal* **66** (3): 243-256.

Lai AE. 1995. *Meanings of Multiethnicity: A Case Study of Ethnicity and Ethnic Relations in Singapore*. Oxford and Singapore: Oxford University Press.

Leong WT. 1997. Commodifying ethnicity: State and ethnic tourism in Singapore. In M Picard, R Wood (eds) *Tourism, Ethnicity and the State in Asian and Pacific Societies*. Honolulu: University of Hawaii Press; 71-98.

LISHA. 2012. The Association. http://www.little-india.sg/Lisha.aspx

Ng SK, Poh V, Zhang F. 2011. *Ethnic Tourism in Singapore*. Unpublished undergraduate dissertation. Nanyang Business School, Nanyang Technological University, Singapore.

NHB. 2011. Public exhibition of shortlisted designs for the new Indian Heritage Centre. National Heritage Board Media Advisory, 21 April. http://www.news.gov.sg/public/sgpc/en/media_releases/agencies/nhb/press_release/P-20110421-1/AttachmentPar/0/file/Media%20Advisory%20(IHC%20Public%20Exhibition)%20FINAL.pdf

NHB. 2008. *Renaissance City Plan III: Heritage Development Plan*. Singapore: National Heritage Board.

Ong C. 2009. Little India. Singapore Infopedia. http://infopedia.nl.sg/articles/SIP_14562009-02-11.html. Accessed 15 January 2012

PMB. 2012. National Monuments. http://www.pmb.sg/?page_id=6

Quek JY, Quek, LX, Tay HJ. 2012. *Little India*. Unpublished undergraduate dissertation. Nanyang Business School, Nanyang Technological University, Singapore.

Rahim LZ. 1998. *The Singapore Dilemma: The Political and Educational Marginality of the Malay Community*. Kuala Lumpur: Oxford University Press.

Shaw S, Bagwell S, Karmowska J. 2004. Ethnoscapes as spectacle: Reimaging multicultural districts as new destinations for leisure and tourism consumption. *Urban Studies* **41** (10): 1983-2000.

Siddique S, Sholam, NP. 1982. *Singapore's Little India: Past, Present and Future*. Singapore: Institute of Southeast Asian Studies.

STB. 2010. *Annual Report on Tourism Statistics 2009*. Singapore: Singapore Tourism Board.

STB. 2011. *Singapore Tourism Board Annual Report 2010/2011*. Singapore: Singapore Tourism Board. www1.yoursingapore.com/annualreport/pdf/stb_ar_2012.pdf

STB. 2012a. Visitor arrivals statistics. https://app.stb.gov.sg/asp/tou/tou2.asp

STB. 2012b. Little India. http://www.yoursingapore.com/content/traveller/en/browse/see-and-do/culture-and-heritage/cultural-precinys/little-india.html

Teo P, Huang S. 1995. Tourism and heritage conservation in Singapore. *Annals of Tourism Research* **22** (3): 589-615.

Tng S. 2010. Enhanced lighting and walkways for Little India. *Skyline*, November-December: 3.

URA. 2012. Listing of conservation areas and maps. http://www.ura.gov.sg/conservation/mod2.htm

URA. 2005. URA reviews guidelines for core areas in Historic Districts in consultation with stakeholders. Urban Redevelopment Authority Press Release, 26 September.

URA. 1995. *Little India Historic District*. Singapore: Urban Redevelopment Authority.

Walker AR. 1994. Indians in Singapore: The background. In AR Walker (ed.) *New Place, Old Ways*. Delhi: Hindustan Publishing; 1-46.

Yeoh B, Huang S. 1996. The conservation-redevelopment dilemma in Singapore: The case of Kampong Glam Historic District. *Cities* **13** (6): 411-422.

Yuen B, Ng TH. 2001. Urban conservation in Singapore: Tradition or tourist bane? *Planning Practice and Research* **16** (1): 39-50.

Ancillary Student Material

Further reading

Diekmann A, Maulet G. 2009. A contested tourism asset: The case of Matonge in Brussels. *Tourism, Culture and Communication* **9** (1-2): 93-105.

National Geographic 2013. Singapore walking tour: Little India temples. http:// travel.nationalgeographic.com/travel/city-guides/singapore-walking-tour-2/

NHB 2013 Trails. http://www.nhb.gov.sg/nhbPortal/Trails

Rath J. 2007. *Tourism, Ethnic Diversity and the City.* New York: Routledge.

Shaw SJ. 2010. Marketing ethnoscapes as spaces of consumption: 'Banglatown – London's Curry Capital'. *Journal of Town & City Management* **1** (4): 381-395.

Related websites

LISHA (Little India Shopkeepers and Heritage Association) Little India: http://www. little-india.sg/

STB (Singapore Tourism Board) Official Singapore Tourism Website: http://www. yoursingapore.com/content/traveller/en/experience.html

Self-test questions

Try to answer the following questions to test your knowledge and understanding. If you are not sure of the answers, please re-read the case study and refer to the suggested references and further reading sources.

1	What is the appeal of Little India for tourists?

2	Who are the principal actors in the management and marketing of Little India as a tourist attraction and what are their respective roles?

3	What is the official approach to managing and developing Little India as a tourist attraction?

4	Have any actual or potential conflicts arisen from the development and promotion of Little India as a tourist attraction?

Key themes and theories

The key themes in the case study relate to the following areas:

◆ Cultural heritage as a tourism resource

◆ Management of ethnic districts as tourist attractions

◆ Interpretation, presentation and marketing of cultural heritage

◆ Impacts of tourism

◆ Sustainable development

The key themes in the case study relate to:

◆ Meanings and uses of heritage

◆ Heritage interpretation and presentation

◆ Visitor attraction development and marketing

◆ Management of heritage sites

◆ Sustainability

If you need to source further information on any of the above themes and theories, then these headings could be used as key words to search for materials and case studies.

5

Managing Religious Heritage Attractions

The Case of Jerusalem

Daniel H. Olsen and Amos S. Ron

Management at religious heritage sites

For centuries, pilgrims and tourists have traveled to sites of religious and spiritual significance for many reasons, including curiosity, worship, and participation in initiatory or cleansing rituals (Morinis, 1992). Shackley (2001) classifies sacred sites into a number of categories (see Table 1). While most of these types of site are considered holy or sacred in the eyes of adherents and leaders of different religious faiths, they are also seen as heritage tourism attractions by government and tourism officials, and are therefore often used in local, regional and international tourism marketing efforts (Olsen, 2003). Because of this interest in using religious heritage sites as tourist attractions, travel to religious sites has become widespread and popularised in recent decades, probably more so than at any other time in human history, with millions of people traveling every year to visit sacred sites both ancient and modern in origin (Olsen and Timothy, 1999; McKelvie, 2005).

One of the main tasks of religious heritage site managers, or their 'core business' as Shackley (2001) puts it, is to create and maintain a 'sense of place', with the managerial focus being on providing an atmosphere of worship and meditation, and enhancing the aesthetic qualities of the site in order to help visitors meet their religious expectations and goals. As such, site managers need to supervise and mediate the interactions between visitors on the one hand and the natural and built environment on the other, so as to preserve both the site's structural integrity and its ambiance. However, this has become increasingly difficult, as increasing numbers of tourists and religious adherents to these sacred sites threatens their integrity and character, with the sheer number of visitors degrading the aesthetic qualities of religious heritage sites and disrupting worship rituals (Shackley, 2001; Olsen, 2006).

Table 1: A classification of sacred sites

Types	Examples
Single nodal feature	Canterbury Cathedral (England), Emerald Buddha (Bangkok, Thailand), Hagia Sophia (Istanbul, Turkey)
Archaeological sites	Machu Picchu (Peru), Chichén Itzá (Mexico)
Burial sites	Catacombs (Rome, Italy), Pyramids (Giza, Egypt)
Detached temples/shrines	Borobudur (Indonesia), Ankgor Wat (Cambodia), Amristar (India)
Whole towns	Rome (Italy), Jerusalem (Israel), Assisi (Italy), Varanasi (India), Bethlehem (Palestinian Authority)
Shrine/temple complexes	Lalibela (Ethiopia), Potala (Tibet), St. Catherine's Monastery (Egypt)
'Earth energy' sites	Nazca lines (Peru), Glastonbury (England)
Sacred mountains	Uluru (Australia), Mt. Everest (Nepal), Tai Shan (China), Mt. Athos (Greece), Mt. Fuji (Japan), Mt. Shasta (United States)
Sacred islands	Rapa Nui (Chile), Lindisfarne (England), Iona (Scotland), Mont-St-Michel (France)
Pilgrimage foci	Mecca (Saudi Arabia), Medina (Saudi Arabia), Mt. Kailash (Tibet), Santiago de Compostela (Spain)
Secular pilgrimage	Robben Island (South Africa), Gorée (Senegal), Holocaust Sites (e.g. Auschwitz-Birkenau, Poland)

Source: Shackley (2001)

At a micro-scale, management issues can range from the mundane, such as garbage collection, the cleaning of public conveniences, and watering gardens and lawns, to the more serious matters of managing the physical impacts of tourism at these sites, such as vandalism and graffiti, accidental damage, general wear and tear/erosion, noise pollution, microclimatic change, and theft (Woodward 2004; Olsen 2006; see Table 2). Crowding, in particular, exacerbates these internal management issues, which leads site managers also to focus on controlling visitor flows to and around the site, whether this is done through limiting visitors through a lack of parking spaces, the charging of entrance fees, or other methods of reducing the potential for the site to receive large numbers of visitors (Shackley, 2001).

Shackley (2001: 8) suggests that national, regional, and local political and social instability can heighten these management problems, arguing that "the easiest sites to manage are those where [socio-political] stability is high even if visitor numbers are high (such as the Vatican or Canterbury Cathedral) since this stability and control permits the development and implementation of effective visitor management systems". Socio-political problems can arise where sacred sites are the focus of competing interests between religious groups over their ownership, maintenance and interpretation. In places which are considered the ancestral homelands of different religious groups, competing discourses over how to interpret the "multiple levels of sedimented history" and "layers of meaning" (Yeoh and Kong, 1996: 55) at particular sacred sites can lead to violence. Examples of such include the Al Aqsa Intifada in (or second Palestinian uprising) September 2000 between Israel and Palestine (Collins-Kreiner, Kilot, Mansfeld and Sagi, 2006) and Ayodhya (India), where Hindus tore down a 16th century Muslim mosque (Shaw, 2000). In these and other instances of religious violence, travelers will seek alternative religious sites to visit, as tourists choose other, safer destinations to visit when political conditions deteriorate (Richter and Waugh, 1986; Collins-Kreiner et al., 2006), thereby hurting the travel industry in that area. As such, religious heritage sites can be both logistically and politically difficult to manage effectively.

Table 2: Physical impacts of visitor activity

Agent of Change	Physical Impact	Example
Theft of artefacts	Loss of resource	Removing tiles from the Taj Mahal
Vandalism/graffiti	Damage to resource	Carving of initials on Nativity Grotto
Accidental damage	Wear and tear	Fabric erosion in cathedrals
Pollution (fouling)	Damage to resource	Urine at Giza Plateau
Pollution (noise)	May undermine atmosphere	Church of Holy Sepulchre
Pollution (litter)	Reduced attractiveness	Mt. Everest area
Microclimatic change	Damage to resource	Egyptian tombs
Crowding	Leads to physical damage	Notre Dame Cathedral

Source: Shackley (2001)

These internal and external management issues are exemplified in the city of Jerusalem, which forms the focus of this case. Not only are there multiple religious heritage attractions within the city, themselves with their own management issues and problems, but these attractions are also divided among the three Abrahamic religions – Christianity, Judaism and Islam – each of which view Jerusalem as a sacred space. This is a unique situation, considering that most sacred cities (e.g. Mecca, Medina, Salt Lake City, The Vatican, Assisi, Lourdes, Fatima and Varanasi) tend to be sacred to just one religious faith. As such, Jerusalem has long been contested by these three religious faiths, each of which historically has competed against the other to possess, control and defend their sacred spaces through the material and visual articulation of religious and political ideology within the city's landscape and architecture (Azaryahu, 1999; Olsen and Guelke, 2004). Furthermore, the central importance of Jerusalem for both Israeli and Palestinian nationalistic movements – both of which unequivocally view Jerusalem as their one and only capital city – also adds a complexity to management that is not usually seen at other religious heritage attractions in holy cities (Collins-Kreiner et al., 2006).

The purpose of this case is to discuss the management challenges related to some of the main religious heritage attractions in Jerusalem, which has traditionally been divided into three areas since 1948: the Old City[1], East Jerusalem and West Jerusalem. The tourism management issues in the city of Jerusalem as a whole are discussed, after which the management issues at four specific case-study sites will be examined: the Temple Mount, the Western Wall, the Church of the Holy Sepulchre, and the Garden Tomb.

The case of Jerusalem

Jerusalem has historically served and continues to serve as a popular pilgrimage and tourism destination. In 2010, approximately 2.8 million visitors came to Israel, creating $3.7 billion in tourism-related income for the country. Of these 2.8 million visitors, 66% came for either pilgrimage or tourism-related reasons (38% pilgrimage; 28% touring). With 77% of these 2.8 million visitors visiting the Western Wall in 2010 (approximately 2.17 million), it is safe to assume that a majority of visitors to Israel make a stop in Jerusalem, making Jerusalem a 'must-see' attraction within Israel (Israel Central Bureau of Statistics, 2012).

Jerusalem is, however, an unusual case when it comes to urban tourism management, in part because it is one of most contested cities in the history of the world, with not only three religious faiths claiming territory within the city but also having a long history of being controlled by foreign powers (e.g. the Greek, Roman, Ottoman and British empires). For Israeli Jews, Jerusalem is their national capital historically, politically, and spiritually, while for Christians, Jerusalem is the historical setting for the life, teachings, death and resurrection of Jesus. For the Islamic world, Jerusalem is the third most holy city after Mecca and Medina, and is associated with the Prophet Mohammed's Night Journey to Jerusalem.

---

1   The Old City is technically part of East Jerusalem.

Each faith has a number of religious sites that mark the material, symbolic, ideological and spiritual significance of Jerusalem to their adherents (see Table 3). Jerusalem is also seen by Palestinians as their political economic, cultural and spiritual centre. For Palestinians, there can be no Arab Palestine without Jerusalem (Albin, 2005). Jerusalem also acts as a civic centre, an everyday lived-in city, a city split by two nations, and a universal sacred city (Nitzan-Shiftan, 2005).

Table 3: Selected Jewish, Islamic and Christian sites in Jerusalem

Judaism	Western Wall, Temple Mount (Haram al-Sharif), Yad VaShem Memorial and Holocaust Museum, Tomb of King David, Tombs of the Prophets
Islam	Al-Aqsa Mosque, Dome of the Rock, Tomb of King David
Christianity	Via Dolorosa, Garden Tomb, Church of the Holy Sepulchre, Church of All Nations, Last Supper Room, Tomb of St. Mary, Chapel of the Ascension, Church of Dominus Flevit, Church of John the Baptist

As such, there exist multiple competing visions and ideologies of Jerusalem at a number of scales:

♦   **Local** – conflict between visions of Jerusalem's development by different groups living in the city

♦   **National** – Israeli and Palestinian conflicts

♦   **Regional** – conflict between Israel and surrounding Arab states

♦   **International** – conflict between representatives and followers of the Abrahamic religions (Albin, 2005)

These competing visions and ideologies can make it difficult for all interested parties or stakeholders to come to a consensus regarding the physical form of Jerusalem and "whose narrative should Jerusalem's image represent" (Nitzan-Shiftan, 2005: 238). For example, prior to 1967, the city's development was a result of historical, topographic, economic and demographic factors, rather than long-term planning policy (Israeli and Mansfeld, 2003). After 1967, however, the Jerusalem city government began to debate how to unite East and West Jerusalem, both formally and symbolically. Israeli planning officials wanted to focus on high-modern, functionalist and progressive urban development, complete with modern infrastructure, modern buildings, extensive road systems, and a more convenient distribution of urban and civic activities. However, this vision of modernising Jerusalem conflicted with the international community, who viewed Jerusalem as an international city (O'Mahony, 2005) which should be developed as a universal spiritual centre with a developmental emphasis on protecting the city from modernisation, so as to maintain the Orientalist and picturesque look of East

Jerusalem that the British had carefully tried to preserve. The end result was a "break with high modernism toward a thematised city, the visual image of which was geared toward religious sentiments and the tourist industry" (Nitzan-Shiftan, 2005: 239).

While some compromise takes place between different stakeholders regarding the physical and ideological development of Jerusalem (Albin, 2005), Olsen and Guelke (2004) suggest that for many stakeholders in Jerusalem, any decision-making effort regarding heritage interpretation or tourism development is seen as a zero-sum game, in which any advantage given to one stakeholder is simultaneously seen to disadvantage other stakeholders. Attempts to develop tourism attractions or infrastructure are therefore intensely negotiated, as stakeholders try to navigate the maintenance of the geographic and ideological status quo, while also acknowledging the need to improve and expand tourism-related spaces and infrastructures. Indeed, in Jerusalem there is a fierce competition between Arabs and Jews, as well as Christian denominations, over the possession of territory and interpretation of the city's history. As Cohen-Hattab (2010: 137) notes, Jerusalem "is an area where tension and conflicts often erupt between religious groups and convictions, where the authority responsible for the holy site tends to establish an official ritual and delineate clear boundary lines that determine what is allowed and forbidden at the site, and where groups not affiliated with the establishment search to find their place. All of this is occurring as modern tourism in the area continues to grow". As alluded to in this quote, changes to the urban fabric of Jerusalem, particularly in the Old City, which is divided up into five closely guarded areas—the Armenian quarter, the Christian quarter, the Jewish quarter, the Moslem quarter, and the Temple Mount—are generally contested, as religious groups jealously guard 'their' religious spaces from secular or ideological intrusion.

While the diversity of archaeological, cultural and religious and ideological resources is a boon to cultural, heritage and religious tourism markets, the geopolitical tensions at various scales not only make it difficult for stakeholders to come to a consensus regarding how tourism development in Jerusalem should take place, but can, as noted earlier, also discourage tourist visitation to Jerusalem and Israel more generally. This occurred following the Al Aqsa Intifada, between 2000 and 2005, where increased violence between Palestinians and Israelis led visitors to perceive travel to Israel as risky. Consequently there was a drastic decrease in visitors and tourism receipts throughout Israel, with visitor numbers dropping from 2.6 million in 2000 to 862,000 in 2002 (Collins-Kreiner et al., 2006). For a country where religiously motivated journeys are a mainstay for its tourism-oriented economy, any violence or acts of terrorism can be detrimental to its economic well-being or even potentially to the urban fabric of the city itself. In addition these actions can create concerns over the safety of visitors who visit religious heritage attractions in and around Jerusalem.

These multiple and contested religious and geopolitical interests in Jerusalem have spilled over into the politics of tour guiding, where both Israeli and Palestinian tour guides view tourism as a propaganda tool through which they can present their image of the city and views of the Israeli-Palestinian tensions to pilgrims and tourists alike (e.g. Bowman, 1992; Cohen-Hattab, 2004; Brin, 2006; Feldman, 2007; Hercbergs 2009; Brin and Noy, 2010; Noy, 2011, 2012; Hercbergs 2012; Higgins-Desbiolles, n.d). As Brin (2006) notes, while many visitors to Jerusalem are politically oriented and come to show their support to one or the other side in the Israeli-Palestinian conflict, other visitors are more politically neutral or just curious about the conflict. Thus both Israeli and Palestinian official tourism bodies and private tour operators have long seen and used tourism as a way to imparting partisan political and narratives to visitors.

At the same time, visitors who already taken sides in the Israeli-Palestinian conflict, such as fundamentalist Christian Zionists who support the notion of a state for the Jewish people, visit Israel and Jerusalem with the theological view that the establishment of the Israeli state is a sign of the imminent return of Christ. Such visitors would doubtless not be interested in engaging with a tour guide promoting an alternative viewpoint of the Israeli-Palestinian conflict, particularly when religiously-oriented tourists tend to prefer guides of their own faith or who reinforce their theological views (Wilkinson, 1998). As such, they would prefer to come to Israel seeking affirmation of their theological-political views, rather than being confronted by competing and conflicting ideologies as promoted by Palestinian tour guides (Belhassen, 2006, Shapiro, 2008; Belhassen, 2009; Belhassen and Ebel, 2009).

In addition to the ideological battles over the meaning of Jerusalem, the political contest over the physical form of Jerusalem has constrained tourism development and growth in the city as a whole. For example, the transportation systems to and within Jerusalem make it difficult for tourists, particularly large tour groups, to get to the attractions they wish to visit. Israeli and Mansfeld (2003) outline a number of these transportation issues in the context of tourism development:

♦ International visitors access Jerusalem via the Ben Gurion Airport, which is located 45km northwest of Jerusalem. Due to the lack of alternative mass transportation, tourists must use an automobile to get to Jerusalem, which results in chronic congestion at the city's entrance.

♦   The Old City is accessible only via Jerusalem's local transportation system. While the bus system in Jerusalem is highly developed, increased private car use in the city makes the local roads around the Old city highly congested.

♦   Jerusalem suffers from severe budget constraints, making it difficult to fund necessary transportation upgrades and additions.

Within the Old City, only small vehicles are allowed through four of the seven open city gates. The road system and parking outside the Old City are inadequate, leading to congestion and illegal parking at the entrances around the Old City. Furthermore, the lanes in the Old City are narrow and congested, and cannot handle vehicular traffic due to the overcrowding caused by overall tourist numbers.

Israeli and Mansfeld (2003) also make a number of recommendations in their study to alleviate many of these transportation issues, including:

♦   **Reduce traffic flows** – through an updated traffic plan, limiting access to private cars, enhancing the road network, creation of a park-and-ride system, and a new parking payment policy

♦   **Flexible urban transportation services** – through taking into consideration significant seasonal variation

♦   **Spread of tourist demand over spaces** – through the creation of a city tour line, cable car, a land train known as the 'fun train', pedestrian trails around the Old City, and tourist information systems

♦   **Tourist coach management** – through establishing parking lots specifically for tour buses near the Old City

♦   **Tourist demand management** – through distributing tourist demand in various time periods to reduce demand during peak hours, and managing tourist behaviour at tourist attractions to diminish the length of stay and overcrowding of tourists

♦   **Reduction of environmental and social impacts** – through the use of electrical vehicles to move people through the old City

Since Israeli and Mansfeld's paper, a number of transportation-related improvements have been made. For example, the Israeli government has recently begun the construction on a modern train line from Ben Gurion Airport to Jerusalem, new tour-bus parking lots have been built near the Old City, a new city light rail system now passes close by the Old City of Jerusalem, and a new 800-car underground parking garage has been built outside of the Jaffa Gate.

Israeli and Mansfeld (2003: 478) do note that "adequate and workable solutions to the transportation problem of the old city of Jerusalem must also take into account the existence of external constraints". The one external issue they highlight relates to the Israeli-Palestinian conflict, which, with the resulting decline in tourism demand, can result in a less-immediate need to upgrade and expand transportation to and around Jerusalem. In the context of this case, another external issue would be the difficulties of negotiations between the different stakeholders in Jerusalem regarding where new roads or railways would be built, considering the contestation over property rights and archaeological concerns within Jerusalem.

One other issue related to tourism that needs to be considered is the important of religious calendars. The three Abrahamic religions use at least five different religious calendars (Jewish, Gregorian for most Christian denominations, Julian and Revised Julian for Eastern Christian denominations, and Muslim). For example, the common Christian calendars (Gregorian and Julian) are solar (Parise, 2002; Doggett, 2012.), whereas the Muslim calendar is lunar (Ziade, 1970) and the Jewish calendar is lunisolar (the years being solar and the months lunar) (Wisenberg, 1970). Certain Christian denominations use a multiplicity of calendars for various ecclesiastical reasons. For example, certain Orthodox churches use the Julian calendar, while others use the Revised Julian calendar (Parise, 2002). Table 3 and Table 4 show the different feast days for Catholics, Orthodox, Jews and Muslims for the year 2012.

Table 3: Catholic and Orthodox feast days, 2012

Catholic: Gregorian	Orthodox: Standard Calendar
Holy Mother of God: January 1	The Nativity of our Lord: January 7
Epiphany: January 6	New Year, Circumcision: January 14
Baptism of the Lord (River Jordan): January 8	Blessing of the Holy Water (River Jordan) (Greek): January 18
Ash Wednesday (Lent time): February 22	Blessing of the Holy Water (River Jordan) (Syrian & Copts): January 19
Annunciation: March 25	Epiphany: January 19
Palm Sunday: April 1	St. John the Baptist: January 20
Good Friday: April 6	Presentation: February 15
Easter Sunday: April 8	Lent - Orthodoxy Sunday: March 4
Ascension: May 17	Veneration of the Hl. Cross: March 18

Pentecost: May 27	Palm Sunday: April 8
Trinity Sunday: June 3	Easter Sunday: April 15
Corpus Christi: June 7	Ascension: May 14
Nativity of St. John the Baptist: June 24	Pentecost: June 3
Sts. Peter and Paul: June 29	Transfiguration: August 19
Sacred Heart of Jesus: June 15	Procession with Icon of the Virgin Mary: August 25
Assumption: August 15	Burial Ceremony of the Virgin Mary: August 27
Exaltation of the Holy Cross: September 14	Assumption: August 28
All Saints: November 1	New Year of the Church: September 14
Advent - 1st Sunday: December 2	Exaltation of the Holy Cross: September 27
Immaculate Conception: December 8	St. George: November 16
Christmas Day: December 25	1st Sunday of Advent: December 2

Source: Christian Information Centre (2011)

Table 4: Jewish and Muslim feast days, 2012

JEWISH (Jewish Year: 5772 – 5773)	MUSLIM (Hegira: 1431 – 1432)
Purim (Esther): March 8-9	Birth of Mohammed: February 4
Pesach (Passover): April 7-13	Miraj (Ascension of Mohammed): June 16
Yom HaShoa: April 19	First day of Ramadan: July 20
Memorial Day: April 25	End of Feast of Ramadan (Eid El Fitr): August 19
Yom HaAtzmaut (Independence day): April 26	Lailatul-Qadr (Night of Power): August 14
Shavuot (Pentecost): May 27	Feast of the Sacrifice (El Adha): October 26
Tishat BeAv: July 28	New Year - Hegira 1434: November 15
Rosh HaShana 5773: September 17	
Yom Kippur (Day of Atonement): September 26	
Succot (Feast of Tabernacles): October 2-7	
Simchat Torah (Rejoicing the Law): October 8	
Chanukah (Feast of the Light): December 9-14	

Source: Christian Information Centre (2011)

The simultaneous use of several calendars with moveable and unmovable feast days is a great managerial challenge for authorities, sites and visitors to Jerusalem. There are many rules regarding opening hours and days of major pilgrimage sites, and ordinary visitors to Jerusalem can find themselves in a feast, procession and celebration, or reach a site that they are unable to enter because of the multiplicity of calendars. Ordinary guide books are unable to handle these issues adequately because of the complexity of the issue and because of what may be called the 'last minute effect'. This term, particularly relevant in the context of Islam, refers to the fact that because the Muslim calendar is lunar, some final holiday dates and calendar details may be provided only the evening or mere hours before a proposed visit because of the reliance on eye witnesses. For example, the exact day that a certain Muslim holiday is celebrated in Jerusalem can be advanced or delayed by one day, depending on the first sighting of the lunar crescent in Jerusalem (Reiter, 2013), or in competing Muslim centers of hegemony such as Mecca (Trawicky, 2000) or Cairo (Praise, 2002).

The main implication for tourism is the impossibility for long-term planning. Because of the uncertainty of feast days visitors are often forced to 'go with the flow' and change their original plans. Another implication involves effective crowd management through the streets of the Old City, particularly on days or weeks of popular feast days such as Easter and Christmas. At the same time, rather than having large crowds for one Easter week, because of the calendar differences there are two Easter weeks for Catholics and Orthodox Christians respectively. The Pentecost and Assumption feast days also illustrate the differences in these two religious calendars.

Religious heritage site management in Jerusalem

The foregoing discussion has focused on some of the broader issues in Jerusalem with regard to tourism development and management. However, each sacred site within Jerusalem deals with its own complex management issues that arise because of both the spatial and temporal variations of visitors to those sites and the contested nature of Jerusalem as whole. While there are hundreds of sacred sites that could be selected to be discussed in this section, the following focuses on the management issues at four of the larger and more popular pilgrimage/tourist attractions in Jerusalem: the Temple Mount, the Western Wall, the Church of the Holy Sepulchre, and the Garden Tomb. These sites will be discussed in the context of the internal and external managerial challenges site managers face in the midst of pilgrim and tourist visitation.

Temple Mount

The Temple Mount is probably the most important and contested site in Old Jerusalem, with all three Abrahamic religions viewing this site as sacred. In Judaism, the site is important because it is where Solomon's temple was built (957 BCE) and then later rebuilt after its destruction by Zerubbabel in 516 BCE. Within these temples lay the Holy of Holies, where Jews believe God's divine presence dwelt and still dwells today (Isaiah 8:18). For Muslims, the Temple Mount (better known as Har a Sharif) is where the prophet Muhammad ascended into heaven as a part of his Night Journey in 621 AD, when he travelled from Mecca to Jerusalem and from Jerusalem into heaven, and then back to Mecca within the space of a few hours. In addition, Jerusalem was the place toward which Muslims turned in prayer, prior to Muhammed changing the direction of the prayers towards Mecca. While the Temple Mount is important for Christians because of its association with the activities of Jesus Christ during his ministry, the site does not play an important role in Christian theology or practice, with the exception of the belief by some Christians that the Third Jewish Temple will be built there prior to the Second Coming of Jesus Christ (Gonen, 2003).

Presently there are two main buildings on the site: the Al-Aqsa Mosque in the southwest corner of the Temple Mount, and the Dome of the Rock in the northern portion of the site. The site itself is controlled by a Muslim Waqf or Islamic trust that controls the entrance into the Temple Mount as well as the buildings on the site. While Muslim visitors are welcome to enter the site and the buildings at any time, non-Muslim visitors are only allowed to enter the site from one gate, and even then they can only visit the site on certain days and at certain times of the day in between Muslim prayers. In addition, while the Temple Mount Waqf is willing to share access to the Temple Mount with visitors, they must adhere to a certain code of conduct. For example, Christian visitors are welcome to the site as long as they not bring Bibles with them, do not pray, worship or consume alcohol while on-site, and must dress modestly (see Figure 1). While Jewish visitors are also welcome as long as they follow the same rules, Jewish law stipulates that Jews are not permitted to enter the Temple Mount in case they inadvertently walk through the Holy of Holies, where, as noted above, God's divine presence is still present. Therefore, the Chief Rabbinate of Israel has erected signs around the entrance to the Temple Mount to warn Jewish visitors of this religious stipulation (see Figure 2). These conditions, coupled with the fact that only Muslims are allowed into the Dome of the Rock and the Al-Aqsa Mosque, can cause frustration among visitors who have travelled a long distance to visit the site, only to be turned away because of special Muslim feast days or prayer times, or are denied access to the buildings at the site or are not allowed onto the site because of religious prohibitions or lack of appropriately modest attire.

Figure 1: Tourists wanting to enter the Temple Mount are asked to cover up because they are not modestly dressed by Muslim standards. Photo credit: Amos Ron

Figure 2: A sign outlining the Jewish law prohibiting Jews from entering the Temple Mount. Photo credit: Amos Ron

In addition to these challenges, there is also the issue of crowd management during the four Fridays of the month of Ramadan (the ninth month of the Islamic calendar), when approximately 250,000 Muslims come to this site to attend prayers. Not only does this affect crowd management at the site but also throughout the entire old city of Jerusalem. Another management issue concerns difficulties with site maintenance. For example, some technical or maintenance issues may require Jews to come onto the site to fix these problems. Not only do these Jewish workers have to enter from a particular gate and only during particular hours, but, if they are a practicing religious Jews, can only walk around the circumference of the site in order to avoid stepping on the site of the holy of holies. This then raises the question of how any technical or maintenance issues can be fixed, demonstrating how seemingly simple things can become difficult and complex in this setting.

Western Wall

The Western Wall (also known as the Wailing Wall) in Jerusalem is the most recognized and important religious site in modern Judaism. The Wall is a remnant of a wall that was part of an expansion of the Second Temple by Herod the Great around 19 BCE. Today, the Western Wall today serves as "a symbol embodying the memory of the destruction of the Holy Temple, the Jewish Diaspora, and the yearning for a return to Zion" (Cohen-Hattab, 2010: 136).

The site is multi-functional, in that it serves as a holy site, a historical landmark, an archaeological site, and a tourist attraction (Cohen-Hattab, 2010). The Western Wall is the holiest site in all of Judaism, and serves as a substitute for the Second Temple: a sacred space where Jewish men and women come to pray, swear oaths (*nedarim*), make requests, and place notes or supplications between the stones of the Wall to increase their chances of their requests being granted by God (Collins-Kreiner, 2010). The Western Wall is therefore the central sacred site for Judaism, and as such is the most anticipated holy site that Jewish pilgrims from around the world seek to visit (Cohen, 2006). The Western Wall also serves as a place that embodies the historical and national ideologies of Israel, with military inductions, Memorial Day services, and national prayer ceremonies taking place at the Wall (Cohen-Hattab, 2010). Archaeological digs are present at certain areas of the Wall, with the Israel Antiquities Authority engaging in both archaeological and aesthetic projects along the Wall with the aim of both learning about the history of the site and enhancing displaying any ancient archaeological findings for religious and tourist consumption (Greenberg, 2009). Tourists, as noted previously, also visit the Western Wall in large numbers.

The Western Wall site (see Figure 3) is managed by the Ministry of Religious Services, in much the same way as a Jewish Orthodox synagogue. For example, according to mainstream Jewish custom, during prayer men and women must be separated by a wall or a curtain. This is for a variety of reasons, including the need to focus on prayer. Therefore, at the Western Wall there is a separation of male and female prayer spaces (see Figure 4). The existing separation of men's and women's worship spaces is uneven, in that the women's prayer space is much smaller and lacks shade, whereas the men's prayer space is much larger and is partly shaded. In addition, there are strict rules as to what constitutes modest dress, particularly for women, much like at an Orthodox synagogue.

Figure 3: Tourists, pilgrims, and worshippers in front of the Western Wall. The structure to the right of the wall is the ramp where visitors to the Temple mount climb. Photo credit: Amos Ron

Figure 4: The separation wall between men's and women's worship space. Photo credit: Daniel Olsen

These religious prescriptions can impact on the experiences of non-Orthodox Jews and non-Jewish visitors to the Western Wall, as visitors have to adhere to these same religious standards. If couples, families, and groups wish to touch the Western Wall they must separate from each other on the basis of gender and enter either the male or female side of the partition before approaching to the Wall. Furthermore, guards throughout the site enforce certain modesty standards, such as covering bear arms and legs. While guards offer wrap-around skirts for women visitors who are in shorts, cardboard yarmulkes or skullcaps for visiting men, and shawls and wraps for both genders who are deemed to be dressed immodestly, anyone either unwilling or unable to comply with the required modesty standards are asked to leave the site.

This surveillance of the site also extends to the behavior of visitors on the Jewish Sabbath. Because of the sanctity of the Jewish Sabbath and the special worship services that take place at the Wall, visitors are asked to observe particular behavioral standards when entering the site on that day, including no smoking, taking of photographs, or using of cell phones (see Figure 5). Even with the presence of these signs, there are special 'Sabbath Inspectors' who enforce these special rules.

Figure 5: A sign outside the Western Wall Plaza that lists the behavioural rules of the site. Photo credit: Daniel Olsen

Other management challenges at the Western Wall include ensuring people can quickly get through security checkpoints as they enter the site, maintaining zoning boundaries between prayer areas and archaeological excavations, and limited parking spaces and shade at the site. With regard to the lack of shade, while there are indoor areas in the men's and women's sections of the wall, the Plaza itself is lacks permanent shading. This lack of vegetation is due to the scriptural injunction in Deuteronomy 16:21 which reads, "Thou shalt not plant thee an Asherah of any kind of tree beside the altar of the Lord thy God, which thou shalt make thee". As can be seen in Figure 3 above, temporary shade can be set up at the site: however these shelters are generally set up during special ceremonies rather than for tourists.

One other important management challenge relates to conflicts within Judaism, particularly regarding women reading from the Torah at the Wall. Sharkansky (2000: 231; see also Raday, 2009) summarizes this conflict well:

> "The issue of religious freedom is perhaps most stark in the case of non-Orthodox Jewish movements that want to perform their rituals at the Western Wall. In practice this is likely to mean prayers involving men and women together, with or without women carrying the Torah and reading from it. … The [Supreme] court has ruled that women should receive police protection for their prayers at the Western Wall on condition that they refrain from reading from the Torah and wearing prayer shawls."

There have been increasing calls for non-Orthodox prayers spaces at the Wall. However, that would include a mixing of men and women praying in the same space (e.g. Charmé, 2005; Cohen-Hattab, 2010), which has increased management tensions at the Wall regarding what types of activities and behaviors are considered out-of-place.

Church of the Holy Sepulchre

The Church of the Holy Sepulchre (also known as the Basilica of the Holy Sepulchre or the Church of the Resurrection) is located in the Christian Quarter of the Old City of Jerusalem, and has been an important Christian pilgrimage site since the fourth century. This site is accepted by most Christian groups (with the exception of some Protestants, Anglicans and Mormons, who prefer the Garden Tomb as an alternative; see below) to be the site where Jesus Christ was crucified (Golgotha or Calvary), buried (the Sepulchre), and resurrected.

The site itself is controlled by a number of Christian groups. According to the 1852 'Status Quo' agreement, the three dominant Christian groups in Jerusalem at the time – the Eastern Orthodox, Armenian Apostolic, and Roman Catholic Churches – were given different 'possessory rights' over the property, upon which temporary and spatially regulated rights of usage (superimposed over these 'possessory rights') were given to other Christian groups, including the Syrian Orthodox, the Coptic Orthodox, and the Ethiopian Orthodox (Bowman, 2011). This has given rise to various chapels and altars, and a diversity of architectural styles within the Church itself. Furthermore, in terms of management, the spatial division of the site among these various Christian denominations is highly contested, with each group protectively guarding the invisible lines that mark their territory. As such, any changes to the interior of the site must be agreed upon by every religious group, as occasional clashes between religious groups do occur over real or perceived transgressions when one group does something to upset the spatial status quo (Cohen, 2008). For example, in 2004 a fistfight broke out when a door to the Franciscan chapel was left open during the Orthodox celebration of a procession to mark the discovery of the True Cross (the Exaltation of the Holy Cross), which was seen by Orthodox Christians as a sign of disrespect (Fischer-Ilan, 2004).

With regard to the Church itself, the most important areas of the Church relate to the events of Jesus' crucifixion, death, burial and resurrection. In front of the entrance to the Church lies the Stone of Unction (also known as the Stone of Anointing or the Rock of Embalmment), a limestone slab which marks the spot where the body of Jesus was prepared for burial, with a mosaic depicting Christ's anointing for burial directly on the wall behind the slab. This site is controlled by the Armenian Apostolic, Coptic Orthodox, Greek Orthodox and Roman Catholic Churches, each of which has contributed to the construction of the lamps that hang over the Stone of Unction (see Figure 6). To the right of the entrance and up a narrow flight of stairs lies Golgotha (or Calvary). A lavish altar has been placed by the Greek Orthodox Church in front of the Rock of Calvary (see Figure 7). Glass windows on either side of the altar allow visitors to see the Rock, and beneath the altar is a place that allows visitors to touch the Rock itself. This location under the altar is also believed to be the place where the original cross was placed. As such, many visitors crawl underneath the altar to both touch the Rock and pray at the feet of where Jesus was crucified.

Figure 6: The Stone of Unction. Photo credit: Amos Ron

Figure 7: Golgotha inside the Church of the Holy Sepulchre. Photo credit: Amos Ron

The focal point of the Church is the Sepulchre or Tomb of Christ (see Figure 8). Contained within the Rotunda or Anastasis (a dome-like structure), the Sepulchre is housed within a larger shrine, which is then housed within a box-like structure known as the Edicule, which, although very unappealing considering the other ornate decorations throughout the Church, provides support for the shrine in the event of earthquakes. Within the shrine is the Chapel of the Angel, which contains a piece of the stone the angel rolled away from the entrance of the Sepulchre, and the Chapel of the Holy Sepulchre, which contains the Tomb of Christ. The Armenian Apostolic, Roman Catholic and Greek Orthodox Churches hold a daily Liturgy or religious ceremony within the Sepulchre.

Figure 8: Lighting candles by the Sepulchre. Photo Credit: Amos Ron

Outside of the inter-faith 'turf war' (Bowman, 2011), a number of management issues can be found at this site. For example, the entrance to the Church itself is found on the south side of the Church. The entrance is very small, as is the courtyard where visitors wishing to enter the Church must wait (see Figure 9). Therefore, the logistics of handling visitor flows to and from the Church are difficult, and congestion is common in this courtyard as well as inside the Church itself, particularly on special holidays or when religious celebrations occur. At these times, thousands of visitors wish to enter the Church. In the courtyard there is also no shade, which can be problematic when large crowds sometimes have to wait for hours to get into the Church. In addition, there is no parking available near the site, so tour buses are required to park a fair distance away. Furthermore, because of the diverse nature of visitors, providing for the various spiritual and religious interpretational needs can be difficult at this site. There is also a lack of security, even though, as shown in Figure 10, armored bins can be found nearby in the event of suspicious objects being found on the premises. Finally, with three Liturgies taking place throughout the day in the Sepulchre, there can be long delays for visitors who wish to enter the Sepulchre.

Figure 9: Entrance to the Church of the Sepulchre. Photo credit: Amos Ron

Figure 10: An armored bin outside of the entrance of the Church of the Holy Sepulchre for suspicious objects. Photo credit: Amos Ron

The Garden Tomb

In contrast with the Church of the Holy Sepulchre, the Garden Tomb, located just north of the Old City, by the Damascus Gate, has since the eighteenth century been favored by Evangelical Protestants and Anglicans, along with Latter-day Saints (or Mormons), to be the location of Jesus' crucifixion, burial and resurrection. During the nineteenth century, doubts began to arise about the authenticity of the Church of the Holy Sepulchre as Jesus' place of death and resurrection. During this time, General Charles Gordon (1883) came to Jerusalem and proposed that it was this site, rather than the Church of the Holy Sepulchre, where Jesus Christ had died and been resurrected. Believed by others to be the garden and sepulchre of Joseph of Arimathea, this site today encompasses what is believed to be both the Hill of the Skull (Golgotha) and the 'rolling stone' burial tomb (see Figures 11 and 12).

Figure 11: Golgotha, also known as the Hill of the Skull. Photo credit: Daniel Olsen

Figure 12: Tourists having their picture taken while waiting to enter the Garden Tomb. Photo credit: Daniel Olsen

The Garden site itself has been controlled since 1894 by a charitable trust called The Garden Tomb (Jerusalem) Association, which is based in the UK. Comprised of a board of persons from various denominations, this Association does not claim that the site is indeed where Jesus was crucified and buried. However, because over time the site has become a focus of popular Protestant piety, the mission of the Association is to create a tranquil location for visitors to reflect upon the death and resurrection of Jesus Christ. To accomplish this, the site is not only enclosed by a wall to dampen the noise of the city, but also has been developed into a garden setting, including numerous small enclaves with park benches and trees to provide shade and privacy for groups wishing to hold worship services or religious discussions at the site (see Figure 13). Bajc (2006) suggests that Christian tour guides prefer to take their groups to the Garden Tomb rather than the Church of the Holy Sepulchre because of the private and shady places within the site as well as the absence of overcrowding. In addition to these private garden settings, the site also contains multilingual signs to cater to the interpretational needs of a diversity of visitor linguistic backgrounds.

Figure 13: Spaces for worship at the Garden Tomb designed to separate groups. Photo Credit: Amos Ron

Even so, as with the other sites mentioned above, management issues do arise. For example, while the walls do insulate the site from much of the noise of the surrounding city, the bus station next door is very loud and can distract from the peaceful atmosphere of the site. While the multilingual signs are an important interpretational tool, difficulties can arise in attempting to meet the diverse spiritual needs of visitors. As well, being a charitable trust, the expenses and time commitment regarding grden maintenance can place a burden on the resources of the Association, in part because there are no entrance fees to the site. However, site managers attempt to overcome this budgetary problem in three ways: there is a book store at the site; groups are reminded that giving money is optional yet welcomed; and volunteers are heavily relied upon in order to save salary costs.

Conclusions

Managing religious heritage sites at any scale – from the single site to the holy city – can be a daunting task because of all the managerial, budgetary, and ministerial issues that need to be considered and dealt with. Jerusalem, as noted earlier, is in a unique managerial position as it is sacred to three religious faiths, each of which control and maintain a variety of religious heritage sites. Furthermore, Jerusalem as a holy city has always been a difficult heritage destination to manage because of the emotion the city evokes in the hearts and minds of people around the world, particularly among adherents to Christianity, Judaism and Islam and their political backers (Efrat and Noble, 1988). While the holy places of Jerusalem have contributed to the overall economic vitality of the city, the conflicts and disputes over the city as a whole, as well as within many of its sacred sites, has contributed to the deterioration of the city, This has included increased segregation of its inhabitants and a division within the social fabric of Jerusalem (Khamaisi, 2010).

This case has explored the difficulties that arise with regards to tourism management in such a situation, both at a city level and at the site level. While the Old City of Jerusalem acts as a quasi 'tourism business district', of a kind that is common in larger urban areas like Las Vegas, Nevada, and Niagara Falls, Ontario (Getz, 1993), tourists from different religions will have different temporal and spatial patterns of movement, along with different spiritual and practical needs, that must all be accounted for in any tourism management plan. In fact, management difficulties can be exacerbated due to presence of both tourists and pilgrims, each of whom will have differing motivations and expectations regarding why they are visiting and the experiences they want to have while visiting the site (Olsen, 2012).

With continual conflicts in this area, particularly between Jews and Palestinians regarding Jerusalem as their eternal capital city, much of this conflict will probably continue into the near future. However, in understanding the management issues at different scales, city and site managers can be proactive in preserving the integrity of their religious heritage sites in the face of ever increasing numbers of visitors to Jerusalem.

References

Albin C. 2005. Explaining conflict transformation: How Jerusalem became negotiable. *Cambridge Review of International Affairs* **18** (3): 339-355.

Azaryahu M. 1999. McDonald's or Golani Junction? A case of a contested place in Israel. *The Professional Geographer* **51** (4): 481–92.

Bajc V. 2006. Christian pilgrimage groups in Jerusalem: Framing the experience through linear meta-narrative. *Journeys* **7** (2): 101-128.

Belhassen Y. 2006. An American evangelical pilgrimage to Israel: A case study on politics and triangulation. *Journal of Travel Research* **44** (4): 431-441.

Belhassen Y. 2009. Fundamentalist Christian pilgrimages as a political and cultural force. *Journal of Heritage Tourism* **4** (2): 131-144.

Belhassen Y, Ebel J. 2009. Tourism, faith and politics in the holy land: An ideological analysis of evangelical pilgrimage. *Current Issues in Tourism* **12** (4): 359-378.

Bowman G. 1992. The politics of tour guiding: Israeli and Palestinian guides in Israel and the occupied territories. In Harrison D (ed.) *Tourism and the Less Developed Countries*. London: Halsted Press; 121-134.

Bowman G. 2011. "In dubious battle on the Plains of Heav'n": The politics of possession in Jerusalem's Holy Sepulchre. *History and Anthropology* **22** (3): 371-399.

Brin E. 2006. Politically oriented tourism in Jerusalem. *Tourist Studies* **6** (3): 215-243.

Brin E, Noy C. 2010. The said and the unsaid: Performative guiding in a Jerusalem neighbourhood. *Tourist Studies* **10** (1): 19-33.

Charmé S. 2005. The political transformation of gender traditions at the Western Wall in Jerusalem. *Journal of Feminist Studies in Religion* **21** (1): 5-34.

Orthodox Wiki. (n.d.) *Church calendar*. http://orthodoxwiki.org/Church_Calendar

Christian Information Centre. 2011. *Christian, Jewish and Moslem Feasts, 2011-2012*. http://www.cicts.org/default.asp?id=446

Cohen EH. 2006. Religious tourism as an educational experience. In Timothy DJ, Olsen DH (eds) *Tourism, Religion and Spiritual Journeys*. Oxford: Routledge; 78-93.

Cohen R. 2008. *Saving the Holy Sepulchre: How Rival Christians Came Together to Rescue Their Holiest Shrine*. New York: Oxford University Press.

Cohen-Hattab K. 2004. Zionism, tourism, and the battle for Palestine: Tourism as a political-propaganda tool. *Israel Studies* **9** (1): 61-85.

Cohen-Hattab K. 2010. Struggles at holy sites and their outcomes: The evolution of the Western Wall plaza in Jerusalem. *Journal of Heritage Tourism* **5** (2): 125-139.

Collins-Kreiner N. 2010. Current Jewish pilgrimage tourism: Modes and models of development. *Tourism* **58** (3): 259-270.

Collins-Kreiner N, Kilot N, Mansfeld Y, Sagi K. 2006. *Christian Tourism to the Holy Land: Pilgrimage during Security Crisis*. Aldershot: Ashgate.

Doggett LE. 2012. *Calendars*. http://astro.nmsu.edu/~lhuber/leaphist.html

Efrat E, Noble AG. 1988. Planning Jerusalem. *Geographical Review* **78** (4): 387-404.

Feldman J. 2007. Constructing a shared Bible land: Jewish Israeli guiding performances for Protestant pilgrims. *American Ethnologist* **34** (2): 351-374.

Fischer-Ilan A. 2004. Punch-up at tomb of Jesus. http://www.guardian.co.uk/world/2004/sep/28/israel.religion

Getz D. 1993. Planning for tourism business districts. *Annals of Tourism Research* **20** (3): 583-600.

Gonen R. 2003. *Contested Holiness: Jewish, Muslim and Christian Perspectives on the Temple Mount in Jerusalem*. Jersey City: KTAV.

Greenberg R. 2009. Towards an inclusive archaeology in Jerusalem: The case of Silwan/The City of David. *Public Archaeology* **8** (1): 35-50.

Hercbergs D. 2009. *Narratives in a Divided City: Childhood and Memory in Jerusalem, 1948-2008*. PhD Dissertation, University of Pennsylvania.

Hercbergs D. 2012. Narrating instability: Political detouring in Jerusalem. *Mobilities* **7** (3): 415-438.

Higgins-Desbiolles F. n.d. *Living Stones and Dead Children: Palestine and the Politics of Tourism*. http://www.scottishpalestinianforum.org.uk/SPF/Visit_Palestine_files/Living%20stones%20and%20Dead%20Children.pdf

Israel Central Bureau of Statistics. 2012. *Tourism 2012*.

Israeli Y, Mansfeld Y. 2003. Transportation accessibility to and within tourist attractions in the Old City of Jerusalem. *Tourism Geographies* **5** (4): 461-481.

Khamaisi R. 2010. Holy places in urban spaces: foci of confrontation or catalyst for development? In Breger MJ, Reiter Y, Hammer L (eds) *Holy Places in the Israeli-Palestinian Conflict: Confrontation and Co-Existence*. Oxford: Routledge; 1-19.

McKelvie J. 2005. Religious tourism. *Travel & Tourism Analyst* **4**: 1-47.

Morinis A. 1992. Introduction: The territory of the anthropology of pilgrimage. In Morinis A (ed.) *Sacred Journeys: The Anthropology of Pilgrimage*. Westport: Greenwood Press; 1-28.

Nitzan-Shiftan A. 2005. Capital city or spiritual center? The politics of architecture in post-1967 Jerusalem. *Cities* **22** (3): 229-240.

Nitzan-Shiftan A. 2011. Frontier Jerusalem: The Holy Land as a testing ground for urban design. *The Journal of Architecture* **16** (6): 915-940.

Noy C. 2011. The political ends of tourism: Voices and narratives of Silwan/the City of David in East Jerusalem. In Ateljevic I, Morgan N, Pritchard A. (eds) *The Critical Turn in Tourism Studies: Creating an Academy of Hope*. Amsterdam: Elsevier; 27-41.

Noy C. 2012. Narratives and counter-narratives: Contesting a tourist site in Jerusalem. In Tivers J, Rakic T (eds) *Narratives of Travel and Tourism*. Aldershot; Ashgate; 135-150.

Olsen DH. 2003. Heritage, tourism, and the commodification of religion. *Tourism Recreation Research* **28** (3): 99-104.

Olsen DH. 2006. Management issues for religious heritage attractions. In Timothy DJ, Olsen DH. (eds) *Tourism, Religion and Spirituality*. London and New York. Routledge; 104-118.

Olsen DH. 2013. Teaching truth in 'third space': The use of history as a pedagogical instrument at Temple Square in Salt Lake City, Utah. *Tourism Recreation Research* **37** (3): 227-238.

Olsen DH, Guelke JK. 2004. Spatial transgression and the BYU Jerusalem Center controversy. *The Professional Geographer* **56** (4): 503-515.

Olsen DH, Timothy DJ. 1999. Tourism 2000: Selling the millennium. *Tourism Management* **20** (4): 389-392.

O'Mahony A. 2005. The Vatican, Jerusalem, the State of Israel, and Christianity in the Holy Land. *International Journal for the Study of the Christian Church* **5** (2): 123-146.

Parise F. 2002. *The Book of Calendars*. New York: Gorgias Press.

Raday F. 2009. Human Rights and the confrontation between religious and constitutional authority: A case study of Israel's Supreme Court. In Kosmin BA, Keysar A (eds) *Secularism, Women and the State: The Mediterranean World in the 21st Century*. Hartford: Institute for the Study of Secularism in Society and Culture; 213-240.

Reiter Y. 2013. Personal Communication, March 7.

Richter LK, Waugh JR. 1986. Terrorism and tourism as logical companions. *Tourism Management* **7** (4): 230-238.

Ron AS. Forthcoming. Gardens and sustainable sacred site management in Christianity: The Case of the Mt. of Beatitudes and the Garden Tomb.

Shackley M. 2001. *Managing Sacred Sites: Service Provision and Visitor Experience*. London: Continuum.

Shapiro FL. 2008. To the apple of God's eye: Christian Zionist travel to Israel. *Journal of Contemporary Religion* **23** (3): 307-320.

Sharkansky I. 2000. *The Politics of Religion and the Religion of Politics: Looking at Israel*. Lanham: Lexington Books.

Shaw J. 2000. Ayodhya's sacred landscape: Ritual memory, politics and archaeological 'fact'. *Antiquity* **74** (285): 693-700.

Trawicky B. 2000. *Anniversaries & Holidays*. 5th Ed. Chicago: American Library Association.

Wilkinson J. 1998. Search of holy places: Then and now. In Fladmark JM (ed.) *Search of Heritage as Pilgrim or Tourist?* Shaftesbury: Donhead; 14-24.

Wisenberg E. 1970. Jewish calendar. In Preece WE (ed.) *Encylopaedia Britannica*, Chicago: William Benton, Vol. 3; 623-625.

Woodward SC. 2004. Faith and tourism: Planning tourism in relation to places of worship. *Tourism and Hospitality Planning and Development* **1** (2): 173–186.

Yeoh B, Kong L. 1996. The notion of place in the construction of history, nostalgia and heritage in Singapore. *Singapore Journal of Tropical Geography* **17** (1): 52-65.

Ziade NA. 1970. Muslim calendar. In Preece WE (ed.) *Encylopaedia Britannica*, Chicago: William Benton, Vol. 3; 626.

Ancillary Student Material

Further reading

Breger MJ, Reiter Y, Hammer L. (eds). 2010. *Holy Places in the Israeli-Palestinian Conflict: Confrontation and Co-Existence*. Oxford and New York: Routledge.

Clarke R. 2000. Self-representation in a contested city: Palestinian and Israeli political tourism in Hebron. *Anthropology Today* **16** (5): 12-18.

Epstein AD, Kheimets NG. 2001. Looking for Pontius Pilate's footprints near the Western Wall: Russian Jewish tourists in Jerusalem. *Tourism, Culture and Communication* **3**: 37-46.

Hassner RE. 2003. "To have and to hold": Conflicts over sacred space and the problem of indivisibility. *Security Studies* **12** (4): 1-33.

Noonan FT. 2007. *The Road to Jerusalem: Pilgrimage and Travel in the Age of Discovery*. Philadelphia: University of Pennsylvania Press.

Poria Y, Butler R, Airey D. 2003. Tourism, religion and religiosity: A holy mess. *Current Issues in Tourism* **6** (4): 340-363.

Singh, RPB. 2008. The Contestation of heritage: The enduring importance of religion. In Graham BJ, Howard P. (eds) *The Ashgate Research Companion to Heritage and Identity*. Farnham: Ashgate; 125-141.

Stein RL. 1998. National itineraries, itinerant nations: Israeli tourism and Palestinian cultural production. *Social Text* **56** (3): 91-124.

Triantafillidow A, Koritos C, Chatzipanagiotou K, Vassilikopoulou A. 2010. Pilgrimage: The 'promised land' for travel agents? *International Journal of Contemporary Hospitality Management* **22** (3): 382-398.

Related websites and audio-visual material

3D Virtual Tours of Israel: 3D Israel: http://www.3disrael.com/jerusalem

Floor plan of the Church of the Holy Sepulchre: Sacred Destinations: http://www. sacred-destinations.com/israel/jerusalem-church-of-holy-sepulchre-plan

Jerusalem – Israel Ministry of Tourism: http://www.goisrael.com/Tourism_Eng/ Pages/home.aspx

Live Kotel Cam, Western Wall: http://english.thekotel.org/cameras.asp

Old City of Jerusalem and its Walls: *UNESCO:* http://whc.unesco.org/en/list/148

The Garden Tomb, Jerusalem: www.gardentomb.com

Self-test questions

Try to answer the following questions to test your knowledge and understanding. If you are not sure of the answers they please refer to the suggested references and further reading sources:

1   Why are religious heritage sites such popular tourist attractions?

2   What are some of the management problems at religious heritage sites?

3   What makes the case study of Jerusalem particularly relevant when considering the issue of religious heritage management? In what ways and at what scales is Jerusalem contested?

4   How does the issue of different religious calendars add to the complexities of managing religious tourism in Jerusalem?

5   What are the common managerial issues that arise in the four site case studies (the Temple Mount, the Western Wall, the Church of the Holy Sepulchre, and the Garden Tomb)?

6   How do you think the competing stakeholders in Jerusalem can best resolve the management issues at their religious heritage sites?

Key themes and theories

The key themes raised in this case study relate to the following areas:

◆   Impact of tourism visitation at religious heritage sites

◆   Management issues at religious heritage sites

◆   Competing visions and ideologies in relation to tourism management decisions

The key theories relate to:

◆   The growth of tourism to religious heritage sites

◆   Motivations for religious travel

◆   Micro- and macro-scale management issues at religious heritage sites

◆   The role of religion in contesting heritage sites and religious space

If you need further information on the above themes and theories, the headings could be used as key words to search for materials and case studies.

6

Indigenous Tourism and Heritage

A Māori Case Study

Ashley R. Puriri and Alison J. McIntosh

Introduction

Indigenous culture often forms an important part of a country's heritage, and in many destination countries, aspects of indigenous culture have become significant attractions for tourists. 'Indigenous tourism' refers to "tourism activities in which indigenous people are directly involved, either through control and/or by having their culture serves as the essence of an attraction" (Butler and Hinch, 2007: 5). While indigenous peoples[1], such as the Māori of New Zealand and Aboriginal people of Australia, are distinct from each another in terms of their social and cultural identities (see Butler and Hinch, 2007), indigenous cultures can generally be depicted as comprising elements of both 'tangible' and 'intangible' heritage. Intangible cultural heritage comprises forms such as folklore, cultural practices and expressions, language, cultural knowledge, skills, oral traditions, performing arts, festivals and events, and traditional craftsmanship. It is transmitted from one generation to the next and is fundamental in perpetuating the sense of identity of the culture concerned. Tangible heritage, meanwhile, refers to the physical environment and places of significance to a culture, including buildings, landscapes, monuments, cultural artefacts, books and works of art.

Much of the scholarly discussion on indigenous tourism centres on the range of opportunities and threats indigenous people may encounter if they choose to become involved in tourism. This case identifies the main motives and challenges for the involvement of indigenous peoples in tourism, and outlines the potential positive and negative impacts of tourism on indigenous

---

1   'Indigenous people' are commonly ethnic groups or communities whose origins are in a region or location, whose traditional cultures are distinct from the mainstream culture, and who have been affected by the processes of colonisation.

heritage and culture. It considers the involvement in tourism of the indigenous Māori people of New Zealand, drawing specifically on a case study of a particular Māori tourism operation, Taiamai Tours, to discuss issues of cultural authenticity and attitudes towards sustainability in the Māori tourism context. In particular, the case study identifies components of the tourism experience offered by Taiamai Tours that are considered culturally 'authentic' and explains why 'authenticity' is an issue of concern for Māori involvement in tourism. In addition, the case study identifies the most important factors that are perceived to achieve 'sustainable' Māori tourism from a Māori cultural view. The opportunities, challenges and contradictions of Māori tourism presented here pose important questions for the future development of tourism based on indigenous cultural heritage.

Indigenous tourism

Tourism is often viewed as a way to address the economic, social and cultural challenges facing many indigenous people, while at the same time preserving their cultural traditions. This strategy is considered to provide an opportunity for indigenous people to achieve economic independence and cultural empowerment, and to provide a source of unique experiences for international tourists. In this way, indigenous tourism is generally supported by governments as policy initiatives to address the needs of indigenous people[2]. In contrast to many other forms of commercial activity, appropriately managed tourism development is seen as a sustainable activity that is congruent with indigenous values towards the sanctity of the environment and indigenous people's relationship with it (Butler and Hinch, 2007). Indigenous culture is seen as a unique competitive marketing advantage (Notzke, 2004), while tourism is a form of cross-cultural interaction that is said to foster greater appreciation and understanding between indigenous and non-indigenous people. This can facilitate changes in attitudes and behaviours, leading to a more equitable relationship between indigenous and non-indigenous peoples (D'Amore, 1988).

Critics, however, argue that indigenous people seldom have control over tourism development and activity in their community: outside interests typically dominate in tourism development. Furthermore, as cultural identity serves as the basic resource for indigenous tourism attractions and marketing, some argue that such culture becomes modified as it is packaged and

---

2   In New Zealand, Te Puni Kōkiri (Ministry of Māori Development) is the principal adviser to the New Zealand government on policy affecting Māori wellbeing and development.

sold to tourists: it can become 'commodified', 'staged' or made 'inauthentic'; sometimes it is abandoned. This can cause the indigenous group involved to become 'stereotyped' and 'othered' in the media in general and in the tourism media in particular. As such, discussion of sustainable approaches to indigenous tourism development has gained popularity (Sofield, 2003). The investigations of sustainable[3] indigenous tourism often involve discussion of how the tourism operation can be infused with authentic cultural values and principles, rather than be dominated by Western economic ideology (McIntosh, Zygadlo and Matunga, 2004). In particular, there is an argument that indigenous people can be empowered to gain much greater involvement and control over the presentation of their culture and their resources, and thereby to correct misleading, incorrect or inappropriate images that may exist (Butler and Hinch, 2007). The ability of indigenous people to enter tourism business on their own terms and in their preferred way is thus essential for sustainable indigenous tourism.

While a sustainable approach to indigenous tourism is commonly proposed, the success rate of this approach is yet to be fully examined. This is important, especially as indigenous culture is often not a primary motivation for tourists to visit a destination, and many indigenous tourism enterprises remain vulnerable in relatively inaccessible areas and offered by people less well-versed in business and management techniques (McIntosh, 2004; Butler and Hinch, 2007). Meanwhile, governments worldwide continue to encourage indigenous tourism development, and private entrepreneurs in indigenous communities remain involved in tourism, especially in places where settlement of land claims has resulted in increasing indigenous control of traditional lands appropriate for tourism development. While indigenous cultures are all distinct from each other, and while there exist no definitive truths to be uncovered about indigenous tourism (Butler and Hinch, 2007), common challenges and strategies for indigenous tourism can be identified. In particular, there are important lessons to be learned with respect to issues of cultural authenticity and the pursuit of 'sustainable' indigenous tourism. These issues will next be illustrated in the specific context of the indigenous Māori people of New Zealand.

---

3   'Sustainable' indigenous tourism generally refers to tourism development that attempts to achieve a balance between commercial success, cultural integrity and social cohesion, and the maintenance of the physical/natural environment. It is commonly associated with developments over which the indigenous people have ownership and control.

Māori tourism in New Zealand

The number of indigenous Māori people of New Zealand choosing to participate in an active role in providing cultural tourism experiences as a product for New Zealand tourists is increasing (McIntosh and Ryan, 2007). Māori tourism is essentially seen as a potentially sustainable activity that can provide a symbiotic relationship between cultural survival and economic success. Due to limited research, there remains the challenge of clearly identifying the value, ranking and economic position that Māori tourism contributes to the New Zealand tourism industry. A Colmar Brunton (2004) report provides a definition of cultural tourism as being those dimensions that enable a more in-depth interaction with Māori people and gaining an understanding of places and cultural identity. Māori tourism according to the Colmar Brunton (2004) report includes Māori art exhibitions, exhibits of Māori history, sites of importance to Māori history, Māori cultural performances (those events that showcase the Māori way of life, including the 'Powhiri' or official welcome ceremony, the Haka, an ancestral war dance, and the Hangi, a traditional clay oven), Māori concerts (music and on-stage performances), Marae (a Māori traditional village) visits, including staying overnight on a Marae. According to Ministry of Tourism statistics, in 2008, 477,000 tourists participated in Māori cultural activities (see Table 1). The majority (76%) were international tourists. The most popular Māori cultural activity for international visitors was Māori cultural performances (experienced by 90% of all international Māori cultural tourists), followed by visiting Marae (30%). Conversely, less than 1% of all domestic tourists (excluding local residents) participated in Māori cultural activities while travelling in New Zealand.

Table 1: Trends in Māori Tourism, 2003-2008

	2003	2004	2005	2006	2007	2008
Māori cultural tourists:						
Total	552,000	482,100	557,400	626,900	529,200	477,000
International	360,000	423,100	471,800	449,100	422,000	361,600
Domestic	192,000	59,000	85,600	177,800	107,200	115,400
Propensity to participate in Māori cultural activities:						
International	18.9%	19.7%	21.5%	20.4%	18.8%	16.3%
Domestic	0.4%	0.1%	0.2%	0.4%	0.3%	0.3%

Source: International Visitor Survey and Domestic Travel Survey

The unique Māori cultural experiences that the Colmar Brunton (2004) report outlines are those which rely on the authenticity[4] of the Māori cultural

---

4   Cultural 'authenticity' reflects beliefs, values, attitudes and traditions that the members of the culture hold to be true.

experience. Ryan and Crotts (1997) argue that appreciating the authenticity in Māori tourism requires an understanding of Māori cosmology, epistemology and ontology[5]. Māori cosmology consists of a specific set of cultural values, principles and beliefs that coherently inform the Māori worldview. It is an intricate set of sensitive and inter-connected cultural elements that are essential principles that underpin the way Māori engage in their thinking process, discussions and planning. Māori ontology is infused with a complex tapestry of cultural beliefs that underpin the management of an authentic Māori cultural tourism experience. Māori ontology, according to Henare and Pene's (2001) paradigm of the Māori worldview, embraces cultural values of Māori cosmology, in which philosophies, theories, cultures, societal and religious elements are bound together by Wairua (spiritual life-force). Wairua is the central element of the Māori worldview insofar as ontology informs assumptions of human nature and for Māori people Wairua enables these assumptions to exist. From the Māori worldview, anything without a Wairua is considered insignificant and no longer to be. These dynamics are discussed by Awatere (2008), who argues that Māori ontology is based on the Mauri (life-force) of a being, and is positioned at the core of philosophical metaphysics. Māori ontology remains constant in that it has always underpinned Te Reo Māori me ōna Tikanga' (Māori language and customary rites).

Māori authenticity

Māori ontology is an essential element of the authenticity of a Māori tourism cultural experience. Ryan and Aiken (2005) argue that there will be some cultural trade-offs or compromises that Māori tourism operators will have had to make in order to cater for the demands of tourists when providing a Tūturu (authentic) Māori cultural experience. This is when the representation of an authentic Māori cultural experience or activity has not been modified, altered or artificially represented. With regard to past research on Māori tourism operators, Mahuta (1987), Poharama (1998) and McIntosh, Hinch and Ingram (2000) suggest that while Māori tourism providers have applied some aesthetic compromise to buildings, infrastructure and costumes, these changes have not impugned the Wairua (spirituality) of the experience and the intention to provide the best for their Manuhiri (arriving visitors) has remained at the forefront of the decision to make these changes.

Tūturu tānga (authenticity) is an imperative aspect of authenticity for Māori. Indeed, more Māori people are choosing to engage and develop cultural tourism experiences that embrace and reflect a more Tūturu or authentic

---

5   This term refers to how Māori people culturally view the world.

Māori cultural experience. This is achieved by culturally integrating and applying beliefs and methods of their Iwi Tikanga (tribal practices) within their business philosophies. These may not be aligned or consistent with the ideals indicated by the strategies and visions outlined by Tourism New Zealand. To achieve Tuturu Tānga or authenticity, Māori tourism operators have adopted the following practices:

◆ The use of authentic traditional costumes.

◆ Building a Marae to host visitors.

◆ The application of Tā Moko (tattoos) by key role-playing presenters.

◆ The use of traditional Taiaha and other traditional weapons during displays.

◆ The telling of local stories in Te Reo Māori (Māori language).

◆ Taking tourists to places of traditional and historical significance.

Māori sustainability

From a Māori worldview, the concept of sustainability takes on a very different perspective in comparison to a Western commercial business model of sustainability. Sustainability in a Western worldview usually has economic sustainability as a key priority. For the Māori, however, economic sustainability is not a primary goal, nor is it the sole driver of sustainability that a Māori tourism business would aim to maintain when planning and when engaging in decision making. In addition to developing economic strategies, Spiller (2010) indicates that Māori tourism operators are also faced with ensuring that their business strategies incorporate relevant spiritual, social, cultural and environmental issues. Māori tourism entrepreneurs believe that business is not about the profiteering of money at all. Rather, it is about looking after the 'Taonga' (precious resources) that they have been entrusted with as guardians to care for and to ensure that they are sustainably replenished; this includes the value that Māori place on their Manuhiri (visitors). Māori cosmology underpins the method through which Māori view the world and effectively make decisions. The key elements of Māori cosmology can be viewed as the spiral of principles (see Figure 1). The spiral of principles demonstrates a set of indigenous principles that interact with each other systematically and have a Whakapapa (genealogy) that interlink Māori into day-to-day thinking. This is a Māori cultural sociological model and it is important to understand that, for a Māori-owned tourism business, sustainability requires them to consider a wider range of cultural factors when strategically planning a sustainable business.

Spirals of principles

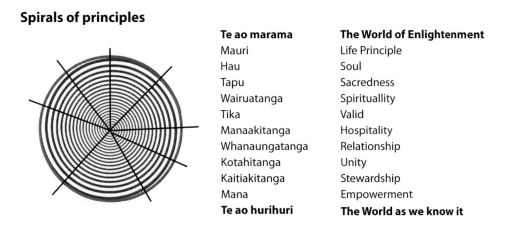

Te ao marama	The World of Enlightenment
Mauri	Life Principle
Hau	Soul
Tapu	Sacredness
Wairuatanga	Spirituallity
Tika	Valid
Manaakitanga	Hospitality
Whanaungatanga	Relationship
Kotahitanga	Unity
Kaitiakitanga	Stewardship
Mana	Empowerment
Te ao hurihuri	**The World as we know it**

Figure 1: Spiral of Māori principles. *Source:* Les and Manuka (2009)

In additional to meeting challenges of sustaining cultural authenticity, Māori tourism businesses are challenged to survive economically. Balancing these two diverse outcomes has proven difficult as many of these businesses struggle to survive past five years. According to quantitative research in the Colmar Brunton (2004) report many Māori tourism businesses self-terminate within the first five-year term. As such, sustainability is a rising concern for the entrepreneur of a Māori tourism business, especially when survival in a competitive environment increasingly requires management skills to be applied in the implementation of a strategy and the fundamentals of business requirements.

Challenges and contradictions of Māori tourism

Māori tourism is culturally distinctive when compared to mainstream New Zealand tourism, yet relatively less significant when defined in terms of visitor statistics. This has an impact on Māori tourism's ability to compete in the larger segments of the tourism market. Māori tourism is limited to the types of cultural tourism they are prepared to engage in and many Māori tourism operators like Taiamai Tours resist the commodification of their cultural heritage by selling it as a commercial product to the market. In this context, many Māori tourism developers and operators are forced to develop their tourism businesses away from their own places of cultural heritage and Marae (traditional communities). Tribal Marae (traditional communities) are often engaged with tribal affairs, including ceremonial occasions like funerals and reunions, and these events in a Māori worldview, take precedence over any other event irrespective of it being planned and pre-booked. This makes it commercially challenging for Māori in tourism to present a totally authentic experience without constructing a purpose-built complex for their tourism concept. Māori in tourism in New Zealand are further met with the challenge of surviving in a narrow seasonal index, as many of their natural resources like forests, rivers, lakes and oceans can become inaccessible in heavy rains and cold winter periods. These natural out-of-season experiences are also hard to provide when visitor numbers are small in the low season.

Taiamai Tours: An authentic cultural experience

Taiamai Tours in New Zealand is a case study of a Māori tourism organisation that delivers an authentic Māori cultural tourism experience by taking tourists on a Waka (Māori canoe) ride (see Figure 2). This business was born out of a complex set of experiences and challenges that the founder, Hone Mihaka (see Figure 3) experienced and was driven by his personal vision and self-determination. The business is located in the Far North of the North Island of New Zealand (see Figure 4). The company was formally registered on 21st August 2009 and operates its own commercial website, and is marketed and published in all major tourism distribution channels throughout New Zealand and overseas.

Figure 2: Taiamai Tours on open sea. Photo credit: Hone Mihaka. Reprinted with permission

Figure 3: Hone Mihaka of Taiamai Tours Heritage Journeys. Photo credit: Hone Mihaka. Reprinted with permission

Figure 4: Taiamai Tours positioned in the Far North or the North Island of New Zealand

Taiamai Tours brand their tourism experience as an interactive Waka experience, wherein the history and stories of the group's heritage are shared during the excursions on the open sea. 'Taiamai' is a pre-European tribal name that identifies this group of Māori descendants to the Ngā Puhi tribe of New Zealand, who live in the Far North. This is a people enriched with a deep history of Māori tribal wars and, more recently, wars with the early 'Pākehā' (European) settlers in New Zealand. Mihaka's ancestral line includes people who aggressively resisted the arrival of the Pākehā but eventually conceded and signed the Declaration of Independence in 1835 and the Treaty of Waitangi in 1840. The Declaration of Independence was signed in 1835 with James Busby, a representative of the British King William IV. The Treaty of Waitangi was also signed by Busby and constituted a formal treaty with the British crown and the Māori in 1840. Hone Heke, from whom Mihaka is a direct descendant, is famous in New Zealand history for the cutting down of the flagpole that flew the British flag. According to Hone Heke, the British flag represented the intrusion of imperialists on his land in that Hone Heke was of a royal chiefly bloodline within Māoridom. Mihaka is known among his peers as being a leader who in many ways resembles the characteristics of his ancestor Hone Heke. In addition to Mihaka's relentless tenacity and determination to make his business survive, he is well grounded in the Māori cultural knowledge of his tribal people and their history.

Both Mihaka and his brother sought the permission and approval of the 'Kaumātua'[6] (tribal elders) to use the sacred tribal name, 'Taiamai', as the name for their company. Although the registered name is Taiamai Tours Heritage Journeys Limited, it is more commonly known and branded simply as Taiamai Tours. Taiamai Tours is operated by both Mihaka and his spouse and, as a family business, has not been exempt from the challenges met by most small- to medium-sized businesses. Mihaka and his spouse both work full time in Taiamai Tours and multi-task by performing all the duties of their business, ranging from administrational tasks to laborious tasks including running the actual tour operation. Their daily routine can include taking the phone calls for bookings, arranging temporary staff as required to fulfil bookings, preparing the Waka and undertaking all the tasks required to launch the Waka safely, teaching and training passengers in preparation for sailing, skippering the vessels on the open water, and maintaining the Waka and all their safety equipment. In common with many owner-operated businesses, the business appears to require their attention for almost 365 days of the year and places a huge strain on the two individuals.

The visitor experience

Taiamai Tours has a fleet of Waka that include both single- and double-hulled vessels; they also have a traditional sailing Waka for their more exclusive cliental. The more common Waka used for larger tours are double hull and offer a more stable and controlled situation on the open sea. Taiamai Tours continue to extend their fleet of Waka to meet the growing demands of tourism during the peak seasonal index of New Zealand's cruise ship tourism trade. Mihaka informs that Taiamai Tours maintain their right to practice their traditions under Article 2 of the 1840 Treaty of Waitangi Act and are exempt from abiding by normal conditions of the Bay of Islands maritime laws. However, Taiamai Tours voluntarily practice the codes of the maritime requirements by way of a written safety charter and comply to such standards that require the use of life jackets and a water   safety induction process (see Figure 5). Taiamai Tours not only drill their passengers how to paddle the Waka properly, but they also perform safety inductions before embarkation of the passengers on-board any of their Waka. Staff employed

---

6   'Kaumatua' are respected tribal elders, or senior members of a tribe, of either gender, who are appointed by their people to teach and guide the current and future generations of Māori. They are the keepers of Māori knowledge and cultural traditions of the family and tribe.

by Taiamai Tours have also completed safety certificates in St. John's first aid and general safety training as part of the requirements of the Qualmark[7] system operated by Tourism New Zealand.

Figure 5: Taiamai Induction with passengers. Photo credit: Hone Mihaka. Reprinted with permission

Each Waka is uniquely decorated with customary patterns and lays ready in preparation for easy manoeuvring. The designs of the Waka have evolved over time, increasing in size to meet the demands of their growing market. At a minimum, each of their Waka can comfortably and safely seat up to 40 people. Their fleet of Waka is now strategically positioned all around the Bay, physically presenting them as a serious Māori business among their competitors. Mihaka notes that their strong position is due to their tenacity in working through and surviving the challenges they have faced in the past which included attempts to sabotage their operations by others attempting to sink their Waka, and having had their equipment stolen on multiple occasions.

Mihaka has constructed his Waka out of modern materials including fiberglass, so that they are durable, light and easy to maintain. He has also modified the hulls so that a small outboard motor could be deployed to escape bad seas and to allow them to cover a greater distance in a shorter time frame. Paddling these enormous Waka can also be exhausting for an older demographic and having the outboard motor has proven to be a good second option. Mihaka has also constructed special trailers to allow the Waka to be moved by road. The changes applied to the design of their Waka makes their Waka totally portable, enabling him the option to operate on nearby lakes, rivers and inland waterways. Although powered by a reasonably silent outboard motor, the rear rudder directs the path of the vessel as it had done in ancient Waka of the past. All of these modifications have been care-

7   Qualmark is New Zealand's official quality assurance organisation.

fully applied so as to enhance the Waka experience and care for their tourists who are considered Taonga (treasures) and are foremost in all the decision-making.

The stories that Mihaka relates to his passengers include the history of his people, the challenges they encountered as a people, and the battles his ancestors fought. Mihaka also teaches his customers about the significance of the Treaty of Waitangi to the Māori people of the Taiamai tribe and points out historical landmarks with a complete commentary of their Whakapapa (see Figures 6 and 7). During the tour, Mihaka teaches his passengers how to Hoe (paddle) the Waka to the rhythm of a simple Waiata (song) (see Figure 8). Once at sea, Mihaka commands everyone to raise their paddles in the air and in the Māori language he instructs his team to anchor the Waka to a reef below the sea. His men then dive into the sea and reappear bearing fresh giant mussels taken from the seabed. Before sharing this bounty of 'Kaimoana' (seafood), Mihaka offers a 'Karakia' (prayer) to 'Tangaroa' (the god of the sea).He then relates a local legend of the sea, which tells us that if we care for the sea, it will provide for us.

Figure 6: Mihaka informing history. Photo credit: Hone Mihaka. Reprinted with permission

Figure 7: Taiamai Whānau workers at Te Haruru Falls. Photo credit: Hone Mihaka. Reprinted with permission

Figure 8: Taiamai Tours paddling in the open sea. Photo credit: Hone Mihaka. Reprinted with permission

In addition to their authentic Māori tourism experience, Taiamai Tours are deeply committed to rendering services to their community. They have voluntarily established and engaged training programmes that have included providing 'Wananga' (Māori training sessions) about Waka, Whakapapa (genealogy) and Māoritanga (Māori beliefs and customary practices) and have extended these training programmes to young adolescent youth from gang affiliations. This has changed the lives of these young persons by enabling them to adopt the visions, aspirations and the leadership of Taiamai Tours, and expanded the potential of them being successful recruits for Taiamai Tours.

Whānau kaimahi (extended family workforce)

Like many of the small- to medium-sized businesses, Taiamai employs 'Whānau'[8] (extended family). It is not uncommon for Māori to form close relationships of trust with work colleagues and Taiamai Tours considers all their workers as 'Whānau'. These Whānau Kaimahi (extended family workforce) members have demonstrated the ability to gain sufficient experience to captain a Waka on their own and become knowledgeable leaders who can deliver all the components of a Waka tour experience (see Figure 9). Whānau Kaimahi workers have indicated that they are prepared to make changes to their lifestyles and are committed to follow the vision and aspirations of Mihaka as their leader, and mutually share the passion and commitment to the 'Kaupapa' (business) of Taiamai Tours. Mihaka is respected as their leader and mentor, and the Whānau Kaimahi demonstrate their commitment by following and supporting his leadership. All Whānau Kaimahi employed by Taiamai Tours have had their bodies tattooed with Tā Moko as a mark of their commitment to the Kaupapa (business) (see Figure 10). This is viewed as a considerably extreme level of commitment of an employee when compared amongst other businesses in New Zealand. Selected Whānau Kaimahi employees have also completed their St. John's first aid courses that have earned credits towards the Qualmark for Taiamai Tours as a further commitment to the Kaupapa of Taiamai Tours. All Whānau Kaimahi workers dress in native apparel for the entire time they are in the presence of their customers, irrespective of the weather conditions. This is how the Whānau Kaimahi workers demonstrate their 'Mana' (empowerment) and commitment to Taiamai Tours and the leadership of Mihaka. Whānau Kaimahi of Taiamai Tours do their upmost to deliver an authentic Māori experience to their tourists.

Figure 9: Whānau Kaimahi presenting their authentic experience by the way they dress and act in front of tourists. Photo credit: Hone Mihaka. Reprinted with permission

---

8   Whanau is an extended family group spanning three to four generations and is the basic unit of Māori society.

Figure 10: Taiamai workers with Traditional Tā Moko. Photo credit: Hone Mihaka. Reprinted with permission

Mihaka explains that before Taiamai Tours begun, they did not even know how to paddle a Waka. Now they feel they have learnt everything that there is to know about their Moana (ocean) and the skills of managing a Waka. According to Mihaka, what once was just a dream had now developed into a complete business operation that has a national and international awareness as an authentic Māori cultural tourism experience.

A Māori perspective of sustainability

According to Mihaka, the underpinning philosophy of sustainability from a Māori perspective for Taiamai Tours was not just a result of his upbringing. For him, sustainability emerged as a result from advice given to him from his 'Kuia' (female Māori elders) and 'Kaumātua' (tribal elders) at the same time that Mihaka sought approval to use the name Taiamai as the name of the company. Mihaka was advised by these prestigious leaders to 'Tiaki te Taonga' (look after the rare treasures) and not to focus on a business strategy, a marketing plan or anything else as a priority. Their complete words to Mihaka and his brother in the Māori language was, "tiaki te Taonga, mā te Taonga e tiaki kia koe." This admonition is further emphasised when translated into English, "look after the Taonga[9] and in turn the Taonga will look after you." These words literally meant that for Taiamai to exist, they needed to look after and care for the rare and precious gifts entrusted to them, and these gifts would in turn provide for them. This seems a simple underpinning

---

9   Taonga in this context encapsulates all precious resources and assets whether tangible or intangible, including people that are required for sustainability.

statement, yet to Taiamai Tours and Mihaka it was powerful and formed the foundation of an indigenous cultural philosophy that embraced an ancient Māori notion of 'Tōhua Te Ao' (to ensure the sustainability of the world).

Mihaka's commitment to respecting the Taonga affects the way that he markets and communicates information about Taiamai Tours. According to Mihaka, the Taonga should never be sold. Mihaka claims, that all he is selling is a plastic seat on a Waka experience. The cultural aspects are not for sale. Although they are a part of his overall Waka experience, they are not sold or planned as a separate scheduled component of the overall experience. Mihaka explains how wholesalers and marketers of his product get frustrated in attempting to commodify his Waka tour by attempting to include a Powhiri (traditional welcome), Karanga (traditional call), Hāka (Māori war dance) and other Māori cultural components, only to be instructed by Mihaka to remove these words from their marketing paraphernalia. Mihaka claims that these cultural components occur as a natural flow of his cultural protocols and are not to be the scheduled or itemised components of his Waka tour experience. When it comes to marketing Taiamai Tours as a product, Mihaka feels that he needs to defragment and change the minds of those who market his business. Mihaka feels that marketers try to market Māori culture like a retail product, rather than accepting that the Māori culture is driven by Wairua (a spiritual connection) and is subject to change as the Wairua dictates and not as a schedule dictates. Taiamai Tours believe that imagery and pictures can demonstrate an experience without having to explicitly state that sacred aspects of their Māori culture are for sale.

Another philosophy held by Taiamai Tours is that Māori tourism is about 'Manaakitanga' (hospitality) and 'Kaitiakitanga' (stewardship) being offered to their Manuhiri. Māori tourism in Mihaka's view is about putting their Manuhiri first and the money last. Mihaka accepts that there are costs in marketing their business in a culturally friendly way, but this is a cost that he is prepared to bear and is not willing to change. The company Taiamai Tours wants to be in control of its 'Tikanga Māori' (Māori philosophy) and their future. Mihaka's resounding deep respect and commitment to looking after the Taonga becomes evident in his resistance to give his permission to marketers to itemise things he considers to be Tāpu (sacred) and that the Taonga (rare precious resources) are not for sale.

Just as the epistemological basis of Mihaka's knowledge was gained through an inter-generational method, whereby knowledge has been passed down from generation to generation, he is also passing on some of these valued lessons to his grandchildren. This includes his vision that an integral component of his mentoring skills is to plant the seed into the minds of the next generation to take the Kaupapa to the next generation while maintaining Tika me Te Pono (absolute truth). Mihaka claims that although he tries to instil these cultural values by teaching his Whānau how to look after the Taonga, he feels that he does not have to try too hard, because he believes that the Taonga (rare precious resource) is something that they inherit through genealogy.

Like most indigenous cultures, the Māori ethos is metaphysically interrelated and interconnected to other things and beings through Whakapapa (genealogy) and history. Taiamai Tours embraces the stewardship placed upon them by their Kuia and Kaumātua, applying it to their everyday thinking and actions. They treat the use of their ancestor's name for their business as a serious responsibility. Traditional Tā Moko (tattooing) is more than a body art form for Māori (see Figure 11). The process not only requires an intense and painful experience, but its permanency is a reflection of the level of commitment to being publically identified as a Māori. To the Whānau of Taiamai, Tā Moko is a code of commitment to their beliefs and Kaupapa (business). The intricate patterns of each Tā Moko tell their own unique 'Korero' (story) and that no Tā Moko are identical. In Mihaka's humble way, this is their commitment to the Taonga (rare precious gifts) and Tikanga Māori (Māori beliefs and customs). Mihaka believes that when it comes to strategy, the Tā Moko (tattoo) markings on his body that start above the ankle and reach across his chest, symbolise his deep commitment to his Tikanga Māori (Māori beliefs and customs). Mihaka claims that his strategy and the cultural meaning are codified in his Tā Moko markings, in a language that predates the European arrival. Mihaka adds that although this may not be a clear articulation of a written strategy in a Pakeha sense, to him and his Whānau workers who have Tā Moko, their strategy is clear and they understand every detail of it from a Māori perspective.

Mihaka recalls that he was told by a competitive tourism operation that he and his staff were 'too authentic' and that they were aggressive-looking. His response was "send them to Rotorua, this is how we are doing it whether you like it or not". He believes that this is his signature in Ngā Puhi territory and that it is not about the gloss and glitz of providing Pākehā what they fell is appropriate for Māori to look like, but feeling passionate and being real and Pono (true) about what one is doing. He claims that cultural authenticity is a subject that Pākehā and Tourism New Zealand do not completely understand but their tourists want.

The attitude of Taiamai Tours towards sustainability appears to relate strongly to the existence of an ancient strategy. Mihaka states that he does not need to plan the path ahead and that he does not have to develop a conceptualised Western strategy. In regards to strategy, he normally does not think any further than waking up in the morning. If anything happens in his day and in his life, to Mihaka it is a result of the Taonga (rare precious gifts) working with the Wairua (spirit). He reiterates how he explains to his customers how their meeting together was a result of him looking after the Taonga (rare precious gifts). He is deeply concerned about the potential damages and affects that can be caused when Western commercial strategies do not address the impacts they have on the natural resources and the local people. For example, Mihaka is mindful of the possibility of unknown viruses that could be transmitted from foreigners and tourists, including the environmental damages to his natural surrounding waterways and precious natural resources. According to Mihaka, these are not only the places where his children and their Whānau retreat, but more importantly these are the places that they gather their food supply and Kaimoana (sea food) for their families to survive on.

In the earlier years of business, Mihaka recalls his strategy was to demonstrate to his competitors and potential customers that he was there to stay. Although the company struggled financially for the first few years, he ensured that he and his employees were there every day, dressed in their traditional costume, ready for potential business. Even though many of those days they made no money, they kept their commitment to their Kaupapa (business), which included giving the impression that they were making money and doing well, which in his view seemed to work. Taiamai Tours and their tenacity to see it through the hard times proved to their competitors that they were serious about their commitment to their Kaupapa (business).

As a quest for sustainability, Mihaka constructed his own purpose built 'Whare'[10] (Māori meeting house) for his tourism experience that he appropriately named after his grandfather (see Figure 11). Mihaka built his Whare so he could bring his Manuhiri (visitors) and tourists into his own Marae (traditional courtyard) and extended his Waka tour to include the Wairua (spiritual) feelings that could be experienced when entering his 'Whare Tupuna' (ancestral meeting house). Having his own Whare meant that he could accommodate this experience without causing any interruption to the 'Tangihanga' (funerals) or other activities going on at his family's traditional Marae. Mihaka strategically positioned his Marae up the river and built it on his own Whānau land that is not interfered by the 'Hāpu' (sub tribe) or Iwi (tribal) entities.

---

10   In this context, a Whare is a constructed building where Māori conduct learning and perform sacred rituals. These buildings are typically named after prominent ancestors.

Figure 11: Taiamai Tours constructed their own Marae and Māori meeting house. Photo credit: Hone Mihaka. Reprinted with permission

From an authentic Māori cultural heritage perspective, as presented in the above case study, Box 1 summarises the key aspects that underpin a Māori perspective of sustainable tourism. These themes reveal that sustainable financial success of the operation is important, but that it is rated second to cultural sustainability and the preservation of cultural heritage from a Māori perspective.

Box 1: Key Themes of Sustainable Māori Tourism

Tiaki Te Taonga	The underpinning strategy for Taiamai Tours is that the primary goal of their organisation is to look after and care for the Taonga (both tangible and intangible)
Tōhua Te Ao	Taiamai Tours assert that their role as guardians of the environment is a responsibility that is paramount in all their business planning and tourism activities
Mahi Tāpoi	Taiamai Tours embraces the role of being a consummate host in providing a safe, authentic cultural, sustainable experience for their tourists.
Te Oranga Pūtea	Māori tourism includes attention to economic sustainability.
Te Hau Pūtea	Making a profit might be a goal of Māori tourism, but it is never to be at the sacrifice of any of the higher values noted above.

Conclusion

This case has examined cultural heritage as the distinguishing feature of indigenous tourism. Indigenous cultural heritage is both a unique attraction for tourists and an opportunity for indigenous people to gain cultural empowerment through tourism. Involvement in tourism, however, also poses a range of threats to indigenous people, including lack of control of tourism development and commodification of cultural identity. As such, discussions of sustainable indigenous tourism are very important. Notably, infusing the tourism enterprise with authentic cultural values and principles, so that indigenous people enter the tourism business on their own terms, is seen as vital for achieving sustainable indigenous tourism. Drawing on the specific context of the indigenous Māori people of New Zealand, this case has examined Taiamai Tours in order to reveal those elements considered to render the Māori tourism enterprise 'sustainable' and 'culturally authentic'.

To be 'authentic', Māori tourism needs to be based on Māori cultural beliefs, epistemology, ontology and cosmology. However, some accepted cultural trade-offs or compromises may be necessary to provide a commercial version of an authentic Māori cultural experience. As such, 'sustainability' for Māori is not premised solely on economic outcomes. Rather, it also encompasses positive spiritual, social, cultural and environmental outcomes. Taiamai Tours offers an authentic and sustainable cultural experience for tourists because it is managed according to the traditions and values of the Taiamai tribal people. For instance, permission was sought from the tribal elders to use the tribal name 'Taiamai' as the name for the business; Waka are decorated with customary patterns; cultural stories and values are told to tourists; the organisation has a Whānau approach to employment and workers share the passion and commitment of the organisation's leader. In addition to maintaining an authentic cultural experience based on tangible and intangible aspects of their heritage, Taiamai Tours hold a deep commitment to giving back to the community. Above all, the sustainability philosophy and strategy driving the enterprise is the stewardship and guardianship of the Māori Taonga.

Glossary of Māori Words

Hāka	Fierce rhythmical war dance
Hāngi	Earth oven
Hapū	Sub-tribe to the main tribe
Hau	Wind, gas, soul, atmosphere, famous, fraction, essence
Hoe	Oar, paddle, to row, to paddle
Iwi	Tribe, people, nation, bone
Kaimoana	Seafood, anything edible from the ocean or waterways
Kaitiakitanga	Guardianship
Karakia	Prayer, incantation, rite, ceremony, church, theology, chant, religious service
Karanga	Traditional call, welcome, hail
Kaumātua	Tribal elder, group of elders, knowledgeable, experienced

Kaupapa	Strategy, theme, level floor, fleet of ships, philosophy, original song
Kōrero	Conversation, story, news, speak, talk
Kuia	Elderly female gender
Mana	Integrity, charisma, prestige, formal, status, jurisdiction, power, control, empower
Manaakitanga	Hospitality
Manuhiri	Official visitor, guest
Māori	Indigenous people and culture of New Zealand
Māoritanga	Māori beliefs and customary practices
Marae	Traditional Māori meeting area, focal community area, settlement, village, courtyard including the buildings, community
Mauri	Life-force, life principle, talisman, special character, moon on night 28, ontology
Moana	Ocean
Pākehā	European, of European descent
Pōwhiri	Official Māori welcome ceremony
Reo	Language, speech, communicate, voice, audio
Taiaha	Weapon of war, ceremonial token, long club Taiamai a sub Tribe of indigenous people Ngā Puhi of the Far North
Tā Moko	Tattoo
Tangaroa	Demi-god of the sea, guardian of the ocean and waterways
Tangihanga	Funeral, bereavement
Taonga	Gift, property, treasure, apparatus, accessory, equipment, thing
Tāpu	Sacred, forbidden, confidential, taboo
Tiaki	To care for, protect, nurture
Tika	Principle of truth, correct, accurate, valid, rights, realistic, reliable
Tikanga	Meaning, custom, obligation and condition, (legal) criterion, convention
Tōhua Te Ao	To ensure the sustainability of the world in which we live
Tohunga	High priest, knowledgeable leader
Tūturu	Principal of truth, post, trust worthy, authentic
Waiata	Song, melody, tune, musical reference
Wairua	Spiritual life force
Waka	Canoe, vessel, case, container, descendants of sacred canoe, confederate of tribes of one canoe
Wānanga	Sacred Māori learning session
Whakapapa	Genealogy, cultural, identity, family tree, recite genealogy
Whānau	Family member, relation (by blood)
Whanaungatanga	Relationship, kinship
Whare	House, homestead
Whare Tūpuna	Ancestral meeting house

References

Awatere, S. B. 2008. *The price of Mauri: Exploring the Validity of Welfare Economics When Seeking to Measure Mātauranga Māori*. Doctoral thesis, University of Waikato Hamilton New Zealand. http://researchcommons.waikato.ac.nz:80//handle/10289/2631

Butler R, Hinch T. (eds) 2007. *Tourism and Indigenous Peoples. Issues and implications*. Oxford: Butterworth-Heinemann.

Colmar Brunton, 2004. *Demand for Māori Cultural Tourism: Te Ahu Mai – He Whao Tāpoi Māori*. Wellington: Tourism New Zealand and the Ministry of Tourism.

D'Amore L. 1988. Tourism – The world's peace industry. In D'Amore L, Jafari J (eds) *Proceedings of the First Global Conference – Tourism a Vital Force for Peace, Vancouver, October 1988*. Montreal: Lou D'Amore Associates; 7-14.

Henare E, Pene H. 2001. Kaupapa Māori: Locating indigenous ontology, epistemology and methodology in the academy. *Organization* **8** (2): 234-242.

Les RTW, Manuka H. 2009. The double spiral and ways of knowing. *MAI Review,* **2009** (3): 1-9.

Mahuta RT. 1987. *Tourism and Culture: The Māori Case*. Center for Maaori Studies and Research University of Waikato. Hamilton, New Zealand.

McIntosh AJ. 2004. Tourist appreciation of Māori Culture in New Zealand. *Tourism Management* **25** (1): 1-15.

McIntosh AJ, Hinch T, Ingram T. 2002. Cultural identity and tourism. *International Journal of Arts Management* **4** (2): 39-49.

McIntosh A, Ryan C. 2007. The market perspective of indigenous tourism: Opportunities for business development. In Butler R, Hinch T. (eds) *Tourism and Indigenous Peoples: Issues and Implications*. Oxford: Butterworth-Heinemann; 73-84.

McIntosh AJ, Zygadlo F, Matunga H. 2004. Rethinking Māori tourism. *Asia Pacific Journal of Tourism Research* **9** (4): 331-351.

Notzke C. 2004. Indigenous tourism development in Southern Alberta, Canada: tentative engagement. *Journal of Sustainable Tourism* **12** (1): 29-54.

Poharama A. 1998. *The Impact of Tourism on the Māori Community in Kaikoura*. Lincoln, New Zealand: Tourism Research and Education Centre, Lincoln University.

Ryan C, Aiken M. 2005. *Advances in Tourism Research: Indigenous Tourism : The Commodification and Management of Culture*. Oxford: Elsevier Science.

Ryan C, Crotts J. 1994. Carving and tourism: A Māori perspective. *Annals of Tourism Research* **24** (4): 898-918.

Sofield THB. 2003. *Empowerment for Sustainable Tourism Development*. London: Elsevier Science and Pergamon.

Spiller C. 2010. *How Māori Cultural Tourism Businesses Create Authenticity and Sustainable Well-being.* University of Auckland: Auckland.

Ancillary student material

Further Reading

Butler RW, Hinch T. (eds) 1996. *Tourism and Indigenous Peoples.* London: International Thompson Business Press.

McIntosh AJ, Johnson H. 2005. Understanding the nature of the Marae experience: Views from hosts and visitors at the Nga Hau E Wha National Marae, Christchurch, New Zealand. In Ryan C, Aicken M (eds.) *Indigenous Tourism: The Commodification and Management of Culture.* Oxford: Pergamon; 33-48.

Related websites

Taiamai Tours: http://www.taiamaiTours.co.nz/

Indigenous New Zealand: http://www.inz.Māori.nz/

New Zealand Ministry of Economic Development: http://www.med.govt.nz/sectors-industries/tourism

Tourism New Zealand: http://www.tourismnewzealand.com/

Self-test questions

Try to answer the following questions to test your knowledge and understanding. If you are not sure of the answers, please re-read the case study and refer to the suggested references and further reading sources.

1   How is 'indigenous tourism' defined?

2   What are the positive and negative impacts of tourism on indigenous heritage and culture?

3   What are the main motives for the involvement of indigenous peoples in tourism?

4   In what ways is the tourism experience offered by Taiamai Tours 'authentic'?

5   What are the key elements of 'sustainability' on which the management of Taiamai Tours is based?

Key themes and theories

The key themes and theories in the case study relate to the following areas:

- ◆ Impact of tourism on indigenous heritage and culture
  - ◆ What are the positive and negative impacts of tourism on indigenous heritage and culture?
  - ◆ What are the main barriers for indigenous peoples' involvement in tourism?
- ◆ Motives for Māori involvement in tourism
  - ◆ What factors are motivating Māori to set up tourism businesses in New Zealand?
  - ◆ What are the different types of tourism products / experiences offered by Māori in New Zealand?
- ◆ Authenticity and Māori tourism
  - ◆ What factors make a Māori tourism business 'authentic'?
  - ◆ Why is 'authenticity' an issue of concern for Māori in tourism?
- ◆ Sustainability and Māori tourism
  - ◆ What factors are perceived to make Māori tourism 'sustainable'?
  - ◆ What possible factors are necessary for 'sustainable Māori tourism' from a Māori cultural viewpoint?

If you need to source further information on any of the above themes and theories, then these headings could be used as key words to search for materials and case studies.

SECTION TWO

MANAGING

HERITAGE SITES

7

The Role of Edinburgh World Heritage in Managing a World Heritage City

Anna Leask, David Hicks and Krzysztof Chuchra

Introduction

"The United Nations Educational, Scientific and Cultural Organization (UN-ESCO) seeks to encourage the identification, protection and preservation of cultural and natural heritage around the world considered to be of outstanding value to humanity. This is embodied in an international treaty called the Convention Concerning the Protection of the World Cultural and Natural Heritage, adopted by UNESCO in 1972" (UNESCO, 2013a: n.p.).

The aim of the Convention is to encourage conservation of the resources within the designated sites and surrounding buffer zones on a local level, as well as to foster a sense of collective global responsibility through international co-operation, exchange and support (Leask, 2006). The Convention introduced the World Heritage List (WHL), upon which designated sites are inscribed. A site that is inscribed on the WHL is known as a World Heritage Site (WHS).

The number of sites with WHS designation has proliferated throughout the world over the last three decades. The WHL has included historic cities from its inception, with Kracow (Poland) being inscribed in the very first World Heritage List in 1978. Since that time an increasing number of urban WHSs have been inscribed, including districts within cities. Examples include the Old Town of Corfu, the historic centres of Bordeaux, Havana and Venice, and Zanzibar Stone Town. It has been argued that the designation brings various conservation and management challenges as a result of the fundamental tensions between the "desire to preserve a sense of the past" on the one hand and "recognising that heritage cities are the product of layers of development and habitation" on the other (Pendlebury, Short and While, 2009: 350). WHS designation can effectively transform places into World Heritage cities, with authorities becoming responsible for managing the site according to

UNESCO's Operational Guidelines requiring consideration of the impact of developments both within and beyond the boundary of the WHS.

The UNESCO World Heritage Cities Programme was established in 2005 to assist States Parties in their efforts to protect, manage and preserve their urban heritage. This was followed in 2005 with the provision of updated guidelines intended to improve the integration of urban heritage conservation into strategies of socio-economic development (UNESCO, 2013b). These include comprehensive surveys of a city's natural, cultural and human resources; participatory planning and stakeholder consultations on what values to protect for transmission to future generations; the prioritising of actions for conservation and development; and the establishment of partnerships and local management frameworks to develop mechanisms for the coordination of activities between the public and private sectors (van Oers and Haraguchi, 2010).

The Organisation of World Heritage Cities was founded in 1993 and currently lists 242 cities (OWHC, 2013), varying vastly in feature, scale, resources and existing conservation support. A non-profit, non-governmental organisation, it aims to create a mechanism to enable member cities to improve the delivery of projects by collecting their experiences, consolidating heritage enhancement, constructing city-to-city partnerships, and contributing to the global debate on urban heritage management and sustainable development. As Pendlebury et al. (2009: 349) state, "the urbanness of WHS presents a series of challenges related to the designation, assessment and management of conservation objects in the context of dynamic and heterogeneous urban systems". Issues identified include the potential tension between authentic conservation and commodification, and the impact on the urban experience as a result of tourism activity (Frey and Steiner, 2011). Even so, it is acknowledged by Assi (2012) that cultural heritage has the capacity to be a powerful engine of economic development.

Numerous studies on the impact of WHS designation exist, mostly focussing on aspects of conservation, tourism development and visitor management, although a few consider the role of local communities and their engagement (Jimura, 2011). The identification, involvement and role of local stakeholder groups within the management of the WHS can be problematic, even from the starting point of identifying who the relevant groups might be (Richards and Hall, 2000; Landorf, 2007). The fragmented nature of some stakeholder groups, such as the tourism industry, further emphasises the need for more formal coordination and broader collaboration in the planning process than is currently the case (Aas, Ladkin and Fletcher, 2005). However, there is a view that local stakeholders have a greater understanding of the economic, environmental and social needs and resources of a community, and that consideration must be made of how these issues might be integrated into more extensive regional and national planning systems (Milne and Ateljevic, 2001). Landorf (2007) argues that WHS partnerships and Site Coordinators have limited collective experience in planning for economic development and tourism. Several studies have investigated how tourism development contributes to the development of a WHS in respect of the links between designation and visitor numbers, the opportunities for a city to develop its heritage tourism business, and how the visitor and resident experience can be enhanced through this international designation (Poria, Reichel and Cohen, 2011; Tze-Ngai Vong and Ung, 2012). A key challenge appears to be the lack of co-ordinating bodies able to undertake the overall management of the multiple and complex nature of managing a World Heritage city.

The purpose of this case study is to explore the challenges of managing the complex urban environment of Edinburgh Old and New Towns WHS. In doing so, it sets out to examine how the organisation that was set up to manage the site, Edinburgh World Heritage, acts as a vehicle to encourage and co-ordinate stakeholder engagement as a means of encouraging the effective management of the whole WHS.

Edinburgh Old and New Towns World Heritage Site

Historical overview

The Old and New Towns of Edinburgh (see Figure 1) were inscribed by UNESCO as a WHS in 1995, in recognition of the contrast and quality of architecture between the medieval Old Town and the Georgian New Town. Specifically, the nomination summarises the reason for inscription as:

> "Edinburgh, capital of Scotland since the fifteenth century, presents the dual face of an old city dominated by a medieval fortress and a new neoclassic city whose development from the eighteenth century onwards exerted a far-reaching influence on European urban planning. The harmonious juxtaposition of these two highly contrasting historic areas, each containing many buildings of great significance, is what gives the city its unique character" (UNESCO, 2013c: n.p.).

The award of WHS status came after a long process of conservation and investment in the city centre. In the late 1960s and early 1970s, awareness of the importance of Edinburgh's Georgian New Town architecture was growing. Concern at its perilous physical state and social decline led to a complete survey of the New Town being conducted by volunteers from the Edinburgh

Architectural Association. Their findings were discussed at a major conference in 1970, as a result of which local and central governments decided to act. The Edinburgh New Town Conservation Committee (ENTCC) was also formed at this time. The ENTCC had a small secretariat charged with disbursing grants for the repair of historic buildings within the New Town, as well as providing advice to owners, both private and public, on the repair and restoration of their properties.

Figure 1: Aerial view of Edinburgh WHS. Source: Reproduced courtesy of EWH

In the 1980s, work on the New Town was well underway and the focus of the authorities turned to Edinburgh's Old Town, perched romantically on a high ridge above the New Town. A comprehensive survey published in 1984 illustrated the depressed state of the area, and made a catalogue of dilapidated buildings and gap sites. The report highlighted that the population had fallen from 23,000 in 1901 to just over 3,000 in 1981, 1,000 of whom were resident in hostels (Old Town Advisory Committee, 1984). To address this challenge, the Old Town Renewal Trust (OTRT) was set up by the City Council and given a broad social, economic and physical remit to begin to address these issues, again through careful investment in the city's buildings and in the Old Town's community. Both the ENTCC and OTRT benefited from professional staff, excellent leadership and the long-term commitment of their local and central government sponsors. They also benefited from communities which organised themselves into associations, be it for a block, a street or an entire area.

By the early 1990s, this investment had enabled the Old and New Towns to recover and attention turned to gaining greater recognition of the importance of the two historic areas. A decision was taken to nominate Edinburgh Old and New Towns to become a WHS, and a working group drawn from

Historic Scotland staff and ENTCC members was established to prepare the nomination documents and define a boundary for the WHS. In his evaluation report for the World Heritage Committee, Professor Herb Stovel, representing the International Council on Monuments and Sites (ICOMOS), highlighted the work of the ENTCC and the OTRT as being central to the success of conservation within the proposed site: "Their working methods (offices set within the Community) have built awareness and sensitivity within the public concerning conservation issues, in the process of achieving more tangible goals. Quite clearly, to a degree not possible within bureaucratic systems, these two agencies have been able to link community development to conservation in substantial and meaningful ways" (Stovel,1996: 32). The site was successfully inscribed on the WHL in 1995.

In 1999 the ENTCC and OTRT were merged to form a new body, Edinburgh World Heritage (EWH). This new organisation continued the work of its predecessors, offering grants for the repair of historic buildings and championing good design, but there were also challenges introduced by the fledgling WHS. The work of EWH was to cover a larger area, including the Dean Village and parts of the West End not previously in the remit of ENTCC or OTRT (Figure 2). The focus of EWH was to be wider than pure building conservation, to consider the social and economic well-being of the site as well.

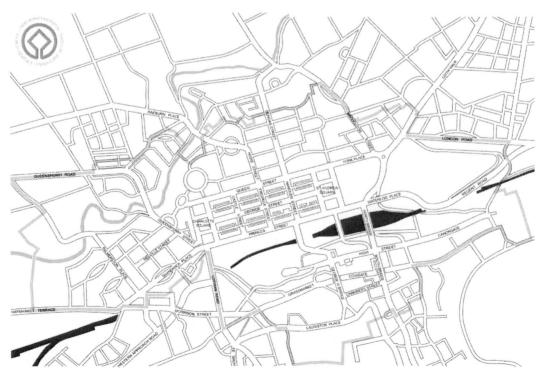

Figure 2: Map of Edinburgh Old and New Towns WHS. Source: EWH

Management issues

Edinburgh WHS encompasses the whole of the city centre, an area of around 1.76 square miles. This sheer scale means that the management of the WHS involves addressing a series of complex issues. The key to WHS status is in maintaining the outstanding universal value and authenticity of the Site, achieved through establishing and retaining a delicate balance between meeting the needs of the built heritage, residents, tourists, businesses, and the cultural and economic well-being of the city.

The WHS has around 22,000 residents, mostly concentrated in the Georgian New Town but also some 5,000 in the heart of the Old Town. This means that the vast majority of the built heritage is in private hands, and makes individual residents and property owners very real stakeholders in the Site. As a thriving city centre the Site is also a place of work for around 69,000 people, employed in everything from retail to professional services, as well as home to national institutions such as the Scottish Government and Parliament.

Protection and management

In terms of planning control, the WHS has a very high level of protection. In the UK, World Heritage status brings no additional statutory controls, with planning authorities instead asked to make it a 'material consideration' in reviewing applications. However, over 75% of all the building stock within the WHS is already Listed with Historic Scotland. All of the WHS is included in designated Conservation Areas (Old Town, New Town, West End, Dean Village). In addition, New Town gardens are protected by being listed Historic Scotland's Inventory of Gardens and Designed Landscapes.

However, there is a balance to achieve, as new development is important in maintaining the economy of the city. The WHS Monitoring Report (EWH, 2011a) emphasised that Edinburgh is a thriving capital city that needs high-quality development to secure its economic and social future. As the political and financial capital of Scotland, and with a WHS covering most of the commercial core of the city, the development pressures in Edinburgh have, until recently, been especially marked (Pendelbury et al., 2009: 354).

In November 2008, a UNESCO World Heritage Centre monitoring mission to the city examined four development proposals. The mission acknowledged the professionalism and skills of the team in place to manage the WHS, but recommended that greater clarity was needed in the management structures and engagement with stakeholders. It also recommended a review of the need for a buffer zone around the WHS.

At a strategic level, protection is also afforded by the Edinburgh Local Plan, adopted in 2009. The Local Plan relates directly to the Edinburgh Old and New Towns WHS: Policy Env1: World Heritage Site (CEC, 2009). This states that development that would harm the qualities that justified the inscription of the Old and New Towns of Edinburgh as a WHS, or would have a detrimental impact on the Site's setting, would not be permitted. This is intended to influence new architecture so as to ensure it is designed with its context in mind, with the size, scale and materials of new buildings drawing inspiration from its historic surroundings, as well as maintaining the contrast of styles between the Old and New Towns

In 2008, a 'skyline policy' was also adopted by the City of Edinburgh Council (CEC). This defined key views across the city with the aim of providing planning control to safeguard them. Such control of tall buildings that might impact on the city centre provides appropriate protection to the setting of the property. It also safeguards the silhouette and views from the WHS outwards to such crucial topographic features as Arthur's Seat and the Firth of Forth.

The authenticity of Edinburgh's built heritage is also critical to maintaining WHS status. This involves factors as varied as the use of materials, the design of new buildings and the public realm, traditional building skills and the core function of the city centre. Both the Old and New Towns were built from local sandstone, which is simply no longer available. The majority of the building stock in the WHS is now over 100 years old and so the need for repairs will be on-going into the future. Great care has to be taken in repairing historic fabric in order to ensure that the correct stone is used, matching the colour and characteristics of the original. In addition, most properties in the WHS are in multiple ownership, with tenements (multiple-occupancy buildings, see Figure 3) a crucial aspect of the character of the WHS. In a New Town tenement, for example, there are on average 12 individual proprietors, and so getting agreement to carry out maintenance and repairs can be difficult. A new issue is the possible effects of climate change, with a particular concern being greater rainfall, which is likely to accelerate stone decay.

Furthermore, traditional building skills are essential to the maintenance of the WHS. Many of the materials used in historic buildings require specific expertise, as their qualities differ greatly from modern equivalents. Such fundamental things as lime mortar, iron founding, slating, joinery, plasterwork, and lead-work, for example, all need specialists trained in their use.

Figure 3: An example of tenement building in Edinburgh. Source: EWH

Economic sustainability and liveability

The WHS is inextricably linked to the success of the city as a whole. The values for which the WHS was inscribed create a visually attractive and culturally vibrant city centre in which businesses and individuals want to be based. In turn, the economic success of the city ensures that businesses and individuals are better resourced to maintain their buildings. These same heritage values also attract residents, and the city is consistently rated as one of the best places to live in Britain and Europe in terms of quality of life.

Tourism is a vital part of Edinburgh's economy, and the WHS is a foundation of the city's international appeal. Edinburgh ranks as the second most popular tourist destination in the UK, attracting around 3.27 million visitors per year (ETAG, 2012). Figures from the most recent Edinburgh Visitor Survey (CEC, 2011) clearly illustrate the part the WHS plays:

♦   70% of visitors were influenced to visit because of the city's historic character

♦   82% of visitors found the city's architecture its most impressive feature

♦   94% of visitors said that walking around the city was their favourite activity

A recent survey by TripAdvisor also saw Edinburgh's WHS voted as the fifth most recommended WHS (Historic Scotland, 2010). One of the priorities for action identified in the recent Edinburgh Tourism Strategy (ETAG, 2012) was careful management of the city to support tourism (see Box 1).

Box 1: World class city management

The city centre – in particular the Old and New Towns – is widely recognised as the city's most unique asset and is therefore of fundamental importance to the tourism strategy. The outstanding natural and built heritage of the city centre provides a superb 'theatre' in which the majority of the city's tourism activities take place. In addition to its inherent value for tourism, the fact that it is a UNESCO designated World Heritage Site (WHS) gives the city a global status of huge worth. These are outstanding competitive advantages for the city that must be both celebrated and protected.

The strategy consultations have emphasised the importance of ensuring that the Old Town and the New Town are managed with great care, to standards that are both appropriate to a WHS and worthy of a five-star visitor attraction.

It is important also to address the challenge of maintaining the quality of the cityscape (through the highest standards of spatial planning, architecture, landscaping, design, etc); and agree whether any action is required to support the existing mechanisms or effect improvements.

Core priorities for concerted action over the next three years are:

■ Well-planned and coordinated day-to-day management of the public realm, especially in heavy footfall areas. This includes addressing the issues of litter, graffiti, begging, etc

■ Maintaining and enhancing the quality of the cityscape. Key elements of this are to:

❑ Formulate and deliver a coherent vision for the Royal Mile, enhancing the quality of the streetscape to support retail and improve the visitor experience, managing it as a five-star visitor attraction

❑ Define the identity of Princes Street and its role in the city and implement action to achieve it

■ Cherishing and enhancing the city's many green spaces, which help to make the city attractive for visitors and enhance the city's green credentials

Source: ETAG (2012)

As stated by Travis (2011: 193) "conservation planning in Edinburgh was comparatively successful and this in turn reinforced and generated further tourism appeal". However, the growth of tourism has led to some challenges in achieving a balance of activities, for example in the proliferation of souvenir shops on the main tourist area of the Royal Mile (see Figure 4), which has resulting in a lack of places for residents to buy everyday essentials, and the over-crowding caused as a result of major festivals hosted annually in Edinburgh, such as the Festival Fringe (see Figure 5).

Figure 4: Royal Mile, Edinburgh tenement buildings and tourist retail outlets. Source: EWH

Figure 5: Royal Mile, Edinburgh during the Festival Fringe. Source: EWH

For the WHS to retain its character, it is crucial that it remains a place for people to live. However, even something as fundamental as the collection of household rubbish has proved problematic, with the New Town requiring a different (and more expensive) approach from the rest of the city (BBC, 2011). Fuel poverty (defined as a households which spends more than 10% of its income on energy costs) is also a real issue in the Old Town (CEC, 2012), where traditional buildings are often perceived as hard to beat, but with the risk of the loss of historic fabric if inappropriate measures are taken.

Management solutions in place in Edinburgh WHS

Management plan

These complex issues of management, authenticity and significance are re-solved through the mechanism of the management plan. It provides a link between the international requirements of World Heritage, the local plan-ning process and the wider management issues involved in protecting a complex Site like the Old and New Towns of Edinburgh. UNESCO requires all WHSs to have a management plan or documented management system in place. This ensures that the outstanding universal value is protected and enhanced. The management plan should set out a series of objectives de-signed to ensure the protection of the site in a way that meets international commitments and helps to align the actions of all parties involved the man-agement process. It is also the policy of the Scottish Government that all Scot-tish WHSs should develop a management plan which sets a framework for the protection, promotion and enhancement of the site.

The first Edinburgh Old and New Towns World Heritage management plan was launched in July 2005, with a revised plan formally launched in 2011 (EWH, 2011a) The draft plan was the subject of a detailed consultation, which took the form of direct and email notification, workshops involving stakeholders, a travelling exhibition, an internet survey and a series of open meetings. The first workshop, in February 2010, provided a solid base for the scope of the review, while a second workshop in October was held as part of the public consultation exercise. This allowed the opportunity to con-sider whether the draft management plan reflected the public perception of its vision for the WHS, the proposed statement of outstanding universal value and the objectives for the implementation of the vision. Consultees were asked to comment on the vision, objectives and actions in particular. The results of the consultation then directly informed amendments to the management plan.

The following vision for the site was developed from the workshop sessions:

> "We share an aspiration for the World Heritage Site to sustain its outstanding universal value by safeguarding and enhancing the remarkable and beautiful historic environment. This supports a confident and thriving capital city centre, its communities, and its cultural and economic life" (EWH, 2011a: xiii).

An important aspect in the development of the management plan was the recommendations of the November 2008 joint UNESCO/ICOMOS reactive monitoring mission to Edinburgh. The recommendations covered issues such as stakeholder engagement, handling development pressure, the skyline study and buffer zones, all of which were addressed during the development of the plan.

There are two important documents for the Edinburgh WHS, which form part of any WHS management plan:

♦ **Action plan** – the management plan is a strategic document; the action plan identifies how each objective will be met over the five-year period (EWH, 2012a).

♦ **Monitoring report** – conducted on a bi-annual basis, the monitoring report provides a way of tracking progress on the action plan, as well as the overall state of conservation of the WHS, against a regular set of criteria (EWH, 2012b).

Steering Group

The key organisations for the implementation of the management plan and protection of the WHS's outstanding universal value are the CEC, EWH and Historic Scotland, which form the Core Steering Group. A broader partnership of this group also meets and has included Essential Edinburgh and Scottish Enterprise. The Core Group is responsible for:

♦ Oversight of the drafting and revision of the management plan.

♦ Oversight of the implementation of the management plan through the action programme.

♦ Setting up the scope of indicators of the monitoring report.

♦ Identification of new partners and additional resources within partner organisations to support the progress of the projects.

♦ Engagement and involvement with potential stakeholders.

♦ Supporting fundraising for the implementation of the management plan.

♦   Reconciliation of conflicting initiatives in relation to the outstanding universal value.

Role of Edinburgh World Heritage in the management process

EWH is an independent charity formally charged by CEC and Historic Scotland with facilitating the work of the World Heritage Steering Group and overseeing the implementation of the management plan (EWH, 2013a). It has a small, outward looking and professional team with close links to the different communities within the Site, and the expertise to raise funds and manage a diverse range of projects.

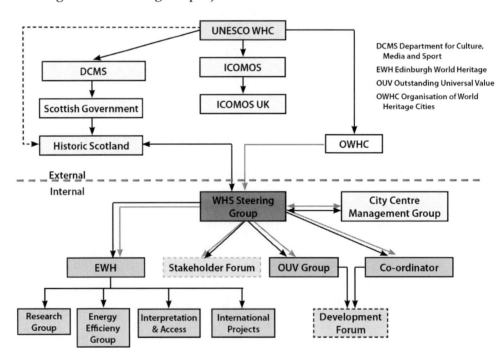

Figure 6: The Old and New Towns of Edinburgh World Heritage Site management structure. Source: EWH

As can be seen in Figure 6, EWH bridges the gap between the wide range of stakeholders in the WHS, acting in an official role as one of the World Heritage partners, developing and implementing the management and action plans for the WHS. However, as a charitable trust it also an independent organisation with a board of trustees and members, drawn from the wider community. EWH acts as the champion on WHS issues across the private and public sectors, residents and external interests, which is very important in co-ordinating initiatives across the city centre. For example, EWH sits on the Streetscape Working Group (a council-led group looking at public realm proposals), City Centre Management Group, Edinburgh Tourism Action Group (ETAG). Having a small but dedicated team in place allows the WHS to benefit from on-going specialist expertise in crucial areas, such as conservation, community engagement and interpretation. In addition, EWH's charitable trust status enables the organisation to attract funding from a wide variety of sources, bringing in investment from charitable trusts, private donations and grants, as well as EU funding to help in maintaining and promoting the site.

The organisation is supported the CEC and Historic Scotland to deliver three core activities covered by Edinburgh World Heritage's business plan which overlaps with the action plan:

♦   **Promote** awareness and understanding of the WHS through learning projects.

♦   **Influence** decision making across the city and the WHS.

♦   **Conserve** and repair of buildings and monuments in the WHS through the Conservation Funding Programme.

Promote

Raising awareness and understanding of the WHS is central to work of EWH, as a key condition of the World Heritage Convention and one of its own charitable objectives. EWH projects aim to encourage everyone to value and enjoy the unique built historic environment of the WHS.

The new Edinburgh Tourism Strategy (ETAG, 2012), which was launched in January 2012, recognised the WHS as one of the main strengths of the city. As a full member of the Edinburgh Tourism Action Group, EWH supports the strategy in a number of ways. A key objective is to enable better exploration of the WHS by visitors, thereby spreading the economic benefits of tourism and providing visitors with a better-quality experience.

EWH aims to encourage everyone to value and enjoy the WHS. However, a variety of studies in recent years have identified a 'missing audience' for heritage, and following a recent survey of Edinburgh residents, a clearer picture of this emerged. In deprived areas of the city, 60% of people were unaware of the status, and between 5 and 7km away from the site, levels of awareness were negligible (Malone, 2010). To help address this, EWH developed outreach projects to engage targeted communities (see Box 2).

Box 2: Promotion of the Edinburgh WHS

World Heritage City app

In October 2011, EWH launched its first smartphone app (see Figure 7). Named 'Edinburgh World Heritage City' (EWH, 2011b), the concept behind the app is to help visitors explore the WHS and to encourage them to engage further with their historic surroundings. The app features city maps and zoomable high-resolution photos, as well as audio clips to help bring the buildings to life with stories of past residents and events. Users can also add their own photos and comments on things they have found, for others to follow and discover for themselves. From October 2011 to March 2012 there were 1,429 new users and 8,092 sessions

Figure 7: Edinburgh World Heritage app. Source: EWH

World Heritage Business Opportunities Guide

In the autumn of 2010, EWH worked in collaboration with Scottish Enterprise and ETAG to produce a Business Opportunity Guide for the city's tourism sector (EWH, 2010). The initiative followed a series of workshops aimed at highlighting the opportunities for businesses in using the WHS for marketing and promotion. The guide explains the concept of World Heritage and the historic qualities that give the Old and New Towns its inscription. It also covers visitor profiles and the importance of the city's built heritage in attracting tourists and shaping their experience while in the city. The guide was launched at an ETAG conference, and was further promoted through briefings for tourism businesses. The guide has proved to be successful in helping businesses engage with their historic surroundings, to see the benefits of WHS status and to acknowledge the requirement to conserve its character.

Heritage Detectives

EWH joined forces with consultants Daisychain Associates and the charity, Circle Scotland, to manage a project aimed at introducing young people to the WHS. Circle Scotland provide community-based support for marginalised children and families, working to improve opportunities for disadvantaged families, and those with children at risk of school exclusion, experiencing neglect or affected by parental drug or alcohol use. Funding of £11,100 came from the Heritage Lottery's Fund's Young Roots programme, which aims to bring heritage and youth organisations together in joint projects. Over a period of eight weeks, a group of 17 young people gathered at the EWH office in

Charlotte Square on Friday afternoons. Divided into small teams, they were tasked to go out and about around the city, to find out the truth behind topics such as Edinburgh's underground city, crimes, famous Scots and traditional myths. The project culminated with several performances of a short piece of drama, inspired by and starring the young people themselves. Titled 'Bondi Brenda and the Heritage Detectives', the piece imagines the group challenging Edinburgh's worst tour guide and exposing her somewhat exaggerated stories. The final performance was held at the Scottish Parliament in November 2011 before an invited audience of parents, project participants and Members of Scottish Parliament.

Auld Reekie Learning Campaign

Auld Reekie (Old Smoky) was a nickname given to the city of Edinburgh in the 17th Century. In 2010, a learning campaign was launched for the year, incorporating a variety of media to attract a wide audience, but with one focused message, enabling each element to support the other. The theme taken was Edinburgh at the end of the eighteenth century, when the New Town was first being planned and built. The campaign was completely funded by a generous gift from a private donor.

A total of 15,000 trail leaflets were distributed between May and November 2010 to venues in the city centre and Edinburgh primary schools. The on-line version of the trail had 3,618 page views between June 2010 and March 2011. Costumed presentations held at the Museum of Edinburgh were led by an interpreter in the character of Mrs Doig, wife of merchant Alexander Doig, a tenant in the building in the 1760s. A series of storytelling events was also organised as part of the Old Town Festival in June 2010.

Six short films entitled '*Edinburgh Adventures of Edward Topham*', looking at everyday life in Georgian Edinburgh, were produced and hosted on the EWH website (EWH, 2013b). The films were based on the accounts of Edward Topham, an English visitor to the city in 1774. Presented by a narrator in costume and shot on location around the WHS, they also featured specially commissioned artwork to help illustrate each topic.

A total of 20 workshops for primary schools were hosted at the Scottish Storytelling Centre, with a total of 482 primary school pupils taking part. '*Tales of Auld Reekie*' was based around three stories featuring the adventures of Jenny and Johnny, young orphans making a living as caddies in Georgian Edinburgh. '*The Old Town Mouse and the New Town Mouse*' was a lively puppet show for younger pupils telling the story of the Old Town Mouse who goes on a journey to visit his New Town cousin. '*Cadie Capers: Tales of Auld Reekie and New Toon*' was a storytelling tour of the Old and New Towns with presenters in character.

Visitor surveys and evaluations all show that the Auld Reekie learning campaign was successful. From the available data, the audience for the campaign has been around 19,600 people.

Influence

As well as conducting its own projects, EWH provides specialist advice on policies and strategies affecting the management of the WHS (see Box 3). The aim is to help ensure that its outstanding universal value, the sum of the key historic features of the city that make it a WHS, is protected for future generations.

Box 3: Influencing the Edinburgh WHS

Energy Efficiency and Sustainability

The EWH Green Heritage Project was awarded a £33,413 grant by the Climate Challenge Fund in 2012 to help energy efficiency in the WHS. Following the success of the previous year's initiatives, this new project delivered community-led regeneration projects and carried out energy-efficiency activities in traditional tenements and historic areas around the site. The Energy Heritage Project was a partnership with Lister Housing Cooperative and Changeworks, involving a pilot study of introducing simple energy-saving measures to a block of Category B Listed Georgian tenements in Lauriston Place. The Renewable Heritage Project followed on from this success, and demonstrated how solar water heating panels could be fitted to the roof of the building.

A new guide was completed in March 2012, advising owners and residents in the WHS about appropriate energy-efficiency solutions for historic buildings. The guide is available in hard copy and on the EWH website, with topics including sustainability and climate change, simple measures to reduce energy consumption, renewable energy, behaviour-changing tips and grants available to help fund improvements. The guide also emphasised the major benefits traditional buildings have in terms of environmental sustainability.

Edinburgh's Historic Graveyards

In 2009, five historic graveyards in the heart of the WHS were included on the World Monuments Fund Watch List. Greyfriars, Old and New Calton, Canongate and St. Cuthbert's graveyards are all recognised as exceptional burial sites, as they have architectural significance and provide a unique record of the transition of Edinburgh from a medieval burgh to an Enlightenment city.

In March 2011, a partnership consisting of the CECC, EWH and the World Monuments Fund commissioned a comprehensive project design for the care of the graveyards. In addition to assessing existing care strategies and identifying potential partners to help in the future management of the graveyards, the recommendations will be informed by a survey of local community interest and visitors to Greyfriars Kirkyard.

Conserve

EWH works to conserve and enhance the WHS (see Box 4), with funding allocated by the CEC and Historic Scotland, and donations from charitable trusts, businesses and the public. Around 80% of the funds are awarded as grants to property owners as part of the Conservation Funding Programme, and around 20% is spent on EWH-initiated public realm projects.

EWH administers a grant programme for repairs. This is unique in the UK by offering repayable grants to the owners of historic buildings. These are for conservation work to privately owned and commercial buildings, with grants offered up to 70% of project costs. These are then repayable on the sale or transfer of the property.

EWH conservation projects help to keep traditional skills alive, and encourage sustainability through the use of locally sourced building materials. Each project starts with a conservation statement, which is invaluable in ensuring that appropriate conservation policies are adopted, resulting in well-informed decisions being made. Through simple legal processes as part of each grant award, owners will continue to maintain their properties, thereby protecting the long-term investment in the city.

Box 4: Conserving Edinburgh WHS

Royal Mile Mansions

Royal Mile Mansions, a block at the junction of North Bridge and The Royal Mile, received a grant of £1.17m, the largest grant awarded by EWH to date. The main North Bridge elevation was part of the Scotsman Buildings, designed by Dunn & Findlay in 1899-1902. The Scots baronial section of the block at 179 High Street and Cockburn Street was built by John McLachlan in 1892-93. The whole project included improvements to the prominent shop-fronts and extensive repairs to the elaborately carved stonework. Royal Mile Mansions is an important feature of the grand entry to the New Town over the North Bridge.

The work involved the agreement of 55 residential owners and 22 commercial proprietors. The impressive teamwork was largely due to the enthusiasm and commitment of the proprietors' committee, as well as the efforts of the design team,

Improvements to the North Bridge Arcade included the repair and reinstatement of original features, including a mosaic ceiling, an ornate leaded-glass dome, and decorative iron gates at each end of the arcade. A more sympathetic lighting scheme was also introduced. Scottish Enterprise Edinburgh and Lothian contributed £120,000 towards the Arcade, and it is hoped that the improvements will help to regenerate the area.

Well Court

Well Court is a Category A Listed courtyard building located in the Dean Village, just within the WHS boundary on the north side of the Water of Leith. In an extensive conservation scheme, carried out by the 55 owners in collaboration with EWH, the appearance and stability of the structure was considerably improved. EWH granted a total of £1.1 million towards conservation work on stonework, roof, windows, clock tower and communal areas. Work in public areas, such as the courtyard, was funded directly by EWH, while the restoration of the main building was paid for partly by the owners and partly through a grant from EWH, which is repayable upon transfer or sales of the properties. Work started in February 2007, following the premise of minimal repair based purely on need. Only traditional materials were used, with great efforts taken to match properties and colour. The characteristic red sandstone was sourced from a quarry in Dumfries and the roof tiles were handmade to match the originals.

Figure 8: Well Court. Source: EWH

Acheson House

Acheson House is a Category A Listed building in the Canongate area of the Old Town, dating back to 1633. Disused since 1997, the building had fallen into disrepair and was on the Scottish Civic Trust's Buildings at Risk Register. In May 2010, EWH awarded a grant of £39,961 for the conservation of the roof, as a first stage in refurbishing the building for use as a museum. The grant not only restored the historic building back to its original character, but also helped promote the use of stone slates as a vital traditional building material. This project is one of only a handful of buildings in the last 50 years to use indigenous Scottish stone as a roofing material. The recently re-opened Denfind quarry in Angus was the only source of the Pitairlie sandstone appropriate for the building.

The project has clearly demonstrated the benefits of stone as a roofing material, and will hopefully encourage others to follow its example. It opens up opportunities for the quarry as a source of future roofing stone, aiding local employment and the development of traditional skills. It also encourages the use of locally sourced traditional materials and shows the potential long-term sustainability of using local materials.

Figure 9: Stone slates on Acheson House. Source: EWH

The Twelve Monuments Restoration Project

The Twelve Monuments Project is a joint initiative of EWH and CEC which aims to restore some of the city's most important statues and monuments. The project started in 2007 and is due for completion in 2013. The project started with restoration of the Bow Well in the Grassmarket and the Melville Monument in St Andrew Square. Perhaps most dramatic of all was the work to the National Monument on Calton Hill in November and December 2008. A key part of the project has been the way it is funded. For each restoration around a third of the cost has been covered by private donations or grants from other public sources, such as the Heritage Lottery Fund. In total, from 2008 to 2012 around £350,000 had been raised from these sources.

The Scotsman Steps

In July 2011, the Scotsman Steps were officially re-opened by Fiona Hyslop, Cabinet Secretary for Culture and External Affairs, following a major conservation project which also included the installation of a new piece of public art by Martin Creed. The project saw EWH and the CEC working with the Fruitmarket Gallery to bring the historic steps back to life, thereby providing a grand public route between the city's Old and New Towns.

Originally built in 1899 as part of the offices of the 'Scotsman' newspaper, the steps had become dilapidated with graffiti on the walls, damage to the stairs and recurring anti-social behaviour. The conservation project started on the Scotsman Steps in September

2010, coinciding with Network Rail's work to improve the Market Street exit from Waverley Station. Using traditional materials, new lighting and lead work was completed, along with the installation of new handrails and iron gates. The interior windows were re-glazed and there were extensive masonry repairs to bring the steps back to use. The Fruitmarket Gallery commissioned the Turner Prize winning Scottish artist, Martin Creed, in a £250,000 special art project. The artwork, called Work 1059, has clad each of the 104 steps in a different colour of marble. The work was supported through the Scottish Government's Edinburgh Festivals Expo Fund, for the Edinburgh Art Festival 2010, as well as individual and corporate donations.

Figure 10: The Scotsman Steps. Source: EWH

Community gardens

A site at MacKenzie Place in the New Town had lain neglected since 1967, when a row of Georgian tenements was demolished, leaving behind only a line of bricked-up cellars. EWH awarded a grant of £41,000 in March 2011 to help transform it into a community allotment and garden.

The project was led by CEC, working in partnership with local residents. Half of the allotments will be offered to local residents and half to a waiting list, with a steering group set up to help manage the site. Local schools were also involved by taking on an allotment space for pupils to use.

In October 2009, EWH awarded a grant of £24,315 to help fund improvements in Coinyie House Close, a residential area of the Old Town which was once the site of the Scottish mint. Working in partnership with the CEC and the local residents, the overgrown garden of the close was re-designed, to provide new facilities and celebrate its long history. The first project involved designing a garden space, reflecting traditional Scottish orchards, parterres and kitchen gardens. Small plots were made available for residents to grow their own vegetables and herbs, and there were workshops in gardening skills such as composting, weed control and planting design. The result is a semi-public space similar to the original function of the close. Residents have benefited not only from the improved facilities, but because the new garden is designed to alleviate anti-social behaviour. An interpretation project is planned, to explain the history of Coinyie House Close to visitors.

Concluding thoughts

Urban WHSs are increasingly complex, with ever more activities and diverse stakeholders to manage. The range of factors to consider and mediate is extensive, including the extent of WHS boundaries and buffer zones, large numbers of landowners and stakeholders, and conflicts between tourism development and planning for the local population. The level of complexity and difficulty in making meaningful decisions about conservation, management and development can result in friction between the different stakeholder groups and those charged with maintaining the authenticity and integrity of a WHS.

As Pendlebury et al. (2009) identify, it is also notable how much UNESCO and ICOMOS have pushed for wider stakeholder engagement in the management of each of the World Heritage Sites. They comment that the wording of reports by UNESCO and ICOMOS suggest a view that better local processes would generate more consensual outcomes, and thus reduce the need for the involvement of the international bodies. The case study of Edinburgh Old and New Towns WHS has been used to demonstrate the challenges in managing urban World Heritage Sites, with the example of EWH, as the body charged with co-ordinating the management of the site, used to emphasise how fruitful the development of such an organisation can be in achieving a mechanism to manage the stakeholders involved effectively.

The case study demonstrates the variety of challenges that World Heritage cities may face in light of potentially conflicting demands from residents, workers and visitors. The examples provided show how an organisation such as EWH can work to address these through their three key aims to promote, influence and conserve the WHS. They do this through an extensive range of innovative initiatives and a structured management framework. One key aspect of the EWH approach is to communicate actively with the huge variety of stakeholders, through a range of both formal and informal mechanisms. Similarly, the decision to seek financial support and initiate projects involving previously disengaged audiences and stakeholders, moves to address some of the common issues of disenfranchised residents. The very nature of a vibrant, multi-dimensional city such as Edinburgh means that the challenges and issues involved in the sustainable development of the city will continue to evolve, there is evidence to suggest that the management structure and initiatives put in in place in Edinburgh Old and New Towns World Heritage provides a positive example for the effective management of World Heritage cities.

References

Aas C, Ladkin A, Fletcher J. 2005. Stakeholder collaboration and heritage management. *Annals of Tourism Research* **32** (1): 28-48.

Assi E. 2012. World heritage sites, human rights and cultural heritage in Palestine. *International Journal of Heritage Studies* **18** (3): 316-323.

BBC. 2011. Edinburgh World Heritage Site set for big bins. http://www.bbc.co.uk/news/uk-scotland-edinburgh-east-fife-15891057

CEC. 2009. Edinburgh City Local Plan. http://www.edinburgh.gov.uk/info/178/local_and_strategic_development_plans/1005/edinburgh_city_local_plan/

CEC. 2011. Edinburgh visitor survey (2009-10) http://www.edinburgh.gov.uk/downloads/file/4104/edinburgh_visitor_survey_2009-10

CEC. 2012. Housing and fuel poverty, http://www.edinburgh.gov.uk/download/meetings/id/35683/item_no_15-housing_and_fuel_poverty

EWH. 2010. ETAG: World Heritage City. http://www.issuu.com/etagbusopps/docs/edinburgh_-_a_world_heritage_city_21.1.11

EWH. 2011a. WHS management plan http://www.ewht.org.uk/uploads/downloads/WHS_Management_Plan%202011.pdf

EWH. 2011b. Edinburgh: World Heritage City app. http://www.ewht.org.uk/visit/edinburgh---world-heritage-city-app

EWH. 2012a. EWHS action plan. http://www.ewht.org.uk/uploads/downloads/Item_17_-_EWHS_Action_Plan_-_KC.pdf

EWH. 2012b. Edinburgh World Heritage Site 2007-8 and 2008-9. http://www.ewht.org.uk/uploads/downloads/Old%20and%20New%20Towns%20of%20Edinburgh%20World%20Heritage%20Site%202007-8%20and%202008-9%20by%20Krzysztof%20Chuchra.pdf

EWH. 2013a. Edinburgh World Heritage. http://www.ewht.org.uk/

EWH. 2013b. Edinburgh adventures of Edward Topham. http://www.ewht.org.uk/learning/auld-reekie/edinburgh-adventures-of-edward-topham

ETAG. 2012. Edinburgh 2020: The Edinburgh Tourism Strategy http://www.etag.org.uk/tourismstrategy.asp

Frey B, Steiner L. 2011. World Heritage List: Does it make sense?. *International Journal of Cultural Policy* **17** (5): 555-573.

Historic Scotland. 2010. *Edinburgh named 5th most recommended World Heritage Site.* http://www.historic-scotland.gov.uk/index/news/mediaresources/edinburghworldheritage.htm

Jimura T. 2011. The impact of World Heritage Site designation on local communities: A case study of Ogimachi, Shirakawa-mura, Japan. *Tourism Management* **32** (2): 288-296.

Landorf C. 2007. Managing for sustainable tourism: A review of six cultural World Heritage Sites. *Journal of Sustainable Tourism* **17** (1): 53-70.

Leask A. 2010. Progress in visitor attraction research: Towards more effective management. *Tourism Management* **31** (2): 155-166.

Leask A. 2006. World Heritage Site designation. In Leask A, Fyall A. (eds) *Managing World Heritage Sites*, Oxford: Butterworth Heinemann; 6-19.

Malone S. 2010. Residents attitudes and perceptions of the World Heritage Site status of the Old and New Towns, Unpublished Masters thesis, International Centre for Cultural and Heritage Studies, Newcastle University.

Milne S, Ateljevic I. 2001. Tourism, economic development and the global-local nexus: Theory embracing complexity. *Tourism Geographies* **3** (4): 369-393.

Old Town Advisory Committee. 1984. *Town Survey*, October.

OWHC. 2013. Organization of World Heritage Cities. http://www.ovpm.org/cities

Pendlebury J, Short M, While A. 2009. Urban World Heritage Sites and the problem of authenticity. *Cities* **26** (6): 349-358.

Poria Y, Reichel A, Cohen R. 2011. World Heritage Site: Is it an effective brand name? A case study of a religious heritage site. *Journal of Travel Research* **50** (5): 482-495.

Richards G, Hall D. 2000. The community: A sustainable concept in tourism Development? In Richards, G. and Hall, D. (eds) *Tourism and Sustainable Community Development*. London: Psychology Press; 1-13.

Stovel H. 1996. *Evaluation Visit to Edinburgh*. ICOMOS report for the World Heritage Centre. ICOMOS Canada Bulletin **5** (3) http://www.icomos.org/~fleblanc/publications/pub_icomos/pub_1996_icomos-canada_bulletin_vol05_no03.pdf

Travis A. 2011. *Edinburgh: Post-war Urban Planning and Conservation in a World Heritage City*. Wallingford: CABI.

Tze-Ngai Vong L, Ung A. (2012. Exploring critical factors of Macau's heritage tourism: What heritage tourists are looking for when visiting the city's iconic heritage sites. *Asia Pacific Journal of Tourism Research* **17** (3): 231-245.

UNESCO. 2013a. World Heritage. http://whc.unesco.org/en/about/.

UNESCO. 2013b. World Heritage Cities Programme. http://whc.unesco.org/en/cities/

UNESCO. 2013c. Old and New Towns of Edinburgh. http://whc.unesco.org/en/list/728

van Oers R, Haraguchi S. (eds) 2010. Managing cities and the historic urban landscape initiative: An introduction. World Heritage Centre, World Heritage Papers 27, *Managing Historic Cities*. http://whc.unesco.org/uploads/activities/documents/activity-47-1.pdf

Ancillary Student Material

Further reading

Aas C, Ladkin A, Fletcher J. 2005. Stakeholder collaboration and heritage management. *Annals of Tourism Research* **32** (1): 28-48.

Garrod B, Fyall A, Leask A, Reid E. 2011. Engaging residents as stakeholders of the visitor attraction. *Tourism Management* **33** (5): 1159-1173.

Leask A, Fyall A. (eds) 2006 *Managing World Heritage Sites*. Oxford: Butterworth Heinemann.

Puczko L, Ratz T. 2006. Managing an urban World Heritage Site: The development of the Cultural Avenue Project in Budapest In Leask A, Fyall A. (eds) *Managing World Heritage Sites*. Oxford: Butterworth Heinemann; 215-225.

van Oers R, Roders A. 2011) Historic cities as model of sustainability. *Journal of Cultural Heritage Management and Sustainable Development* **2** (1): 4-14

Related websites and audio-visual material

Department of Culture, Media and Sport: http://www.culture.gov.uk/what_we_do/historic_environment/4168.aspx

Edinburgh Tourism Action Group: http://www.etag.org.uk/home.asp

Self-test questions

Try to answer the following questions to test your knowledge and understanding. If you are not sure of the answers, please re-read the case study and refer to the suggested references and further reading sources.

1   What were the key motivations for the nomination of Edinburgh Old and New Towns as a World Heritage Site?

2   Who are the key stakeholders in the management of Edinburgh Old and New Towns World Heritage site?

3   What have the implications of the designation been for the following groups: visitors, developers and residents?

4   What role does Edinburgh World Heritage play in the effective management of the Edinburgh Old and New Towns World Heritage site?

5   What does EWH do to encourage the authentic development and enhance the interpretation of Edinburgh Old and New Town for interested groups?

6   Why is it important to balance the needs of residents, workers and visitors to World Heritage cities?

Key themes and theories

♦   Stakeholder involvement and management in urban environments.

   ♦   The complex nature of urban environments

   ♦   The variety of (conflicting) objectives the drive the various stakeholders

   ♦   The level of recognition of tourism activity within the broader cityscape

♦   The role of organisations such as Edinburgh World Heritage in the effective management of heritage cities.

   ♦   Main aim is often conservation rather than tourism

   ♦   The opportunity afforded by resourcing such a central role for a city in terms of improved communication and information exchange between stakeholders

   ♦   Providing a focus for the conservation of a city's heritage resources

   ♦   As a mechanism to work towards achieving the variety of objectives of planning, business, conservation and visitor organisations working within the urban environment

♦   The recognition of role of tourism within wider issues and management of differing stakeholder views within heritage cities.

   ♦   Challenges in balancing the needs of multiple stakeholders within city areas – residents, visitors and businesses

   ♦   Recognition of the role that tourism activity can play in delivering broader objectives within a city without compromising the fabric and historical nature of the resources

♦   Community engagement in World Heritage site management

   ♦   Justification of value of public money being invested in Edinburgh World Heritage via education activities, public benefits, property restorations and research work

   ♦   Engagement with previously disenfranchised sectors of the community

If you need to source further information on any of the above themes and theories, then these headings could be used as key words to search for materials and case studies

8

Managing Megalithic Monuments

A Comparative Study of Interpretation Provision at Stonehenge and Avebury

I-Ling Kuo and Peter Mason

Introduction

At the time of writing, a quick browse through 'Things to do' on the Visit Britain website (VisitBritain, 2012), even in London's Olympic year, reveals the image of Stonehenge appearing on the first page. Stonehenge also ranked third in the Top 10 World Heritage Sites in the UK on the VisitBritain website, after the Tower of London and Westminster Abbey[1]. This raises the question, why is Stonehenge so prominent in the international marketing of Britain? Part of the answer, at least, is that Stonehenge is considered to epitomise British cultural and natural heritage treasures.

One of the most iconic images of prehistoric monuments in the UK and possibly in the world, Stonehenge has fascinated visitors and researchers for centuries (Mason and Kuo, 2007). Its significance is such that in 1986 it was inscribed on the World Heritage List (WHL), together with nearby Avebury and their surrounding sites and monuments (UNESCO, 2012). It is notable that Avebury, which is less than 20 miles from Stonehenge, appears to be almost unknown to non-British visitors, despite the fact that the stone circle in Avebury is much bigger than that of Stonehenge (Mason, 2008). In fact, Avebury Henge[2] is the biggest henge in the world; while nearby Silbury Hill (a massive human-made earth mound) is the largest prehistoric human structure in Europe (English Heritage, 2012a; UNESCO, 2012).

Stonehenge attracted over one million visitors in 2010, more than double the number recorded in the mid-1970s (see Figure 1). This does not include the

---

1   The basis of ranking UK World Heritage Sites on VisitBritain website is unknown to the authors.

2   Henge: a Neolithic monument in Britain, consisting of a circular enclosure defined by a bank and ditch and often containing additional features such as circle(s) of upright stones or wood pillars.

Summer Solstice visitors or the estimated 250,000 visitors viewing the stone circle from the verge of the A344 main road (Young, Chadburn and Bedu, 2009). Even on sunny summer weekends, visitor numbers to Avebury can hardly be described as high and parking is rarely a problem; moreover, most of the visitors to Avebury are British. Stonehenge, in contrast, attracts large numbers of visitors on a daily basis and even the overflow car park can be full at the busiest times; there is an almost continual flow of coaches and tour buses taking international as well as domestic visitors to the site. Stonehenge is a site of industrial scale in visitor volume and popularity, whereas Avebury, set in a sleepy village in rural Wiltshire, is almost genteel. There is on-site interpretation provided through a hand-held audio guide at Stonehenge but this is not available at Avebury. The relevant public agencies strive to improve the surrounding setting and aesthetic values of Stonehenge and plans for its future are put forward and carried out; yet there is little mention of Avebury, where visitor numbers have been in decline in recent years. While both sites are part of this same World Heritage Site, there are great differences in their public profiles, international fame, popularity and prioritisation.

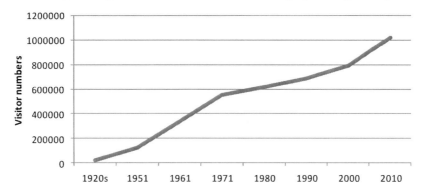

Figure 1: Visitor numbers to Stonehenge World Heritage Site from the 1920s to 2010. *Source:* English Heritage (2012b)

This case explores the reasons for the significant differences in visitor volume, international fame and exposure, future plans and management, and the 'spirit of place' of these two closely related prehistoric megalithic monuments. In doing to it will focus particularly on issues of accessibility, atmosphere, interpretation and the availability of tourism facilities.

Stonehenge, Avebury and associated sites

Stonehenge, Avebury and Associated Sites (see Figure 2) were inscribed on the World Heritage List (WHL) in 1986 for their outstanding importance as prehistoric ceremonial and funerary sites (UNESCO, 2012). The resulting

WHS is made up of two major areas: the sites of Stonehenge and Avebury. Each comprises a focal stone circle and, in addition, numerous monuments and burial mounds in the surrounding landscapes.

Figure 2: Stonehenge, Avebury and Associated Sites WHS. *Source:* Pomeroy-Kellinger (2005). © *Crown Copyright Ordnance Survey. All rights reserved*

The two sites are approximately 17 miles (27km) apart (Young et al., 2009). The monuments near the Stonehenge site (see Figure 3) that are inscribed on the WHL include the Avenue, the Cursuses, Durrington Walls, Wood-henge and numerous burial mounds (Young et al., 2009; UNESCO, 2012). The Avebury site (see Figure 4) lies to the north of Stonehenge. The monuments included in the World Heritage List at this site include Windmill Hill, the West Kennet Long Barrow, the Sanctuary, Silbury Hill, the West Kennet and Beckhampton Avenues, the West Kennet Palisaded Enclosures and various barrows (Pomeroy-Kellinger, 2005; UNESCO, 2012). Although the two sites are inscribed together as a single WHS, English Heritage refers to them as Stonehenge WHS and Avebury WHS respectively. This can be confusing as they may be perceived as two separate World Heritage Sites when in fact they are two sites or locations of the same World Heritage property. For the purpose of this case, in order not to add to any further confusion, the terms used by English Heritage will be used unless stated otherwise.

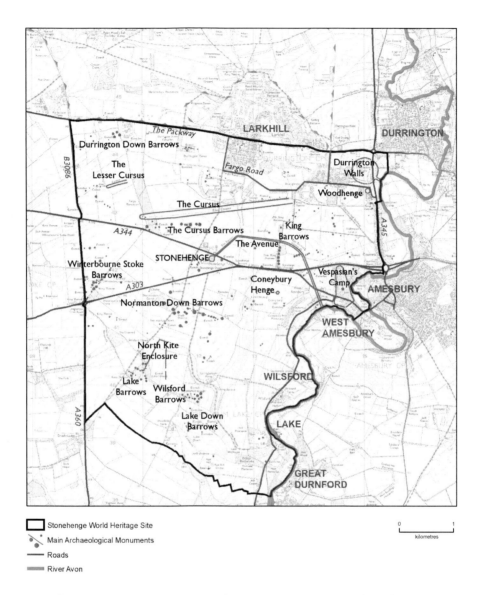

Figure 3: Stonehenge WHS. *Source:* Young et al. (2009). © *Crown Copyright Ordnance Survey. All rights reserved*

According to UNESCO (2012), the Stonehenge, Avebury and Associated Sites WHS is of outstanding universal value as it not only showcases creative, architectural and technological capabilities and achievements in prehistoric times, but it also illustrates the evolution of monument construction as well as the continual use and shaping of the landscapes by prehistoric societies over 2000 years from the Neolithic to the Bronze Age in Great Britain. Moreover, the World Heritage property provides an insight into the funerary and cultural practices of prehistoric Britain due to the inter-relationship between the monuments. In other words, the importance of this WHS is more than just the two stone circles: their roles in ceremonial and funerary practices, as well as their relations with other monuments, are essential in making them one of the greatest prehistoric monuments in the Britain and, indeed, the world. Nevertheless, apart from the actual stone circles at Stonehenge and Avebury, many of the other prehistoric remains of these monuments are only visible either in aerial view or to the trained eyes of historians and archaeologists.

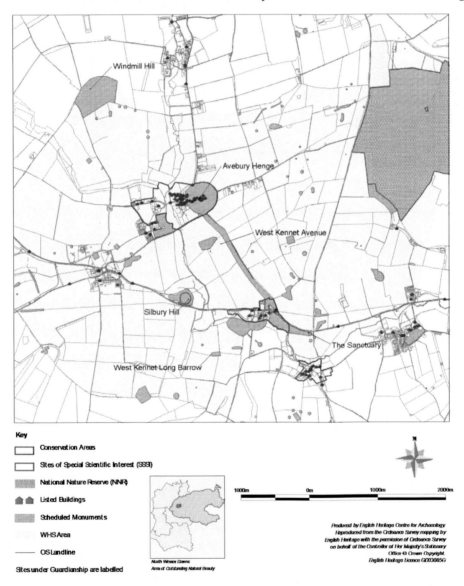

Figure 4: Avebury WHS. *Source:* Pomeroy-Kellinger (2005). © *Crown Copyright Ordnance Survey. All rights reserved*

The stone circle at Stonehenge is small enough to be absorbed in one glance, but its individual stones are large enough to create awe and wonder among visitors, specifically in relation to the 'how' and 'why' of construction and particularly as the purpose of the stone circle and associated landscape is contested and a full explanation remains elusive. This explains, at least in part, why for most visitors, especially the international ones, a visit to the WHS is not about visiting the whole site but just a part of it: this is usually Stonehenge because it is the most striking visual element of the entire WHS. Confirmation of Stonehenge having the highest profile among the monument complexes of the WHS and, indeed, iconic status (see Mason and Kuo, 2007), is that former Olympic sprinter Michael Johnson was asked to carry the Olympic torch to the monument during the build-up to 'London 2012' for a dawn photo shoot. It should also cause no surprise to find that at the Olympic equestrian show jumping events, there was a jump called 'Stonehenge'. Meanwhile at ExCel, one of the Olympic venues, a billboard poster depicting Stonehenge adorned the venue's wall (see Figure 5). As such, the ancient monument of Stonehenge has been used to advertise and promote the major modern global sporting event in the UK; the neighbouring site of Avebury, meanwhile, did not feature at all.

Figure 5: VisitBritain advert of Stonehenge at the Olympic venue, ExCel. Photo credit: I-Ling Kuo

Sense of place and visitor accessibility at heritage sites

Managing heritage sites for conservation and tourism use requires a multi-faceted approach. Management of the site is essential to ensure that the conservation effort of cultural heritage resources is not compromised or jeopardised, responsibilities of various stakeholders are fulfilled and adequate facilities are provided to meet the needs of visitors. It is also imperative to manage visitors' on-site activities and behaviour, and to plan the direction of tourism development in order to generate income for the upkeep of the site (Mason and Kuo, 2008; Leask and Garrod, 2009). Tourism and conservation may, however, be conflicting forces, and the incompatible relationship between resource conservation and the growth of tourism at heritage sites is an issue that is often discussed and written about by academics (see, for example, Leask and Fyall, 2006). As seen in the case of the Stonehenge, increased visitor numbers have led to greater problems of erosion and vandalism, such that access to the inside of the stone circle was fully prohibited in 1978 (Young et al., 2009). Of course, if access control or outright prohibition was the solution to such conflicts, the management of tourism at heritage sites would be much more straightforward. Indeed, highly restrictive access control or denial does not necessarily serve the best interests of the site's various stakeholders (see Leask and Garrod, 2009); rather, it may be wholly counterproductive. Forestell (1993) and Kals, Schumacher and Montada's (1999) research into emotional connections with nature suggest that provision of access to experience nature helps to foster more appropriate and protective behaviour towards nature. Arguably, this suggestion can also be applied to cultural heritage resources; by offering visitors the opportunity to experience cultural heritage sites through managed visitor access, visitors are more able to relate to earlier people, societies and civilisations through an increased knowledge and understanding of their history, archaeology, literature, and social and cultural practices. An increased understanding of cultural heritage resources can be achieved through well-designed and effective information provision and interpretation while the visitor is accessing the heritage site.

Approximately 20 years ago, Bender and Edmonds (1992) advocated a more flexible access to Stonehenge and the provision of more intellectually stimulating, multi-angled interpretation. They argued strongly that visitor access to the stone circle should be made available not just on a limited number of days, as the access policy stood by that time. Further, their paper argued that the presentation of the stones should reflect the complexity and dynamics of human society, both prehistoric and contemporary. They cautioned on the danger of the 'museumisation' of Stonehenge, which would comprise only a one-dimensional, abstracted and stifling presentation and interpretation of the stones by a single entity (namely English Heritage).

Shackley (2004) echoes Bender and Edmonds' concerns in her comparison of the Becharre cedar groves in Qadisha Valley in north Lebanon and the Chouf Cedar Reserve in central south Lebanon. The former were inscribed on the WHL in 1998, while the latter is not. The Becharre cedars in Qadisha Valley grow in a walled grove outside Lebanon's main ski resort and the site is isolated from its surroundings, which is largely a treeless and desolate landscape. In order to protect the cedars, visitors are told not to stray from marked footpaths. There is no access enabling visitors to get closer to the trees, because the path is used to separate visitors from the cedars. In Shackley's words, the construction and maintenance of the footpaths, although intended to look natural, is not visitor friendly and gives visitors "the impression that both they [the footpaths] and the trees are fiercely regimented" (Shackley, 2004: 421-422). Loud music from souvenir shops near the grove entrance is persistent and the site is not "a well-preserved forest grove but a sterile tree museum" and "far from giving the visitor a taste of what it would have been like in the original ancient forest, conveys the impression of an over managed botanical garden. The grove has preserved the trees, but without their spirit of place" (Shackley, 2004: 422). By way of contrast, in the Chouf Cedar Reserve visitors are accompanied by guides to walk through the cedar forest and they get the opportunity to see old cedars as well as newly planted saplings, and the opportunity to spot wildlife. The Chouf Reserve has spectacular landscapes and is quiet: a complete contrast from the busy Qadisha Valley cedar groves. Shackley (2006: 85) also argues for the importance of "maintaining the spirit of place" and the need to avoid the artificiality that can result from excessive or inappropriate management of heritage sites. Shackley (2006) has written specifically about Stonehenge and remarks on the monument being sandwiched by roads, the presence of traffic noise and the low standard of visitor facilities, which she claims contribute to a 'spirit of place'.

Many heritage sites are not a single entity but are part of a wider cultural landscape. Cultural landscapes are defined as "cultural properties [that] represent the 'combined works of nature and of man' … [and] are illustrative of the evolution of human society and settlement over time, under the influence of the physical constraints and/or opportunities presented by their natural environment and of successive social, economic and cultural forces, both external and internal" (World Heritage Centre, 2011: 14). Cultural landscapes differ significantly from objects kept and displayed in glass cases in museums insofar as a cultural landscape is a living environment, with the landscape being shaped and moulded by centuries (perhaps even millennia) of human activity. In order to present and interpret a cultural landscape, there is therefore a greater need to allow visitors to get close to it, to feel it and to be part of it; in other words, to experience it (Prentice, 2001; Richards, 2001; Pine and Gilmore, 2011). Unlike objects, cultural landscapes tend to be much larger in scale and size, and the spirit or sense of the landscape is that of something that is both intangible and living. The presentation of a cultural landscape cannot therefore be detached, fragmented or sterilised; instead it needs to be unabridged, interactive and presented in its entirety wherever possible, so that visitors are able to feel the size and scale of the landscape and involve themselves with the human activities that took place there through the passage of history. This raises an important dilemma between site management and resource conservation on the one hand and the visitor experience on the other. This is by no means to suggest that visitors' direct access to resources should take priority over resource conservation. It is not always possible to strike and maintain a balance between visitors' direct access and resource conservation. There is often also a very real need to protect visitors from dangers (such as, for example, falling stones). When direct access cannot be offered, appropriate and effective interpretation can be employed to fill the gap by providing visitors with a range of information without compromising resource conservation and visitor safety (Kuo, 2002; Mason, 2008). To be effective, this information should be high-quality, educational, interesting and relevant.

Interpretation at a heritage site

Writers such as Tilden (1977) and Beck and Cable (2002) emphasise the importance of relating interpretative information and messages to visitors. To be effective, such interpretation should be relevant and coherent, rather than abstract and disjointed, and should employ excellent communication skills. Interpretation that does not relate to visitors is likely to be dismissed as irrelevant, while disjointed and abstract interpretation will be difficult for visitors to comprehend. It is absolutely essential to provide accurate interpretation to visitors; however, this does not necessarily mean that interpretation should be littered with jargon (Ham, 1992; Moscardo, 1996, 1999; Kuo, 2011). In a tourism destination the audiences are visitors, not scientists, historians or archaeologists. Thus interpretation, although an educational activity, should be written and presented for ordinary laymen and women rather than specialists (Tilden, 1977; Ham, 1992). The challenge lies in maintaining the balance between keeping educational elements of interpretation and the integrity of the site on the one hand, and providing an enjoyable and pleasant visit experience to visitors on the other. Interpretation in heritage and archaeology-rich sites, if not planned and delivered appropriately, is likely to be considered dry, difficult or irrelevant to today's visitor. Facts are necessary and they are the foundation for interpretation; yet merely presenting and delivering facts is not interpretation (Tilden, 1977; Beck and Cable, 2002). Various practitioners and researchers have stressed the importance of using storytelling as a method to deliver interpretation (Ham, 1992; Tilden, 1977; Carr, 2004; Hays and MacLeod, 2006; Kuo, 2011). Storytelling is not about fabrication: it is about presenting facts in a way that can attract visitors' attention and can be understood without prior knowledge about the heritage; it is about delivering interpretation in an interesting and exciting fashion, bringing the past to life and making it relevant to present day (Christie and Mason, 2003).

There is also a need for the managers and custodians of heritage attractions to understand that tourism at heritage sites is unlikely to decline but rather to grow. As such, their responsibility should go beyond preserving the heritage resources to include wise use of the resources for the purposes of education, public access and enjoyment, research and financial sustainability (Garrod and Fyall, 2000). In this context, interpretation is ideally integrated into the site management plan from the start, rather than being added as an after-thought. With the advancement of information technology, there is a wide range of media and techniques available to deliver and present interpretation. The potential of seemingly low-tech media, such as signage, information panels, maps, guides and rangers should nevertheless not be under-estimated. Heritage sites with a number of clusters of monuments would benefit from using a large scale of map or 3D model to give visitors an overview of the site. Maps or models showing the relative sizes and distances of the temple complex of Angkor Wat in Cambodia, pyramids and temples and tombs in Giza and the Valley of Kings in Egypt, or significant and sacred landmarks at Uluru of Australia or Stonehenge and Avebury in Britain would give visitors a clear introduction to the site. Archive photos and artists' impressions of what the ruins must have been like in their prime would help visitors visualise the scale, colour and appearances of the sites, especially where the passage of time has taken its toll. Nevertheless, it is depressing to see how many renowned heritage sites around the world lack simple but high-quality maps or models in their visitor information centres. Indeed, visitor information centres are not even present at many heritage tourism sites.

With the advancement in technology, there is a wide range of media available to deliver interpretation. While large maps, models, photos and films usually require a visitor centre or at least a shelter to house them, modern technology is often pocket-sized and, increasingly, actually owned by the visitor. In the British Museum, for example, smart phones are now being used to host an audio guide, providing interpretation for special exhibitions such as the Hajj exhibition in the first quarter of 2012. Intricate details of exhibited items and objects are often incorporated into the interpretation, and the advantage of using smart phone is that visitors are able to look at the hand-held screen, enlarge images as necessary, and have a good look at the items while listening to the audio guide. The smart-phone audio guide also helps to reduce visitor congestion around exhibits because visitors can look at the screen to view the details of the objects in their hands, rewinding or fast forwarding the interpretive messages as they wish, instead of physically competing with other visitors to see the exhibits.

In addition to interpretation and a visitor information centre, car parks, toilets, cafés/restaurants and souvenir shops are typical facilities at tourism attractions. They fulfil some of the basic biological needs of visitors and provide the necessary conveniences and stress-free experiences provided they are well-designed, clean and fit for purpose. If a visitor attraction cannot meet the basic needs of visitors because, for example, queues for toilets are lengthy, toilets are not clean, car parks are difficult to access or congested, the visitor information centre is crowded, or souvenirs of the appropriate type and value are not offered for sale, then whatever the quality of the interpretation, visitors may feel far from satisfied with their visit. Cafés and souvenir shops offer shelter at outdoor sites in poor weather conditions and a resting place for visitors to relax; they also have the potential to encourage higher visitor expenditure at the site. With good backward linkages with local producers, visitor expenditures can contribute significantly to the local economy. Even so, it is not uncommon to see car parks full to their capacity, dirty toilets, kitsch for sale in souvenir shops, and over-priced food and drinks on the menu at many tourism attractions, including well-known heritage sites.

The cases of Stonehenge and Avebury are presented in detail below to provide a comparative narrative of interpretation provision, facilities, ambience and visitor experiences. Given that both sites are part of the same WHS, the similarity between the two sites – each having a prehistoric stone circle as the focal point – does not prevent there being a number of significant differences between them in these respects.

Stonehenge as a World Heritage Site

Located on Salisbury Plain, in southern England, approximately two hours' travel from London, Stonehenge is considered one of the most well-known icons in Britain (Mason and Kuo, 2007). Archaeological evidence suggests that substantial monuments were built in the area as early as the Mesolithic era (c.10,000-4000 BC), before Stonehenge was created. During the early to middle Neolithic era (c.4000–2000 BC) the earliest ceremonial and funerary monuments were constructed in and around today's Stonehenge WHS area. The earliest phase of construction of Stonehenge began around 3000 BC, as an earth monument comprising a circular ditch, dug using antlers (Richards, 2011). The site went through several phases of modification and construction and prior to Stonehenge as we see it today there may have been other structures on the site: possibly timber posts or stone pillars once stood in a series of holes, now called Aubrey holes, partially encircling today's Stonehenge. Some of the Aubrey holes are marked in white and are visible as one walks along the designated path around the stone circle (see Figure 6). These Aubrey holes are easily overlooked were it not for a brief commentary in the on-site interpretation delivered via the hand-held audio guide. Although there has not been sufficient scientific evidence about the earlier structures to determine their use, cremated human bones have been found in some of the Aubrey Holes, as well as in the bank and the ditch, suggesting that Stonehenge may have been used as a cemetery during its early life (Richards, 2011).

Figure 6: One of the Aubrey holes. Photo credit: I-Ling Kuo

Stonehenge is considered to be the most architecturally sophisticated prehistoric stone circle in the world (Young et al., 2009). Circa 2500 to 2000 BC, the stone circle made up with bluestones and sarsens was erected. The larger stones, called sarsens, each weigh about 25mt, with the largest one weighing over 40mt and standing over 7m high. The outer circle comprises 30 upright sarsen stones and these were topped by horizontal lintels, each weighing approximately 7mt. There are only 17 sarsens still standing today and only five of the lintels are still in place in this part of Stonehenge. Inside the first layer of sarsen stone circle is a concentric circle of bluestones, then there is an additional horseshoe of five sets of sarsen trilithons (meaning three stones) and another horseshoe of bluestones within that (see Figures 7 and 8).

Figure 7: Stonehenge. On the left is the best preserved section of outer stone circle with lintels still intact. One can make out the inner stone circles contained within. The middle upright with a lintel on top is one of the trilithons that form the sarsen horseshoe inner circle. Photo credit: I-Ling Kuo

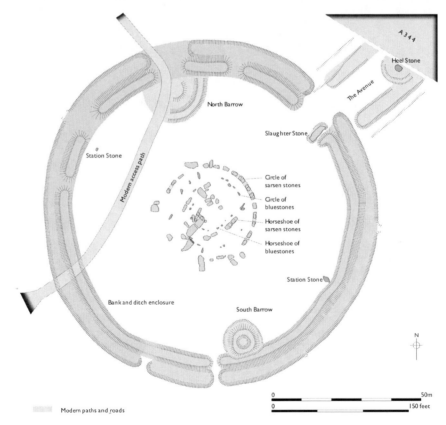

Figure 8: Stone settings at Stonehenge. Note the close proximity of the Heel Stone to the A344 road at the top right-hand corner. The A344 separates most of the Avenue (believed to be the ceremonial approach to Stonehenge) from Stonehenge. *Source:* Carver (2011) © *Copyright English Heritage. All right reserved*

The large sarsens are believed to have come from the Marlborough Downs, about 19 miles (30km) north of Stonehenge, and the transport of each stone would have required 200 men and taken about 12 days dragging it on a wooden sledge running on wooden rails (Richards, 2011). The smaller stones, called bluestones, came from the Preseli Hills in Wales, about 150 miles (240km) away, each weighing up to 4mt. Many of the stones at Stonehenge reveal evidence of stonework that they were shaped and trimmed. The setting of lintels above upright sarsens shows techniques common in modern carpentry such as tenon (a protruding peg on the top of an upright sarsen, see Figure 9) and mortise (a hole under the lintel shaped to fit a tenon), as well as vertical tongue-and-groove jointing so that the lintels are interlocked with the uprights beneath and the other lintels on each side (Richards, 2011).

The diameter of the circular enclosure, marked by the bank and ditch (the actual 'henge') surrounding the stone circle, is approximately 110m and the circumference of the enclosure is about 350m. The diameter of the stone circle is less than 50m (see Figure 8). This represents a very restricted area to accommodate the nearly one million visitors per annum to the site, the vast majority of whom would doubtless wish to stand there.

Figure 9: Evidence of craftsmanship in the shaping and trimming of stones. Photo: I-Ling Kuo

Many burial grounds were built in the area around Stonehenge and they were used until the early Bronze Age. However they were abandoned after 1600 BC (Young et al., 2009; English Heritage 2011). The purpose of Stonehenge is still contested among scholars, but the general belief is that Stonehenge and neighbouring monuments were part of ceremonial and funeral sites. As such, they help us to understand the funeral practices of Neolithic and Bronze Age Britain. The important ceremonial and astronomical attributes of Stonehenge and nearby monuments are denoted by their precise alignment on the axis of the midsummer sunrise and midwinter sunset (see Figure 8). The axis runs northeast to southwest, up the avenue through the circle. These attributes are considered of spiritual value by pagan and druid [3] groups, as well as hippies, who claim Stonehenge as a place for worship.

Stonehenge has always attracted visitors, and throughout the centuries the site has been vandalised, such as chips being knocked of the stones as souvenirs. The stones have also been removed by local farmers and those seeking stone to repair farm tracks or for building purposes. In 1978, access inside the stone circle was prohibited due to increased vandalism as well as physical erosion of the stones and surrounding ground, which it was perceived could destabilise the stones (Young et al., 2009). Since then, the stone circle of Stonehenge has been roped off and direct access has been restricted in some form or other. Since the mid-1970s Stonehenge had been the setting for Free Festivals and by the mid-80s they had attracted a very large number of festival followers. At this time, clashes between the festival goers and police began (Bender and Edmonds, 1992; Harvey, 2004). This led to the infamous Battle of the Beanfield[4] in 1985, just a few miles from Stonehenge, with several hundred arrests being made and 12 festival goers being hospitalised (BBC, 2004). Access to the stone circle by the general public has largely been banned ever since.

Since 2000, 15 years after the Battle of the Beanfield, druids, hippies and festival revellers have been permitted to enter the stone circle to perform religious or spiritual ceremonies at particular times, specifically the Summer Solstice[5] and on occasions the Winter Solstice (Young et al., 2009). The crowd and traffic management of the Summer Solstice has been a persistent issue. There is always a heavy police presence during the Summer Solstice due to the large crowds, and in June 2011 22,000 people gathered at Stonehenge (English Heritage, 2012b). A very recent feature is that visitors can apply for entry into the stone circle outside normal opening hours, although prior application is needed and the entrance charge is also higher.

---

3   Druids were the priests who carried out religious rituals during Iron Age Britain (c.800 BC to AD 43). They did not build Stonehenge: Stonehenge had been abandoned for over a thousand years before the Druids emerged. Modern druids are different to the ancient Druids. They are a diverse body of worshippers, pagan believers, revellers and travellers.

4   Violent clashes between police and festival goers on 1 June 1985 erupted when police attempted to block the way of a convey of vehicles travelling to Stonehenge for Stonehenge Free Festival, a festival started in 1974 on Summer Solstice day.

5   Summer solstice is the longest day of a year; winter solstice is the shortest. In the Northern Hemisphere, the Summer Solstice usually falls between 20 and 22 June, while the Winter Solstice falls between 20 and 22 December.

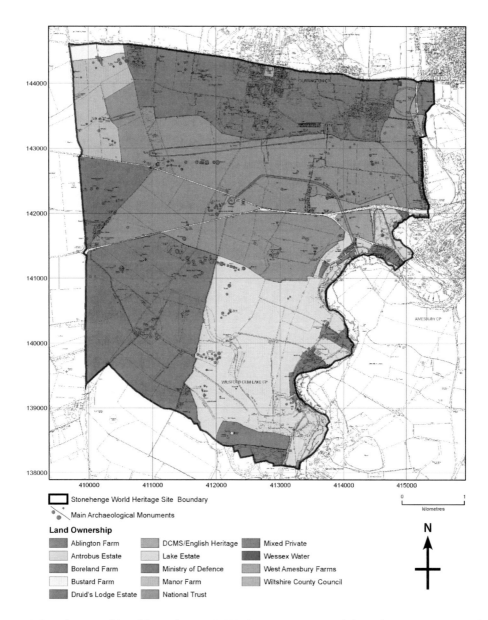

Figure 10: Land ownership of Stonehenge WHS. *Source:* Young et al. (2009). © *Crown Copyright Ordnance Survey. All rights reserved*

The ownership of Stonehenge is far from simple, mainly because it does not have just one single owner (see Figure 10). Most of the land surrounding Stonehenge is used for farming and areas farmed for arable crops are subject to EU's Common Agricultural Policy. The Ministry of Defence owns Larkhill Military Base and surrounding farmland in the northern part; the National Trust owns a sizable portion of the WHS; while the Secretary of State for Culture, Media and Sport is the owner of the specific site of the Stonehenge circle and 15 hectares of land around it. On behalf of the Secretary of State, English Heritage manages Stonehenge, the land around it and nearby Woodhenge. English Heritage operates the existing visitor facilities, including a car park, shop, kiosk and interpretation provisions. There are a number of private houses within the WHS boundaries (Young et al., 2009). One can also say that Stonehenge is surrounded by modernity rather than the ancient: it is sandwiched between the A303 main road to the south and the A344 to the north (see Figure 3). Both are busy roads, surrounded by modern-day farming and periodically a fighter jet from the nearby Larkhill military base will over-fly the Neolithic stone circle. It is hence virtually impossible to ignore the modern when visiting the prehistoric site.

Car parking facilities in Stonehenge are limited, and in peak times in the summer the volume of visitors exceeds capacity. At present, there is space for eight coaches and 123 cars in the permanent car park (with a hard surface). There is an additional fenced overflow car park (with a grass surface), with spaces for a further 150 vehicles. This is now in use for six months of the year. When the visitor volume in peak times exceeds even the capacity of the overflow car park, an adjacent field is used for additional parking (Young et al., 2009). Visitors parking their vehicles on the roadside is not an uncommon practice on busy summer days. Although it is possible to visit Stonehenge using public transport, it is not a common mode of arrive due to its inconvenience and lack of flexibility; one would have to go to Salisbury then change to the special 'Stonehenge Tour Bus' at Salisbury railway station (The Stonehenge Tour, 2012). The majority of visitors thus arrive in their private cars or in coaches as part of package tours. The parking spaces turn over several times in a day during peak times and the flow of visitor and vehicle traffic is continuous, with queues of vehicles looking for space to park and visitors frequently waiting in line for toilets, refreshments, entry to the ticket office, admission via the turnstile and to pick up audio guides (for on-site interpretation). In 2012, English Heritage implemented refundable parking charges of £3.00 during peak times (from June to the end of August, plus school half-term and Easter holidays), where visitors are asked to pay parking attendants upon arrival at the car park and the charge is then refunded when entrance into Stonehenge is purchased at the ticket office. Managing the volume of visitors (and thereby vehicle traffic) is of paramount importance in the Stonehenge area to ensure road safety and the aesthetic integrity of the site.

Entrance charges and access to Stonehenge World Heritage Site

The entrance charge to Stonehenge in 2012 was £7.80 for adults and £4.70 for children between five and 15 years of age (see Figure 11). Members of English Heritage or the National Trust may enter without charge. However, a report for English Heritage (Young et al., 2009) estimates that approximately 250,000 visitors view the stones from the A344 roadside without paying (see Figure 12). The use of the hand-held audio guide is included in the entrance fee. Nevertheless, it is surprising to see the number of people who opted not to use the audio guide. English Heritage also offers the option of purchasing an Overseas Visitors Pass, priced at £23.00 for a nine-day pass or £27.00 for a 16-day pass for an individual, which allows unlimited admissions to all English Heritage properties. In addition to visiting Stonehenge during normal opening hours, access into the Stonehenge stone circle is available outside the normal opening times, subject to availability. Prior booking is required and the charge in 2012 was £15.80 for adults and £12.60 for English Heritage or National Trust members. The number of people permitted in the stone circle is limited to 26 at any one time and the duration of stay is restricted to one hour. Although access to the stone circle is granted, touching the stones is not allowed. Visiting the inner stone circle is proving to be popular and in the summer months places are booked up well in advance. No audio guides are provided for these private visits, as they are outside the normal opening hours. In the summer months, when daylight hours are longer, there can be a variety of groups entering the stone circle in the early mornings and in evenings.

Figure 11: Opening hours, available languages for audio guide and entrance charges at Stonehenge WHS. Photo credit: I-Ling Kuo

Figure 12: People viewing Stonehenge from the A344 roadside. The stone on the right is the Heel Stone, a large unshaped sarsen. From the Heel Stone parallel banks and ditches of the Avenue (believed to be the processional, ceremonial approach to Stonehenge) leads across the field on the other side of A344. Note how close the Heel Stone is to the road and how the Avenue is cut and separated from Stonehenge. Photo credit: I-Ling Kuo

Interpretation at Stonehenge World Heritage Site

Despite the fact that Stonehenge is part of the surrounding wider prehistoric landscape, it is the site that attracts the largest number of visitors. Other prehistoric features in the area, although part of the World Heritage property, are less dramatic and seemingly insignificant to untrained eyes (Carver, 2011). For many international visitors, Stonehenge is a 'must-see' attraction (see Mason and Kuo, 2007); however, their awareness of other monuments in the surrounding landscape is limited (Carver, 2011). Although Stonehenge, Avebury and Associated Sites is not actually inscribed as a 'Cultural Landscape' on the WHL, at present only the focal stone circle of Stonehenge is presented and its relationship to other prehistoric monuments is not explicit in the site setting or in on-site interpretation. Figure 3 has shown the monuments, sites and landscapes that form this part of Stonehenge, Avebury and Associated Sites WHS. However, visitors are rarely explicitly made aware of the wider landscape and other monuments during their visits to Stonehenge.

Interpretation about Stonehenge is almost exclusively delivered through the audio guide provided immediately after the visitor had entered through the turnstile. It is available in 10 languages: English, Chinese, Japanese, French, Spanish, German, Swedish, Italian, Russian and Dutch, as well as a more detailed commentary in English for partially sighted visitors (see Figure 11). The hand-held audio guide is about the size of a smart phone. Visitors follow the footpath around Stonehenge and listen to respective commentary at designated points and visitors can fast-forward, skip or rewind different sections of interpretation at will. The current audio device is an improvement on its previous version, an audio wand, which was approximately 30cm long – much bigger and clumsier than the current device – and frequently out of order. English Heritage has identified the need to improve the presentation, visibility and interpretation of Stonehenge and key archaeological monuments and sites (Young et al., 2009). With the open expanse of Stonehenge and the scattered monuments in the surrounding landscape, sufficient interpretation provision would be a challenge in both financial and practical terms. Signage would have to be able to sustain the natural elements, such as sun and rain, and regular maintenance would be needed. There is also concern about aesthetic values: some visitors may argue that the signs or information panels destroy the atmosphere of the setting. English Heritage may not be able to utilise iPhones, such as the ones used at British Museum, for delivering interpretation, because of the outdoor setting of the site: on rainy days the iPhone would risk being damaged. Moreover, most of the prehistoric monuments in the surrounding Stonehenge landscape are not as dramatic and visible as Stonehenge. In order to explain and interpret the relative locations and distances, shapes, sizes and purposes, a large map or a 3D model is needed. Alternatively, films or audio-visual presentations may be more appropriate and effective. Either way, such interpretation would require a visitor centre as the focal point for interpretation provision.

Although the interpretation commentary explains the stonework and the relationships between the outer sarsen stone circle and the inner bluestone circle on the one hand and the inner horseshoes of bluestones and sarsens on the other, it is certainly not easy to grasp (Figure 6 shows visitors listening to the hand-held audio guide). Stonehenge was constructed in several phases, over a very long period of time, and was in use for several thousand years: a brief commentary without visual aids such as aerial photos or a map or information panel does not do much justice to the complexity and architectural achievements of Stonehenge.

Some interpretation at Stonehenge is undoubtedly difficult for visitors to understand for a variety reasons, including the use of jargon, lack of visual aids and/or poor choice of media. For instance, it is doubtful that the interpretive commentary using terms such as 'barrows', 'avenue', 'north-south position of the station stones' or 'ceremonial procession' would be fully understood by most visitors, especially international ones. For example, visitors may have little or no understanding of what a barrow is for or what it might look like. Moreover, there are no visual aids available on the hand-held audio guide, and unless taken to the air it is difficult for visitors to visualise the relative location, distance and scale of the various monuments spread across the landscapes surrounding Stonehenge.

Other than the audio guide, there is no exhibition and no maps, photographs or archaeological finds are displayed at Stonehenge. It is difficult for a visitor, especially an international one, to grasp the historical significance of Stonehenge and its relationships to other monuments dotted around in the surrounding landscape. To date, the Stonehenge WHS has been presented as a circle of stones in the interpretation, with very limited information on the nearby surroundings and the relations between various monuments. To most international visitors[6], and even to many British visitors, these interpretive commentaries of how it might have been used, the settings of the stones and its relationship to other monuments can be difficult to comprehend, especially considering Stonehenge was built and used for several thousands of years by numerous peoples and cultures. Such a long history is likely to be complex and diverse.

The lack of models, large maps and information panels/signage as visual aids to the audio guide exacerbates the inadequacy of on-site interpretation at Stonehenge. The lack of appropriate interpretation and educational provision may be a more considerable weakness than the traffic congestion, noise pollution or low aesthetic value in the current management of the site. In addition, anecdotal evidence suggests that a significant number of visitors do not use the hand-held audio guide on site. This may be because it does not have a language that they understand, or perhaps it is that the current presentation and setting of Stonehenge is perceived as being nothing more than a spectacular stone circle, in which case there is no reason to listen to the interpretation. It is disheartening to see crowds of visitors, usually relatively young (in their teens to early 20s), both international and British, walking around the stones chatting away to each other and barely paying attention to the site, failing to use the interpretive audio guide even when the entrance fee includes hire of it. It sometimes appears that there is little difference between visiting a renowned WHS and shopping with friends on the high street. This is, however, not uncommon in many heritage sites today, where some visitors appear indifferent to the heritage resources.

---

6   At least half of the annual visitors to the site are international according to Young et al., (2009), although more recent research suggest more than 70% of the visitors are from overseas (English Heritage, 2011).

The spirit of Stonehenge

The magical, mystical or magnificent spirit of Stonehenge and its surrounding landscape is arguably diminished during normal opening hours by a number of factors (Shackley, 2006): it is often crowded with visitors, some of whom are being noisy or appear uninterested; there is continual road-traffic noise; provision of on-site interpretation is inadequate; visitor facilities are insufficient, so that after walking around the stones there is no place to sit to take in the views and absorb atmosphere of the surrounding landscapes; the route around the site takes the form of a one-way-only route march, in which visitors must follow the footpath encircling the stone circle and view the stones at a distance; the interpretive commentary, albeit educational and informative, lacks detail, and comes across as being rather one-dimensional and dry. As such, it differs little from Becharre cedar grove (also a WHS), which was criticised by Shackley (2004; 2006) for much the same reasons. The interpretation provides a brief explanation of the origins of the site but not its development throughout the passage of time; nor does it cover the relationship between people and the landscapes over the centuries including latter day legends and myths about the site (Bender and Edmonds, 1992). Although the custodian role and contribution of key stakeholders such as English Heritage in the management of Stonehenge cannot be underestimated, one cannot help but wonder how the mere 40 minutes or so interpretation provided through the audio guide could ever be sufficient to present the complexity and histories of the 5000-year-old Stonehenge. The visit to Stonehenge WHS is almost the same as a production-line style of manufacturing: highly standardised, structured and regulated.

Documentaries on Stonehenge can be found on British television and some have been aired in other countries. However, research findings suggest mixed viewer opinions on these programmes (Carver, 2011). It seems they have not been watched by a majority of the British, and even fewer international visitors. Indeed, many international viewers could not remember much from the documentaries they saw. No doubt these documentaries were informative and educational; however, the effects of these programmes as interpretation are questionable. Moreover, recent research suggests a continuing low level of knowledge and confusion over the wider Stonehenge landscape among tourists, even after they have visited the stones (Carver, 2011). This indicates a need for improvement in interpretation and presentation of Stonehenge, not as an isolated stone circle but as part of a prehistoric landscape. This also implies an over-emphasis in the marketing and promotion of the site of Stonehenge itself, to the exclusion of other elements of the wider prehistoric landscape, individually and in its totality

Future plans for Stonehenge WHS

The current visitor centre is not a visitor centre as such but a souvenir shop, although publications and guidebooks relating to Stonehenge and other monuments and archaeological sites in Wiltshire are available for purchase. The traffic congestion around the site, made worse by regular traffic accidents, and inadequate visitor parking, interpretation, catering and toilets have been identified as not doing justice to Stonehenge, even though it is considered to be an "internationally significant cultural site" (Chris Blandford Associates, 2000: 3/23) and overall the facilities at Stonehenge have been referred to as a 'national disgrace' by the UK Parliament (see Mason and Kuo, 2007).

In 2000, English Heritage published the Stonehenge WHS Management Plan (Chris Blandford Associates, 2000), in which a bold vision was set out for improvements to the access roads (the A344 and A303) and visitor facilities, including a proposal for a state-of-the art, world-class visitor centre. A scheme for the road network surrounding Stonehenge was proposed, including closure of the A344 and putting the adjacent part of the A303 into a tunnel to run directly underneath the WHS, making it much less visually intrusive to the landscape. The intention was to unify Stonehenge with other archaeological sites in the surrounding landscape and to reduce traffic congestion and noise pollution while enhancing the aesthetic integrity of the area. In addition, a new visitor centre located away from the stone circle was proposed to be the focal point of interpretation for Stonehenge, as well as a promotional point for other attractions and sites in the region (Chris Blandford Associates, 2000). The purpose of constructing a new visitor centre on the edge of the WHS, away from the core of Stonehenge area was to reduce traffic congestion, with visitors either using a shuttle bus from the new visitor centre or walking to the stone circle. The idea was that the new visitor centre should be located "on a site that is clear of significant archaeology [;] allows for access on foot to the Stones and the wider WHS and/or by other sustainable means of transport via a drop-off point or points on the edge of the core zone; is outside the boundary of the WHS to avoid undermining the values and significance of the WHS landscape, and to facilitate managed visitor access…" (Chris Blandford Associates, 2000: 4/17-18).

The proposed plan of putting the A303 in a tunnel was abandoned in December 2007 due to its high cost, estimated to be over £500 million (BBC, 2007). Immediately after the announcement of this decision, a brief news item was published on the UNESCO website indicating that "UNESCO regrets the UK government's decision to cancel the A303 road improvement scheme for

Stonehenge World Heritage property" (UNESCO, 2012: n.p.). In the meantime, English Heritage stated that "the setting of the stones and a visitor centre [are] still a priority" (BBC, 2007: n.p.). Nevertheless, the future of constructing a new visitor centre and other facilities is far from straightforward. In 2009, the UK government announced a £25 million plan for building a new visitor centre at Airman's Corner (on the A344), approximately 1.5 miles away from the existing visitor car park and shop cluster. Sources of funding were to include the central government, English Heritage, the Heritage Lottery Fund and various other private and public sources (BBC, 2009a,b). In mid-2010, however, the announcement by the coalition government of £10 million of funding cuts cast considerable doubt over this funding package (BBC, 2010a). However in November 2010, the Heritage Lottery Fund announced an extra £10 million of funding for the Stonehenge visitor centre plan, which more than doubled the funding it had initially allocated for the scheme (BBC, 2010b). In June 2012 preparation began for the building of a new Stonehenge visitor centre at Airman's Corner (BBC, 2012a; see Figure 13) and in July 2012 the planned A344 road closure occurred, signalling the start of the project.

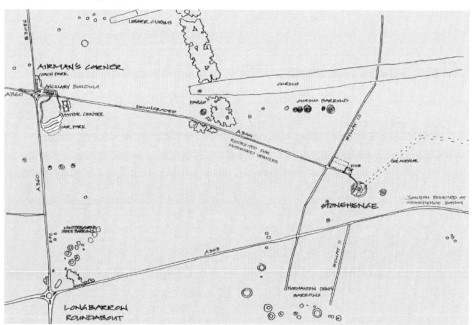

Figure 13: Proposed location of the new Stonehenge visitor centre. Source: English Heritage (2011). © *Copyright English Heritage. All right reserved*

The new visitor centre and parking facilities will replace the existing ones and a shuttle service will ferry visitors between the new visitor centre/car park and the stone circle. The land reclaimed through the closure of the A344 will be grassed over (BBC, 2012b; English Heritage, 2012c). Since 2000, efforts in turning farmlands surrounding Stonehenge into permanent grassland have been successful, with the aims of improving the ecological diversity and enhancing the aesthetic values of the site (Young et al., 2009). With the additional closure of the A344, Stonehenge will finally be reunited with its surrounding monuments, including the Avenue, the ancient processional approach to Stonehenge (BBC, 2012b). The new visitor centre is expected to open in autumn 2013. English Heritage has made a short video depicting the envisaged improvements from the plan (English Heritage, 2012c). It would seem that the improvements to the facilities, setting and presentation of Stonehenge that were promised when it became a WHS in the mid-1980s have finally started.

The plan for the new visitor centre, including the new traffic arrangements, has an estimated cost of £27 million, and aims to provide appropriate interpretation and education to visitors. The existing facilities and visitor centre, which is little more than a souvenir shop, were erected in the 1960s as a temporary measure. As such they are now out of date and barely able to cope with the year-on-year increase in visitor numbers. Visitors can be forgiven for thinking that when they reach Stonehenge they have arrived at an outdoor temporary event: the toilet blocks on the corner of the car park are temporary Portaloos and the ticket booths are housed in temporary Portakabins, rather than permanent, purpose-built structures (see Figure 14).

Figure 14: The queue at the temporary ticket offices (since the 1960s) and the crowds just after the entry turnstile. Photo credit: I-Ling Kuo

The new visitor centre will house displays and exhibitions, including objects found in the area. The expectation is that since visitor car parks and the new visitor centre will be located away from the stones, visitors will take the opportunity to go to the visitor centre first. Here, they can receive information and interpretation prior to their actual arrival at the stone circle. The distance between the new visitor centre and Stonehenge also affords visitors a chance to journey through the landscape in order to appreciate what the place might have been like thousands of years ago. This impression will be very much enhanced since the closure of the A344 in June 2012. There is also a plan to erect three replica Neolithic houses using recently unearthed evidence of domestic dwellings near Stonehenge (English Heritage, 2012c; see also Leask and Garrod, 2011). The overall intention is to improve the visibility of various other monuments in the landscapes and present a more complete and fully integrated picture of Stonehenge (Carver, 2011) both as a focal ceremonial location for the people at the time, and as part of a living and working environment for those communities. Such interpretation of the site, assuming it is well-planned and well-presented, would reduce the presently abstract and disjointed feel of Stonehenge, reuniting the stone circle with various other archaeological monuments located in the nearby landscape and a holistic rather than merely partial story of Stonehenge and the people who used it (Tilden, 1977). English Heritage is also considering offering a portable audio-visual device for use in the open landscape around Stonehenge (Carver, 2011).

According to various English Heritage reports (Chris Blandford Associates, 2000; Young et al., 2009; Carver 2011), the average length of visitor stay at Stonehenge is between 45 and just under 100 minutes. Since Stonehenge is three miles away from the nearest settlement of Amesbury, visitors rarely visit and spend money there. In other words, besides the entrance charges to visit the stone circle, there is very limited local economic impact, despite Stonehenge receiving over a million visitors per annum. With the intention of making the new visitor centre a focal point for not only the whole WHS but also other regional visitor attractions, it is hoped that visitors may spend a longer time at the Stonehenge WHS and Amesbury itself, with the effect of increasing visitor expenditure into the local economy. It is planned that there will be a larger shop and a café in the new visitor centre, and English Heritage has pledged to use local produce whenever possible. English Heritage together with other stakeholders has put forward a document entitled '*Stonehenge World Heritage Site: A Strategy for Interpretation, Learning and Participation 2010-15*', setting out their plans for improving the delivery and presentation of interpretation (Carver, 2011). This seems to be an important step in the right direction to justify the significance of Stonehenge and the surrounding landscapes.

Avebury World Heritage Site

Also part of the WHS, Avebury is very both literally and metaphorically in the shadow of Stonehenge, which is located only a short distance to the south, and being less well-known, despite being the largest stone circle in the world. Avebury WHS consists of a series of ceremonial and burial sites, with the earliest monument in the area believed to be the West Kennet Long Barrow (burial chamber), built around 3700 to 3600 BC and located approximately 1.2 miles (about 2km) south of Avebury. Human remains have been found in the burial chambers, showing that the use of the long barrow spanned several centuries (National Trust, 2008). In around 2400 BC the building of Silbury Hill began (National Trust, 2008). This is the largest prehistoric earth mound in Europe, being 37m high, 30m across the top and about 500m around the base (National Trust, 2008). It is approximately half way between Avebury and the West Kennet Long Barrow in the valley of the River Kennet (see Figure 4 for relative location and distance of various monuments at Avebury). No burials have found within the mound and the purpose of Silbury Hill is still a mystery. It is at present off limits to the general public.

Unlike the stones of Stonehenge, where many have been hewn and shaped, Avebury's stones were not shaped and vary greatly in size. Similar to the construction of Stonehenge, Avebury Henge was built and modified over centuries, starting from approximately 2850 BC and continuing to around 2200 BC (English Heritage, 2012d). A vast circular bank and ditch (see Figure 15) was made around 2600 BC, using no more than antlers to break into solid chalk to create a ditch as deep as 9m and form a bank as high as 4m. The circumference of the enclosure is approximately 1200m, covering an area of 11 hectares (National Trust, 2008). The vast, circular henge area cuts through part of Avebury village (English Heritage, 2012d; National Trust, 2008), with more recent houses, farmland and roads enclosed in this prehistoric monument.

Within this circular bank and ditch is a circle of large standing stones of about 100 in number, with two additional smaller stone circles enclosed within, each with a central feature (English Heritage, 2012d; National Trust, 2008). Most stones were erected a couple of centuries after the construction of the circular enclosure. Two stone avenues are visible leading to and from Avebury Henge: the West Kennet Avenue and the Beckhampton Avenue. Visitors can follow the former easily and it is also identifiable from the road, with its paired stones standing approximately 15m apart and each pair around 20 to 30m from the next pair (National Trust, 2008). In addition to Avebury Henge, there are other stone circles and henges in the close vicinity, such as the Sanctuary (see Figure 4), although they are no longer easily visible. Taking an aerial view of the landscape is the best way to identify the locations, sizes and shapes of this myriad of prehistoric monuments. Like Stonehenge and its surrounding landscape, Avebury Henge is the most obvious and identifiable evidence of Neolithic Britain in this part of the WHS as a whole. However, unlike the alignment of the Stonehenge stones to the Summer Solstice sunrise and Winter Solstice sunset, Avebury Henge has no such an alignment.

Figure 15: The bank and ditch encircling Avebury. Photo credit: I-Ling Kuo

Ownership of Avebury WHS

As with Stonehenge, the ownership of Avebury is multiple and the different interests of the various owners can create certain challenges for the management of the WHS. There are several farm estates and private landowners, while the National Trust is the largest landowner in the Avebury WHS, holding one third of the area for permanent preservation (Pomeroy-Kellinger, 2005). Management and ownership of various monuments in the site may involve several agencies: for example Silbury Hill is privately owned but managed by English Heritage, while the Sanctuary at the end of West Kennet Long Barrow is managed by the National Trust under an agreement with English Heritage (National Trust, 2008). Other agencies with statutory responsibilities may also exert an influence over the future management and protection of Avebury WHS, including the Countryside Agency, the Department for Environment, Food and Rural Affairs and various parish councils (Pomeroy-Kellinger, 2005).

The lesser fame of Avebury

Unlike Stonehenge, Avebury Henge does not have the horizontal lintels capping the stones. Although Avebury's outer circle is vast in comparison with the compact size of Stonehenge, Avebury Henge is not as visually striking as

Stonehenge at first glance (see Figure 16). Two further facts do not help Avebury's status as 'little sister in the shadow of Stonehenge': visitor numbers and its awareness among international visitors. For a long period of time, ranging from the Middle Ages to possibly the 16th century, many of the stones at Avebury were damaged, destroyed and removed. It was estimated that in the 11th century, around the time of the Battle of Hastings, most of the stones of the stone circles and West Kennet and Beckhampton Avenues were still standing. However, when the first large- scale excavation began at the beginning of the 20th century, only 15 stones were still standing upright in the Avebury Henge, with only two at Beckhampton Avenue and four at West Kennet Avenue. Many stones were buried or broken into pieces to use in the construction of local building over the centuries (National Trust, 2008).

Figure 16: Avebury Henge: unshaped stones, without lintels, and a much larger outer stone circle containing two inner circles. Unlike at Stonehenge, visitors have unrestricted access. Photo credit: I-Ling Kuo

Amateur archaeologist Alexander Keiller not only conducted archaeological digs for several years at Avebury, he also re-erected many of the buried or fallen stones as close to their original positions as possible when he found them. Where stones had been destroyed, he marked their positions with concrete posts (see Figure 17). In total, Keiller re-erected 50 stones in Avebury and the West Kennet Avenue; he also opened a museum on site, housing records and artefacts found during his digs and from later work around Avebury (National Trust, 2008). Due to the destruction and the disappearance of many stones at Avebury, the visual effect of Avebury Henge is less striking than Stonehenge. Moreover, the popularity of Stonehenge is reinforced through its continual use in the public media. While Avebury may be mentioned, often it is placed behind Stonehenge. This combination of being in the runner-up spot, with a less striking visual image, consigns Avebury WHS to being the less-visited prehistoric megalithic monument. The prevailing iconic image of Stonehenge dominates and hence represents the prehistoric cultural heritage of Britain among tourists, especially international ones.

Figure 17: Concrete pillars marking the position of the missing stones. Photo credit: I-Ling Kuo

It is difficult to visit Avebury using public transport and due to its less well-known status relative to Stonehenge, bus tours to Avebury can be difficult to find. It is possible to use a train and bus combination between Swindon and Avebury; however, on weekends and bank holidays, public transport services are less frequent. In Stonehenge car park, the number of coaches is high and there are usually many occasions of turnover in coach parking bays daily during summer months. There are also tour companies operating day tours from London to Stonehenge on a daily basis. This is not the case at Avebury. Bus tours to Avebury are usually offered by specialist tour operators and often this is on a private-hire basis. On several occasions when the authors visited Avebury, not one coach was in the car park. It is therefore not surprising that the majority of the visitors have to use their private vehicles to reach Avebury (Pomeroy-Kellinger, 2005). This may pose potential crowding and traffic congestion in the visitor car park on special occasions such as the summer solstice.

The annual visitor number to Avebury is not clear because of the open-access nature of the site. However, the National Trust estimates that Avebury attracted around 350,000 visitors per annum in the early 2000s (Pomeroy-Kellinger, 2005). The visitor number appears however to have been in decline since the mid-2000s and the estimated visitor volume in 2009/10 was around 250,000 (Pomeroy-Kellinger, 2005; Carver, 2011). Although English Heritage states in its Avebury WHS Management Plan that a large percentage of visitors to the site are of international origin (Pomeroy-Kellinger, 2005), the ratio of international to domestic visitors to Avebury is likely to be lower than that at Stonehenge WHS, where as many as 70% of its 1 million annual visitors are from overseas (Carver, 2011). The lesser fame of Avebury is not necessarily a disadvantage to the visitors to the site. Unlike the restrictions on access to the stone circle at Stonehenge, visitors to Avebury enjoy literally unlimited access to the stones (see Figures 16, 17 and 18). Since part of Avebury village is encircled within the Avebury Henge, the opening hours of the site are unlimited, although it is advisable to enter during daylight hours.

Figure 18: Unrestricted access to stones at Avebury. Photo credit: I-Ling Kuo

Visitor facilities and atmosphere at Avebury World Heritage Site

The current visitor parking facility is about a five-minute gentle stroll away from the entrance to the stone circle and the National Trust shop, museums and tea room cluster (known as the Old Farmyard). The parking charge is £5.00 per day 'pay and display' or £3.00 after 3pm in the summer months. The parking charge is cheaper in the winter, at £2.00 per day. There is a manned mobile National Trust information hut in the corner of the car park at the head of the trail leading towards the stone circle entrance, the Old Farmyard and the village high street. Basic leaflets about Avebury Henge and Avebury Manor (discussed later in this case), as well as other monuments in the county, are available

At the Old Farmyard there are two museums: at the Stables Gallery is the Alexander Keiller Museum, named after the archaeologist who carried out excavations and re-erected a number of stones. He opened this museum in the stable block of his residence Avebury Manor to house and display the finds from his excavations. In the Barn Gallery are interactive models and computers for children to learn more about the Stone Age and the Avebury area. There is also a dressing-up area, where children can try on Bronze-Age clothing (National Trust, 2012). The hands-on approach to interpretation is considered to be a good way to attract and retain visitors' attention, especially that of children (Tilden, 1977; Ham, 1992).

There is no entrance charge for the Avebury Henge, other than a pay-and-display parking charge. The fact that Avebury village is enclosed within the circle and roads run through it makes implementing an entrance charge difficult at present and unlikely to happen in the future. Visitors are able to roam freely among the stones, and it is common to see visitors touching and hugging the stones. Groups of worshippers can be seen meditating or praying near stones, another activity which is not permitted at Stonehenge other than on the summer or winter solstice days (see Figure 19).

Figure 19: A group of worshippers at Avebury. Photo credit: I-Ling Kuo

The facilities at the Old Farmyard enable visitors to stay and linger on site for a longer and more relaxed visit. This is much in contrast with the lack of resting places or café at the Stonehenge site, where visitors have little else to do other than leave once they have walked around the site. The atmosphere at the car park and the Old Farmyard is more relaxed and leisurely relative to the Stonehenge site, with no competition for parking spaces, toilets or ticket offices. The stress-free ambiance also extends to the stone circle, where visitors stroll and roam among the stones at their own pace, in any direction they wish to go. It is normal to see visitors lying on the grass, having a picnic or worshipping at Avebury Henge (when the weather permits it). This is in complete contrast to the highly structured, 'ushered-through' visits at Stonehenge. Due to the vast size of Avebury Henge, with its circumference of 1200m and a much smaller number of visitors, together with the backdrop of rural Avebury village, the site has a genteel atmosphere in contrast to the high-density visitor volume at Stonehenge site, with its circumference of about 350m and over one million visitors, with a backdrop of roads and temporary facilities.

With part of Avebury village encircled within it, the Avebury WHS is clearly a lived-in environment. There is still traffic noise, but it is not persistent and it is relatively quiet. Instead, the 'noises' come from villagers' daily lives. Using one's imagination, the setting projects images of how earlier people and societies living in the area would have lived among the stones as they are set within the landscape, and how they may have interacted with the stones or changed the landscape for farming or other purposes. However, this advantage of open, unrestricted access to ancient stones and the surrounding landscapes is not utilised to its full potential the in interpretation at Avebury WHS.

Interpretation at Avebury World Heritage Site

There is very limited interpretation on site at Avebury Henge. A range of guide books is available but there is no hand-held audio guide for visitors as self-guide. Nor is there signage or information panels in the open, aside from the two museums at the Old Farmyard and two information panels (with limited contents, see Figures 20 and 21) along the trail linking the visitor car park to the stone circles and Old Farmyard. There are some guided walks and events available but they are not offered on a regular basis. If a visitor is hoping to participate in such activities, it would be advisable to check the National Trust website first.

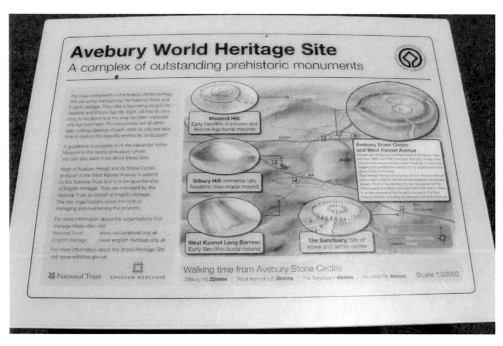

Figure 20: One of the two information panels depicting Avebury Henge and various other prehistoric monuments at Avebury World Heritage Site. Photo credit: I-Ling Kuo

Figure 21: Information panel depicting the Alexander Keiller Museum, Avebury Manor, the Old Farmyard, shop and café, and the setting of Avebury Henge. Note the limited amount of interpretation on the information panels. Photo credit: I-Ling Kuo

The potential contribution of interpretation to visitors' enjoyment and to effective visitor management is, however recognised. Moreover, the National Trust acknowledges that there is scope to improve presentation and interpretation of other monuments as well as Avebury Henge, particularly the overall landscape of the WHS (Pomeroy-Kellinger, 2005). Since there is no entrance charge to Avebury Henge, once visitors have parked their car they may go directly to the stone circles without visiting the museums. This is an opportunity missed in offering interpretation and information about Avebury Henge and the surrounding landscapes. In the Avebury WHS Management Plan, improvements in interpretation have been recommended for Avebury Henge and village as well as the many other monuments such as the West Kennet Avenue (Pomeroy-Kellinger, 2005).

Opportunities at Avebury Henge: Interpretation and 'spirit of place'

Avebury Manor and Garden became Alexander Keiller's residence in the 1930s and it is open to the public for an entry charge (£10.00 in 2012). In late 2011, a documentary series of how a group of historians, experts and volunteers refurbished Avebury Manor was aired on the BBC and this documentary made Avebury Manor a significant tourism attraction during 2012. Unlike the usual approach of the National Trust in its management of stately homes, visitors are allowed – even encouraged – to touch the objects and furniture on display in the Manor house: "you can go lie on the bed but please take off your shoes first" was announced to one of the authors upon entering the manor house. Families crowded on the bed having their photos taken, children opened and closed secret doors in awe, young visitors stitched their names in the embroidery set and visitors handled the unfamiliar kitchen utensils. All these activities are uncommon in National Trust properties but afford wonderful opportunities in interpretation of the Manor house. Members of staff are on site to chat to visitors and to explain various features and histories of the house. Nevertheless, at present the Avebury Manor experience is detached from the Avebury Henge, other than that it was once Alexander Keiller's residence.

The two museums are unique features of Avebury WHS. The Alexander Keiller Museum houses many archaeological finds discovered in the area and the close vicinity between the Museum and Avebury WHS is unusual in Britain (Pomeroy-Kellinger, 2005). It offers great opportunities for research, as well as playing a pivotal role in education and interpretation provision at Avebury and the Alexander Keiller Museum. The Manor House should also be a focal point in the provision of education and interpretation for Avebury Henge and its people.

There is great potential to create a unique and fitting 'spirit of place' (Shackley, 2006) at Avebury WHS, given that it was the home of one of the key archaeologists of the site, and that many of his discoveries are also housed and displayed in an on-site museum. Being a contemporary figure, there are many archive photos, documents, items and equipment that Alexander Keiller used in his daily life and for his archaeological digs kept in the house. These are from the not-so-distant past and visitors have little difficulty relating to the lifestyle of this era and the items he used such as clothing, walking canes and equipment he used. His role in archaeological work in the area, especially his efforts in positioning and erecting fallen stones, has made Avebury Henge as we see it today. Furthermore, the unrestricted access to the stones affords visitors a close encounter with evidence of prehistoric Britain, as well as the opportunity to through walk the landscapes in which the people and civilisations throughout the centuries walked, worked, shaped and changed. Avebury Henge and the surrounding landscape is rich in both tangible and intangible heritage and steeped with the 'spirit of the place' spanning nearly 5000 years, as well as being sufficiently visible and easily accessible to visitors. With appropriate planning and well designed interpretation (see Tilden 1977; Ham, 1992; Beck and Cable, 2002) Avebury Henge could and should be a prominent heritage site offering insightful, educational and experiential visits. During such visits, visitors could have direct, first-hand experience of the real, tangible objects, as well as the broader landscape, in a well-managed but not regulated or stifling setting. Avebury Henge possesses these unique attributes that Stonehenge site does not: they are what could help Avebury to step out of the shadow of Stonehenge.

Conclusion

This case has attempted to indicate the similarities and differences between the prehistoric visitor attractions of Stonehenge and Avebury. Table 1 provides a summary of these, using a number of different headings.

The case has revealed the iconic status of Stonehenge, which stands in stark contrast to that of Avebury, despite the fact that both are very significant archaeological sites within the same WHS, and located less than 20 miles apart. Although the management of each is in the hands of a variety of bodies and organisations, both sites have at least the active management involvement of the UK's biggest membership organisation, the National Trust. However, matters are more complicated at Stonehenge, with the physical site of the monument being managed by the government body, English Heritage, while the National Trust manages much of the surrounding land.

Despite its iconic status, it has been argued that interpretation at Stonehenge is far from satisfactory and could be greatly improved. It is hoped that the building of a new purpose-built visitor centre close to the site of Stonehenge will assist in improving visitors' understanding not just of the significance of Stonehenge itself but also of the importance of the surrounding prehistoric landscape. There has been a more low-key approach to management and interpretation at Avebury, with some commentators suggesting that it should not be exposed to the same volume of visitors as Stonehenge. Indeed, the site has actually been de-marketed in the past, particularly to international visitors (see Mason, 2008). Nevertheless, Avebury has the potential to offer stimulating interpretation experiences, particularly if lessons from the approach at neighbouring Avebury Manor under the auspices of the National Trust can be applied to interpreting the site's prehistoric monuments.

Table 1: Comparison between Stonehenge and Avebury

Stonehenge	Avebury
Age:	
Construction of early phase began c.3000 BC	Construction of early phase began c.2600 BC
Evidence of human settlements and civilisations in the surrounding landscapes before the first phase of Stonehenge construction	Archaeological finds unearthed from other monuments in the surrounding landscapes were dated as early as c.3700 BC
Purpose:	
Unknown: the common belief is that it forms part of funerary and ceremonial practices	Unknown: like Stonehenge, it is believed to be part of funerary and ceremonial practices
Materials:	
Built with local sarsen stones and bluestones from south-east Wales	Built with local sarsen stones
Craftsmanship:	
Some stones were shaped and trimmed and stonework similar to carpentry was evident	Stones were not shaped
Features:	
Consists of upright stones and some were topped with horizontal lintels	Upright stones, no lintel capping
An outer stone circle (sarsens), a concentric inner circle (bluestones) and two horseshoes, one each of sarsens and bluestones	An outer stone circle and two inner circles with more stones stood within. All stones are sarsens
Small and compact, visually impressive	The biggest stone circle in the world
	Many stones have been damaged and removed; too big a stone circle to be visually imposing

Settings, presentation and relation to surrounding landscape:	
Busy roads dissecting through the landscape Persistent traffic Stonehenge is presented in isolation relative to other monuments in the landscape Other monuments on the landscape are not discernible to untrained eyes Restricted access to the stone circle; visitors are kept away by ropes	Roads dissect Avebury Henge and the surrounding landscape, although they are less busy and relatively quiet Part of Avebury village is encircled by the Henge Avebury Henge is the most prominent site among the monuments on the landscape; at least one other is clearly visible and easily accessible from Avebury Henge (West Kennet Avenue) Open, unrestricted access; with Avebury village in the middle of the Henge, the site blends in with the surrounding rural landscape
Tourism:	
Continual increase in visitor numbers; currently over one million per annum Well known domestically and internationally; highly exposed in international marketing High density of visitor volume in a small area Highly regulated and structured visit experience; visitors follow the footpath encircling the stone circle; no direct access to the Avenue (processional route) because the A344 separates it from the stone circle Visitor facilities such as ticket office, toilets and refreshment kiosk are housed in temporary buildings A kiosk selling snacks and beverages; no sitting or resting area Inadequate car park capacity Visitor arrive in private vehicles, coaches and tour buses Incessant flow of visitors in a small area Entrance charges; £7.80 for adults in 2012 Interpretation delivered though hand-held audio guide; available in 10 languages No signage or information panel on-site; a leaflet of Stonehenge is available on entry Archaeological finds are not displayed on site but housed at museums in towns such as Salisbury and Devizes	Visitor numbers have been in slight decline in recent years Lesser known domestically and possible unknown internationally; rarely featured in international marketing Low density of visitor volume in a large area Open and unrestricted access to the stones; visitors can walk to and along West Kennet Avenue leading away from Avebury Henge A cluster of facilities including a restaurant, National Trust tea room, souvenir shop, two museums and toilets are located in the Old Farmyard, about 200m away from the car park Almost all visitors arrive in their private vehicles; very limited public transportation link No entrance fee to Avebury Henge; pay and display at car park, £5.00/day in 2012 A trickle of visitors; visitors are spread out across a much larger area No on-site interpretation No signage or information panel on-site; two panels with brief information at car park; a leaflet of Avebury Henge is available from the National Trust hut at car park Archaeological finds are displayed on site (Stables and Barn galleries) as well as in the museum in Devizes

References

BBC. 2004. Revisiting Britain's biggest free festival. http://news.bbc.co.uk/1/hi/entertainment/music/3662921.stm

BBC. 2007. Stonehenge tunnel plans scrapped. http://news.bbc.co.uk/1/hi/england/wiltshire/7130666.stm

BBC. 2009a. Stonehenge centre gets go-ahead. http://news.bbc.co.uk/1/hi/england/wiltshire/8047968.stm

BBC. 2009b. Stonehenge centre plans unveiled. http://news.bbc.co.uk/1/hi/england/wiltshire/8302561.stm

BBC. 2010a. Government funding for Stonehenge visitor centre axed. http://www.bbc.co.uk/news/10343945

BBC. 2010b. Stonehenge visitor centre backed by £10 million from lottery. http://www.bbc.co.uk/news/uk-england-wiltshire-11792484

BBC. 2012a. Stonehenge visitor centre preparation work begins. http://www.bbc.co.uk/news/uk-england-wiltshire-18590301

BBC. 2012b. Stonehenge visitor centre and road closure project starts. http://www.bbc.co.uk/news/uk-england-wiltshire-18782893

Beck L, Cable T. 2002. *Interpretation for the 21st Century: Fifteen Guiding Principles for Interpreting Nature and Culture*, 2nd ed. Champaign: Sagamore.

Bender B, Edmonds M. 1992. Stonehenge: Whose past? What past? *Tourism Management* **13** (4): 355-357.

Carr A. 2004. Mountain places, cultural spaces: The interpretation of culturally significant landscapes. *Journal of Sustainable Tourism* **12** (5): 432-459.

Carver E. 2011. *Stonehenge World Heritage Site: A strategy for interpretation, learning and participation 2010 – 15*. Report for English Heritage. http://www.english-heritage.org.uk/content/publications/publicationsNew/stonehenge-whs-interpretation-learning-participation-strategy/stonehenge-whs-interpretation-learning-participation-strategy.pdf

Chris Blandford Associates. 2000. *Stonehenge World Heritage Site Management Plan*. Report prepared for English Heritage. http://www.english-heritage.org.uk/content/imported-docs/p-t/stonehengemgtplanfull.pdf

Christie M, Mason P. 2003. Transformative tour guiding: Training tour guides to be critically reflective practitioners. *Journal of Ecotourism* **2** (1): 1-16.

English Heritage, 2012a. Silbury Hill, Avebury. http://www.english-heritage.org.uk/daysout/properties/silbury-hill/

English Heritage. 2012b. Stonehenge World Heritage Site facts and figures. http://www.english-heritage.org.uk/daysout/properties/stonehenge/world-heritage-site/why-is-stonehenge-a-world-heritage-site/facts-and-figures/

English Heritage. 2012c. Our proposals for Stonehenge. http://www.english-heritage.org.uk/daysout/properties/stonehenge/our-plans/our-proposals/

English Heritage. 2012d. Avebury. http://www.english-heritage.org.uk/daysout/properties/avebury/

Forestell PH. 1993. If Leviathan has a face, does Gaia have a soul? Incorporating environmental education in marine eco-tourism programes. *Ocean and Coastal Management* **20** (3): 267-282.

Garrod B, Fyall A. 2000. Managing heritage tourism. *Annals of Tourism Research* **27** (3): 682-708.

Ham SH. 1992. *Environmental Interpretation: A Practical Guide for People with Big Ideas and Small Budgets*. Golden: North American Press.

Harvey G. 2004. Endo-cannibalism in the making of a recent British ancestor. *Mortality* **9** (3): 255-267.

Hays D, MacLeod N. 2006. Packaging places: Designing heritage trails using an experience economy perspective to maximise visitor engagement. *Journal of Vacation Marketing* **13** (1): 45-57.

Kals E, Schumacher D, Montada L. 1999. Emotional affinity toward nature as a motivational basis to protect nature. *Environment and Behavior* **31** (2): 178-202.

Kuo I. 2002. The effectiveness of environmental interpretation at resource-sensitive tourism destinations. *International Journal of Tourism Research* **4** (2): 87-101.

Kuo I. 2011. Management strategies in geotourism sites: A comment. In Lin JC (ed.) *Landscape Conservation*. Taipei: Department of Geography, NTU; 143-156.

Leask A, Fyall A. (eds.) 2006. *Managing World Heritage Sites*. Oxford: Butterworth Heinemann.

Leask A, Garrod B. 2011. Visitor management at a World Heritage Site: Skara Brae Prehistoric Village, Orkney, Scotland. In Garrod B, Fyall A (eds) *Contemporary Cases in Tourism* Volume 1, Oxford: Goodfellow; 81-98.

Mason P. 2008. *Tourism Impacts, Planning and Management*. 2nd ed. Oxford: Butterworth-Heinemann.

Mason P, Kuo I. 2008. Visitor attitudes to Stonehenge: International icon or national disgrace? *Journal of Heritage Tourism* **2** (3): 168-183.

Moscardo G. 1996. Mindful visitors: Heritage and tourism. *Annals of Tourism Research* **23** (2): 376-397.

Moscardo G. 1999. *Making Visitors Mindful: Principles for Creating Quality Sustainable Visitor Experiences through Effective Communication*. Champaign: Sagamore.

National Trust, 2012. Avebury. http://www.nationaltrust.org.uk/home/item257376/

National Trust, 2008. *Avebury: Monuments and Landscape*. Swindon: National Trust.

Pine BJ, Gilmore JH. 2011. *The Experience Economy*. Updated edition. Boston: Harvard Business Review Press.

Pomeroy-Kellinger M. 2005. *Avebury World Heritage Site Management Plan*. Report for English Heritage. http://www.wiltshire.gov.uk/amp05_a4.pdf

Prentice R. 2001. Experiential cultural tourism: Museums and the marketing of the New Romanticism of evoked authenticity. *Museum Management and Curatorship* **19** (1): 5-26.

Richards G. 2001. The Experience industry and the creation of attractions. In Richards G. (ed.) *Cultural Attractions and European Tourism*. Wallingford: CABI; 55-69.

Richards J. 2011. *Stonehenge*. London: English Heritage.

Shackley M. 2004. Managing the cedars of Lebanon: Botanical gardens or living forest? *Current Issues in Tourism* **7** (4 & 5): 417-425.

Shackley M. 2006. Visitor management at World Heritage Sites. In Leask A, Fyall A. (eds) *Managing World Heritage Sites*. Oxford: Butterworth-Heinemann; 83-93.

The Stonehenge Tour. 2012. http://www.thestonehengetour.info/index.shtml

Tilden F. 1977. *Interpreting Our Heritage*. 3rd ed. Chapel Hill: The University of North Carolina Press.

UNESCO. 2012. Stonehenge, Avebury and Associated Sites. http://whc.unesco.org/en/list/373

VisitBritain. 2010. http://www.visitbritain.com/en/GB/

World Heritage Centre. 2011. *Operational Guidelines for the Implementation of the World Heritage Convention*. Paris: UNESCO World Heritage Centre. http://whc.unesco.org/archive/opguide11-en.pdf

Young C, Chadburn A, Bedu I. 2009. *Stonehenge World Heritage Site Management Plan 2009*. Report for English Heritage. http://www.english-heritage.org.uk/content/publications/publicationsNew/stonehenge-management-plan-2009/sh-manplan09-full-print.pdf

Ancillary Student Material

Further reading

Ballantyne R, Packer J, Sutherland LA. 2011. Visitors' memories of wildlife tourism: Implications for the design of powerful interpretive experiences. *Tourism Management* **32** (4): 770-779.

Frauman E, Norman WC. 2004. Mindfulness as a tool for managing visitors to tourism destination. *Journal of Travel Research* **42** (4): 381-389.

Gilmore A, Carson D, Ascenção, M. 2007. Sustainable tourism marketing at a World Heritage Site. *Journal of Strategic Marketing* **15** (2/3): 253-264.

Guiver J, Lumsdon L, Weston R. 2006. Visitor attractions, sustainable transport and travel plans – Hadrian's wall: A case study. *Managing Leisure* **11** (4): 217-230.

Knudson DM, Cable TT, Beck L. 1995. *Interpretation of Cultural and Natural Resources*. State College: Venture Publishing.

Madin EMP, Fenton, DM. 2004. Environmental interpretation in the Great Barrier Reef Marine Park: An assessment of programme effectiveness. *Journal of Sustainable Tourism* **12** (2): 121-148.

Landorf C. 2009. Managing for sustainable tourism: A review of six cultural World Heritage Sites. *Journal of Sustainable Tourism* **17** (1): 53-70.

Shackley M. (ed.) 1998. *Visitor Management: Case Studies from World Heritage Sites*. Oxford: Butterworth Heinemann.

Sharp GW. (ed.) 1982. *Interpreting the Environment*. 2nd ed. New York: John Wiley & Sons.

Taylor K, Lennon J. 2011. Cultural landscapes: A bridge between culture and nature. *International Journal of Heritage Studies* **17** (6): 537-554.

Willis KG. 2009. Assessing visitor preferences in the management of archaeological and heritage attractions: A case study of Hadrian's Roman Wall. *International Journal of Tourism Research* **11** (5): 487-505.

Related websites

English Heritage: http://www.english-heritage.org.uk/

National Trust: http://www.nationaltrust.org.uk/

UNESCO World Heritage Centre: http://whc.unesco.org/

United States National Park Service on-line book *Interpretation in the National Park Service: A historical perspective*: http://www.cr.nps.gov/history/online_books/mackintosh2/index.htm

Wiltshire County Council: http://www.wiltshire.gov.uk/index.htm

Self-test questions

Try to answer the following questions to test your knowledge and under-standing. If you are not sure of the answers, then please re-read the case and refer to the suggested references and further reading sources.

1   What are the similarities and differences between Stonehenge and Avebury Henge?

2   Why does Stonehenge attract a large number of visitors, both domestic and international?

3   Why is the number of visitors at Avebury only about a quarter of that at Stonehenge?

4   How would you suggest maintaining or enhancing the 'spirit of place' at both Stonehenge and Avebury?

5   What are the current approaches to managing visitor volumes and visitor flows at both Stonehenge and Avebury?

6   Using Tilden and Beck and Cable's principles of interpretation (see Appendix), how would you suggest interpretation be provided and delivered at both Stonehenge and Avebury sites?

Key themes and theories

The key themes raised in the case study relate to the following areas:

♦   Management of heritage sites

♦   Interpretation of heritage sites

♦   Spirit or sense of place

♦   World Heritage Site and cultural landscapes

♦   Visitor access to heritage resources

The key theories relate to:

♦   Effective interpretation of heritage sites with complex and long histories

♦   Interpretation and presentation of heritage sites

♦   Visitor experience and atmosphere at heritage sites

♦   The role of tourism facilities in creating visitor experience

♦   The physical presence and appearance of heritage sites and its significance in the popularity and recognition as tourism attractions

If you need to source further information on any of the above themes and theories, these headings could be used as key words to search for materials and case studies.

Appendix: Principles of interpretation

Tilden's six principles of interpreting heritage

1   Any interpretation that does not somehow relate what is being displayed or described to something within the personality or experience of the visitor will be sterile.

2   Information, as such, is not interpretation. Interpretation is revelation based upon information. But they are entirely different things. However, all interpretation includes information.

3   Interpretation is an art, which combines many arts, whether the materials presented are scientific, historical or architectural. Any art is in some degree teachable.

4   The chief aim of Interpretation is not instruction, but provocation.

5   Interpretation should aim to present a whole rather than a part, and must address itself to the whole man rather than any phase.

6   Interpretation addressed to children (say, up to the age of twelve) should not be a dilution of the presentation to adults, but should follow a fundamentally different approach. To be at its best it will require a separate programme.

Beck and Cable's 15 principles for interpreting nature and culture

1   To spark an interest, interpreters must relate the subject to the lives of the people in their audience.

2   The purpose of interpretation goes beyond providing information to reveal deeper meaning and truth.

3   The interpretive presentation – as a work of art – should be designed as a story that informs, entertains, and enlightens.

4   The purpose of the interpretive story is to inspire and to provoke people to broaden their horizons.

5   Interpretation should present a complete theme or thesis and address the whole person.

6   Interpretation for children, teenagers, and seniors – when these comprise uniform groups – should follow fundamentally different approaches.

7   Every place has a history. Interpreters can bring the past alive to make the present more enjoyable and the future more meaningful.

8 Technology can reveal the world in exciting new ways. However, incorporating this technology into the interpretive program mush be done with foresight and thoughtful care.

9 Interpreters must concern themselves with the quantity and quality (selection and accuracy) of information presented. Focused, well-researched interpretation will be more powerful than a longer discourse.

10 Before applying the arts in interpretation, the interpreter must be familiar with basic communication techniques. Quality interpretation depends on the interpreter's knowledge and skills, which must be continually developed over time.

11 Interpretive writing should address what readers would like to know, with the authority of wisdom and its accompanying humility and care.

12 The overall interpretive program must be capable of attracting support – financial, volunteer, political, administrative – whatever support is needed for the program to flourish.

13 Interpretation should instill (*sic*) in people the ability, and the desire, to sense the beauty in their surroundings – to provide spiritual uplift and to encourage resource preservation.

14 Interpreters can promote optimal experiences through intentional and thoughtful program and facility design.

15 Passion is the essential ingredient for powerful and effective interpretation – passion for the resource and for those people who come to be inspired by it.

Sources: Tilden (1977), Beck and Cable (2002)

9

Heritage as a Development Resource in China

A Case Study in Heritage Preservation and Human Rights

Robert Shepherd

Introduction

Government efforts to preserve cultural heritage sites during times of rapid economic change invariably have particular challenges. These can range from commercialisation and tourist overcrowding to the forced displacement or the pricing-out of local residents. A common response is to define local residents as active stakeholders in debates, discussions and negotiations about heritage planning. In theory, this inclusive approach will lead to optimal outcomes in the development, promotion, and regulation of a site. Such an inclusive approach is not only cognisant of the desires of different stakeholders such as preservationists, private business people, government regulators, visitors and local residents, but it also takes these desires into account in the resulting plans and practices.

What happens, though, in situations in which residents are permitted limited influence over heritage policies and plans? For example, sometimes local authorities are assumed to speak for local residents. When formal means of questioning or contesting heritage policies and plans are either limited or non-existent, local residents may turn to informal means of action: what James Scott (1985) has referred to as the 'weapons of the weak' and French social theorist Michel de Certeau (1984) as the 'art of getting by'. This is the case in contemporary China, where a one-party political system and an intense state-directed emphasis on modernisation has limited the ability of people to question or contest development projects in their communities, including heritage campaigns. This case examines the state-directed transformation of Mount Wutai, a Buddhist pilgrimage destination in eastern China, first into a government-endorsed scenic spot, then into a national park, and finally a UNESCO World Heritage Site, and how these changes have affected local residents, including shopkeepers, farmers, and members of monastic communities. From a macro-level perspective, this project has resulted in a demarcated space that protects both built heritage and the local environment while also managing tourist arrivals. It has also fractured the local community, however, rewarding some monastic authorities, displacing most farmers, and leaving shopkeepers in a state of limbo as they anticipate the demolition of their homes and businesses.

This forced displacement, however, has not originated with the Chinese government. Instead, its origins are found in the United Nations Education, Scientific and Cultural Organization (UNESCO) perceptions of heritage space, while its expression is found in how such perceptions intersect with everyday life and tourism. From a UNESCO perspective, large-scale tourism is an inherent threat to material heritage sites, particularly when used as a development tool, because this has the potential to reduce heritage to a "tourist resource" (WCCD, 1995: 176). Similarly, Valery Patin of the International Council on Monuments and Sites (ICOMOS) has warned of "heritage supermarkets" filled with copies of "authentic heritage" as a result of unchecked tourism (Patin, 2002: 138-139).

These concerns are understandable at a time of rapid global economic change and the ongoing removal of both political and cultural borders between states. However, efforts to identify and protect a global archive of World Heritage Sites in the face of rapid globalisation may at times contribute to the flattening out of actual cultural diversity. This leads to a paradox: top-down efforts to preserve and protect material culture through universal prescriptions of how heritage space should be organised can lead to the erasure rather than the protection of cultural diversity.

Tourism, heritage and development

In the last two decades, the Chinese government has embraced tourism and, by extension, cultural and natural heritage projects, as key development tools. State-funded museums have been built at an astonishing pace, quadrupling in number between 1980 and 2000, and now standing at more than 1,400 (Denton, 2005). The country had no national parks until 1982, yet now it has 208, as well as more than 1,000 official nature reserves (Weller, 2006). The People's Republic of China (PRC) is also ranked third in the world in terms of the number of World Heritage Sites (43 as of 2012), despite not becoming a member party to the 1972 World Heritage Convention until 1986. Finally, the State Administration of Cultural Heritage (SACH), which has oversight over all heritage sites in China, estimates that as of 2010 the PRC had approximately 400,000 cultural heritage sites. However, less than 20% of these have been formally recognised and provided state protection. These include 2,351 nationally recognised sites, 9,300 provincial sites, and 58,000 municipal or county sites (Chen and Chen, 2010).

While the recognition, formalisation, and funding of cultural and natural sites has increased in China, it is important to realise that Chinese heritage policies are not aimed primarily at preservation. Instead, these policies have clear economic and political goals. First, the economic reforms that began in 1978 have required more citizen mobility. The most obvious result of this has been the emergence of a class of transient factory and construction workers, mainly peasants. Numbering as many as 200 million, these 'new economy' labourers have been the focus of much academic research on worker rights as well as the subject of debates in China over questions of health, education, and exploitation (Gaetano and Jacka, 2004; Lee, 2007). In addition to a marginalised class of exploited peasants, however, economic reforms have also created a growing class of citizens with disposable incomes and a desire to travel.

The emergence of a domestic tourism industry lagged behind initial economic reforms by a full decade, largely because of a continued government effort to monitor and control the movement of citizens through the *hukou* (internal passport) system. Although the origins of the *hukou* system have been traced to the Ming Dynasty, it was during the Maoist era (1949-1976) that surveillance of citizens reached its height, with employment, housing and travel all tightly controlled by state authorities. Consequently, tourism for most of the early decades of the PRC consisted almost solely of workplace-centred trips to either natural sites, such as the seaside resort of Beidaihe to the east of Beijing, or revolutionary sites linked to the Communist Party, such as Mao's birthplace at Shaoshan in Hunan Province. International arrivals during this period were largely non-existent. Initial economic reform policies, beginning in 1979, sought to encourage international tourist arrivals as a means of increasing foreign exchange earnings. However, following student and worker protests and the subsequence military crackdown centred on Beijing's Tiananmen Square in 1989, international tourist arrivals flattened out. This sparked a turn to domestic consumers to boost the tourist industry.

Subsequently, tourism was included for the first time in the Chinese government's five year development plans in 1998, an indication of its growing importance, largely driven by domestic demand. As a result of the removal of domestic travel restrictions and the growth of a middle class with disposable income, the overwhelming majority of tourists in contemporary China are either PRC citizens or overseas Chinese, despite the fact that international arrivals have more than doubled since 1998.

Between 1997 and 2008, international tourist arrivals rose from 23.7 million to 53.1 million, before leveling off to 55.6 million as of 2010 (World Bank, 2011). However, significant numbers of these arrivals were in fact overseas Chinese. Chinese government statistics for 2009 indicate that of approximately 126 million overseas arrivals[1], 104 million visitors were citizens of Hong Kong, Macau, or Taiwan. In 2010, total overseas arrivals reached 133 million, of which 107 million were overseas Chinese (CNTA, 2011). In contrast, by 2007 (a decade after travel restrictions were loosened), approximately 1.6 billion domestic trips were recorded, according to China National Tourism Administration statistics (CNTA 2009). This figure includes 998 million trips by rural residents, presumably while seeking employment as migrant labourers or returning home from migrant jobs. Nevertheless, 612 million urban residents travelled that year, spending on average 907 Yuan ($131), far more than the average 223 Yuan ($33) spent by rural residents (CNTA, 2009). In 2011, 2.6 billion domestic trips were recorded, of which approximately 20% involved a hotel stay (UNWTO, 2012).

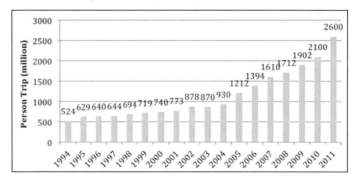

Figure 1: Domestic Tourism in China, 1994-2011. Source: National Tourism Administration of China

In summary, after separating out excursionists (international arrivals crossing the Hong Kong and Macau borders on day trips, and domestic travelers who did not stay in hotels) from tourists, a conservative estimate indicates that between 450 and 500 million domestic tourists travelled in China in 2011, compared to 57.5 million international arrivals, most of whom were regional tourists (UNWTO, 2012). As noted above, this rapid increase in domestic tourism has been fueled by increased disposable incomes, better transpor-

---

1   Chinese official statistics include people crossing the quasi-international borders separating the special administrative zones of Hong Kong and Macau from China proper on day trips, accounting for the discrepancy between World Bank and government figures.

tation links and hotel facilities, and a government promotion of tourism as an economic development tool. At the same time, the central government has ceded more decision-making authority to provincial and local officials, while simultaneously slashing direct budget subsidies. This has led government officials at the local level to seek to develop heritage sites as tourism destinations as a way of raising revenue.

Politics have also played a key role in Chinese heritage projects. The narratives deployed at heritage sites are often aimed at demonstrating a unified Chinese past by downplaying or ignoring ethnic, linguistic, religious, or regional differences (Gladney, 2004; Hevia, 2001). Heritage is also a key part of a national campaign to promote Party-sanctioned modern behaviour among citizens: what in Chinese is termed a 'civilised' (*wenming*) consciousness. This state effort to cultivate a modern sensibility among its citizens is not new, echoing similar campaigns conducted during the Maoist (1949-1976) and Nationalist (1911-1949) eras, as well as foundational Confucian ideas about role models and correct public behaviour. What is new is the linking of civility campaigns with tourism. From a central state perspective, urban visitors to rural tourist sites can serve as role models for peasants, who are regarded by Communist Party officials as not yet modern, while these same peasants are exposed to modern life as migrant workers in urban areas.

State-encouraged tourism at heritage sites thus has several objectives. At the local level (the primary source of funding for heritage projects), these include economic growth and job creation. At the national level, heritage projects are supposed to contribute to the development of a modern class of citizen-subjects. Finally, these projects are one element in a Chinese Communist Party narrative asserting that China is both a revolutionary state and a country with 5000 years of unified history and culture, despite any empirical evidence that may suggest otherwise.

Developing a World Heritage Site

Mount Wutai, known in Chinese as *Wutai Shan*, consists of a broad mountain valley in Shanxi province in Northern China. Located midway between Shanxi's two major cities, Taiyuan and Datong, and approximately 400km southeast of Beijing, Wutai takes its name from five (*wu*) surrounding peaks (*tai*) that range in elevation from 2,700 to 3,000 metre s. Originally a Daoist meditation area during the Han Dynasty (206 BCE – 220 CE), the Wutai valley became a Buddhist pilgrimage destination in the fifth century when several temples dedicated to the Buddha of Wisdom, Manjusri (*Wenshu*) were constructed during the Northern Wei Dynasty (386-534 CE) (Gimello, 1992).

Box 1: Buddhism in China

Scholars dispute when Buddhism appeared in China, although most agree this was likely in the second or third centuries BCE. While some argue that Buddhism reached China via sea routes, the consensus is that monks crossed the Himalayas from India. The first translation of sacred texts into Chinese occurred in the second century CE, but the faith faced a number of obstacles. The Buddhist emphasis on monasticism, withdrawal from social affairs, and individual enlightenment all ran counter to Confucianism's focus on filial relationships and social rituals. It was not until the seventh century CE that the religion began to spread widely, following a journey to India by the celebrated Chinese monk Xuanzang (602-664 CE). Over the course of a 16-year journey (629-645CE), he collected and translated scores of texts, visited iconic sites, and studied with famous monks. Upon his return to China, he helped popularise the faith. However, renewed opposition at the Tang Imperial Court led to a harsh crackdown under Emperor Wuzong in 845CE. Citing Buddhism's foreign origins, the Emperor ordered the destruction of tens of thousands of monasteries and temples, imposed grain taxes on practitioners, and forced an estimated 400,000 monks and nuns to become peasants. This was the severest attack Chinese Buddhism would face until the Cultural Revolution began in 1966.

For further information, see Wright (1959).

While Buddhism had long been known in China (Box 1), it was not until the thirteenth century that Tibetan Buddhism was introduced to the Shanxi area, with the Mongolian establishment of the Yuan Dynasty (1271-1368). During the Manchu-dominated Qing Dynasty (1644-1911) it became very influential (Kohle 2008). The Wutai area survived the collapse of Qing authority in 1911, the Japanese invasion and occupation of northern China (1933-1945), and the subsequent Chinese civil war (1945-1949). However, as Box 2 explains, many temples and monasteries were attacked and ransacked by Maoist Red Guards during the chaotic years of the Cultural Revolution (1966-1976).

Following the start of economic reforms in 1979, the Chinese government permitted limited religious practice at Wutai, although, as was the case at all religious sites in China, state authorities viewed Wutai's temples and monasteries as historical, not religious sites. Mount Wutai was designated a national park by the State Council in 1982 and a national forest preserve in 1992. By 2005, annual arrivals had reached 2.5 million, the vast majority of whom were domestic visitors. In 2002, local government officials, seeking to capitalise on this popularity, announced a master plan aimed at achieving world heritage status. They also increased admission fees from 65 Yuan to 90 Yuan (approximately $14 or €11) in 2004, and then to 168 Yuan ($27 or €20.5) in 2007, which remains the rate as of 2012.

Box 2: The Cultural Revolution

The Great Proletarian Cultural Revolution began in May 1966, when Mao Zedong, China's pre-eminent ruler, issued a proclamation calling for the country's youth to lead an ideological cleansing of the Communist Party. Organised into Red Guard factions, students and working youth attacked party and government officials, teachers, and other symbols of authority. Heeding Mao's call to destroy the 'four olds' (customs, culture, habits and ideas), Red Guards looted and damaged thousands of historic sites, particularly religious buildings and private collections.

The impact on cultural heritage, while devastating, was also complicated. Mao's 'four olds' campaign was launched in August 1966, peaked in the following month, and was largely abandoned by late 1967. In March 1968, national authorities and the Central Military Commission ordered Red Guards to protect all state property, including cultural relics, and to turn over all objects seized from private homes. In 1969 Mao announced the end of the Cultural Revolution. Simultaneously, the government began resettling millions of radicalised urban youth in rural areas. However, instability continued until Mao's death in 1976, when pragmatists in the Party led by Deng Xiaoping seized power and arrested Mao's key supporters. These included the so-called 'Gang of Four', who became the official scapegoats for the chaos of the Cultural Revolution. These were Jiang Qing, Mao's wife; Zhang Chunqiao, Second Deputy Premier; Yao Wenyuan, a member of the Party's Politburo; and Wang Hongwen, Vice-Chairman of the Politburo.

The Cultural Revolution remains a highly sensitive political topic in contemporary China and is glossed over in textbooks and history museums. The chaos and destruction of 1966-1967 certainly was in part a result of Mao's obsession with continuous revolution and political maneuverings against his political opponents. But this was also indicative of a long state campaign for modernisation that framed 'traditions' as the enemy of progress. This modernisation movement can be traced back to Sun Yatsen's attack on Qing rulers as foreign occupiers before the 1911 Revolution, the New Culture Movement's critique of Chinese traditions beginning in 1919, and Nationalist Party campaigns against Confucianism and Buddhism during the early years of the Republican era (1911-1949).

For further information see Gao (2008) and Ho (2006).

Mount Wutai was added to China's tentative list of UNESCO heritage sites in 2001[2]. In the original application, the State Administration of Cultural Herit-

---

2   World Heritage Sites go through a four-step process to inscription on the World Heritage List. First, national authorities place a site on their tentative lists: an inventory of sites to be proposed in the next decade. During this time, sites are formally proposed to the World Heritage Council (WHC). The WHC in turn delegates the evaluation process for cultural sites to the International Council on Monuments and Sites (ICOMOS) and natural sites to the World Conservation Union (IUCN). If approved, a site is then evaluated and voted upon by the World Heritage Committee:

age cited Wutai's Buddhist heritage, its unique environmental features, and its strategic importance during the anti-Japanese War as reasons for inclusion on the World Heritage List. This application was upgraded to a formal nomination in March 2008, this time as an exclusively cultural site consisting of a core zone of 13 temples located near the town of Taihuai. References to the anti-Japanese struggle were eliminated. Instead, the provincial authorities described Wutai as the global centre for the worship of Manjusri, the Buddha of Wisdom, as well as the centre of what the official nomination report called 'Sino-Tibetan Buddhism' (UNESCO, 2009, 121). In the spring of 2009, Wutai Shan was formally approved by UNESCO as a cultural World Heritage Site.

The region of the Mount Wutai National Park included in the World Heritage Site contains 68 Buddhist temples from seven Chinese dynasties, over 150 pagodas, and approximately 146,000 religious statues (Nomination Report, 21-24). The park is also home to more than 2,500 monks and nuns, making this the largest concentration of Buddhist monastic personnel in China outside of the Tibetan Autonomous Region (Nomination Report, 234)[3]. The religious buildings are clustered around the small town of Taihuai, in the centre of the Wutai Valley. For centuries, local residents have farmed the valley, provided labour for monastic construction projects, and run businesses geared towards a pilgrimage economy, including restaurants, teahouses and hostels, as well as shops selling foodstuffs, incense, and Buddhist ceremonial objects. In the years immediately following the beginning of the reform era, local business boomed as pilgrims began to return to the area, but the decision to seek formal recognition as a World Heritage Site in 2001 began a process that has resulted in the forced displacement of at least 10% of Taihuai's 7,700 residents (UNESCO, 2009), a figure local residents argue is vastly under-stated. What all agree on is that the Master Plan for Wutai National Park will eventually relocate most secular residents to a newly built satellite community outside the Park's south gate.

---

an inter-governmental body with a rotating membership. For a list of criteria for nominations, see http://whc.unesco.org/en/criteria/. For an explanation of the tentative list process, see http://whc.unesco.org/en/tentativelists/.

3   Government-controlled national associations oversee China's five official faiths (Daoism, Buddhism, Islam, Catholicism, and Protestant Christianity) under the overall authority of the State Religious Affairs Council. Under a decree issued by the State Council in 1982, citizens have a right to believe in any of the five officially tolerated religions. In 1991, the State Council issued a second decree that reaffirmed state tolerance of religious orthodoxy but warned against heterodoxy, such as non-sanctioned Muslim, pro-Dalai Lama Tibetan, Vatican-tied Catholic, and charismatic Christian groups.

Displacement and preservation

In 2005, the local authorities issued a revised Master Plan in response to UNESCO's evaluation of the original nomination for World Heritage status. This divided the proposed heritage area into four zones: a 'strict protection zone', where any construction that threatens the 'authenticity of cultural resources' would be prohibited; an 'ecological coordination zone' surrounding the core area; a 'visitor utilisation zone' for managing tourist arrivals; and a 'community utilisation zone' to house relocated residents (GOC, 2008a, 240-241; GOC, 2008b: 211). In less technical terms, the plan called for a preserved heritage core surrounded by green space, which would serve as a buffer between the actual heritage site and commercial facilities. Most residents of the core zone around Taihuai would be relocated to the new community of Jingangku, approximately 20km south of Taihuai, near the main entrance to the National Park. In addition, shops and guesthouses in the core zone would be demolished and tourist facilities relocated to a new service complex, also near the south gate (GOC, 2008b). While some residents have taken part in small-scale protests about compensation rates and the loss of their farmland and businesses, planners insist that they will benefit from better housing, education opportunities, and interaction with visitors, leading them to value cultural heritage (GOC, 2008b).

The local authorities justify this relocation project as necessary to protect the material culture of historic temples from uncontrolled tourism, as demonstrated in the official nomination report sent to UNESCO:

> "The largest threats to the physical conditions of the temples and ancient buildings lie with unauthorised constructions of tourist service facilities in the surrounding area of the Taihuai Proposed Core Zone, which have seriously marred the historical and environmental integrity as well as the religious ambience." (GOC, 2008a, 228)

This depiction of tourists and residents as threats to Wutai's heritage is not unique to China or the Chinese state. Instead, it reflects underlying assumptions about the potential dangers of unchecked tourism shared by UNESCO, the World Union of Conservation, and associated transnational heritage organisations. Indeed, the heritage preservation plan for Mount Wutai mirrors the transnationally dominant blueprint of spatial planning by heritage organisations that divides protected areas into separate zones, ranging from an inner core to an outer fringe area (Weller, 2006). This global model, which is supposed to strengthen cultural diversity, may paradoxically have the opposite effect, transforming World Heritage Sites into remarkably similar spatial zones while displacing local residents in the name of preservation (Shepherd, 2012).

In China, this transnational preservation model has been followed closely. For example, the original intent in designating national scenic areas, which began in the 1980s, was to replicate the national park system model found in Europe and the United States. This is reflected in the English translation of 'national scenic areas' (*guojia fengjing qu*) as 'National Parks of China', and reflects underlying cultural assumptions about the separation of natural and cultural spaces. However, most of these scenic areas are a blend of natural landscapes, cultural heritage, and local communities, such as that found at Mount Wutai. Moreover, unlike in the European and American tradition, park areas in China have historically been built spaces in which the reproduction of both nature and culture in miniature is highlighted, not the marking off and preservation of distinct natural spaces. Two examples of this are Jingshan Park in Beijing and the Imperial Summer Resort in Chengde, Hebei Province. Jingshan ('Coal Mountain') Park, constructed during the early Ming era, is located just outside the north walls of the Forbidden City. Using landfill removed to make a moat around the Forbidden City, builders created an artificial hill in the centre of the park that was designed as a mountain-in-miniature, with winding rocky paths, evergreen trees, and at its summit, a viewing pavilion. Meanwhile the Imperial Resort, built during the reigns of the Kangxi and Qianlong Emperors at the height of the Qing era, replicated the Empire itself. It was filled with scale models of illustrious material and natural sites, including the Great Wall, famous monasteries, and temples, lakes, rivers, and mountains.

These examples illustrate the absence of a clear distinction between nature and culture in traditional Chinese philosophy. The word 'nature' is most often translated as *zi ran*, literally 'all being' (Li and Sofield, 2009). This Chinese sense of nature does not infer either a cosmological source for the world or a superior quality (Weller, 2006). In other words, 'nature' as evidence of God or 'natural' as innately superior to human-made is absent from this perspective. So also is the Enlightenment emphasis on a separation of nature and culture. Instead, Confucianism stresses harmony between humans (and Earth) and Heaven (nature), with the world serving as a resource to be used for the improvement of humans. From this perspective, 'civilisation/civility' (*wenming*) is key, not 'nature' versus 'culture'. The edges of civilisation are neither to be feared and conquered nor embraced as more faithful to an original human nature; instead, the periphery is simply further from civility. Confucianism situates humans within a web of mutual dependency with each other and the world itself, linking humans with both the past and the present in mutual dependence premised on a desire to tame and control not nature but *qi*, the energy force that emanates everywhere (Weller, 2006). In contrast, the spatial segregation of either culture or nature, in the form of gated heritage sites, nature preserves or national parks, is based on the fundamentally non-Chinese assumption that heritage of all types is best maintained by removing it from existing social realities.

In summary, how Chinese philosophy has traditionally viewed the relationship between humans and the world, the real and the fake, and nature and culture, is at odds with both advocates of modernisation, who call for the taming of nature and their opponents, who insist we must 'return' to nature. Instead, 'nature' is conceived of as 'all being', including us. This perspective is not however, the norm in today's China. This is because Chinese society has been the subject of an intensive modernisation experiment for more than a century. Beginning in the late nineteenth century and continuing to the present, Qing dynasty reformers, Guomindang (KMT)-affiliated nationalists, and Chinese Communist Party (CCP) members and supporters have all embraced policies and programs aimed at subjugating nature and transcending the past, culminating in the violent attacks on material culture instigated by Mao Zedong during the Cultural Revolution. Under Mao, both nature and the historical past became enemies of progress and had to be conquered. This position was not in itself that unusual during the era of High Modernism that stretched roughly from the First World War until the collapse of the Soviet Union (Scott, 1998). This was a period characterised by a widespread faith in the transformative power of objective science, state planning, and the efficacy of economies of scale that transcended political and cultural divisions, underwritten by a dominant faith that life could be qualitatively and quantitatively improved through state-directed planned interventions (Scott, 1998). Soviet agricultural and industrial projects, energy projects in the United States such as the Tennessee Valley Authority and Hoover Dam, and numerous development projects in post-colonial Africa and Asia sought to at least tame nature, if not to conquer it.

What made Mao's approach unusual (and in hindsight catastrophic) was the Utopian element he added. His dictum that willpower trumps scientific laws, combined with suppression of authentic scientific inquiry and all aspects of public debate, resulted in environmental disasters, cultural destruction, and a population explosion from which Chinese society has yet to recover (Shapiro, 2001). Mao was thus unique because he rejected both traditional norms and scientific laws, effectively ending the *ti-yong* (essence-versus-use) debate that had dominated Chinese politics since the late Qing Dynasty (see Box 3). The question no longer was how to reconcile foreign borrowings with an underlying essence of Chinese culture. Instead, a utopian future could be reached through an all-out attack on the natural world and the cultural past, constant personal sacrifice and self-cultivation in the service of the nation, and the folk wisdom of the peasant masses.

Box 3: Must Modernisation be 'Westernisation'?

Ti-Yong refers to a long intellectual debate in China about the meaning of and means of achieving modernity. In the late nineteenth century, reformers at the Qing Imperial Court advocated a policy that would utilise (*yong*) foreign technology and industry why maintaining the essence (*ti*) of Chinese culture. In the decades immediately before the National Revolution of 1911, a group of public intellectuals centred on Kang Youwei (1858-1927) and Liang Qichao (1873-1929), went further, proposing political reforms within a specific Chinese context. Finally, during the Republican era (1911-1949), a Neo-Confucian movement spearheaded by Zhang Junmai (1887-1969) and Gu Hongming (1827-1928) advocated for the defence of a unique Chinese spiritual (*jingshan*) civilisation against the materialism of the West. The language of Neo-Confucianism has been revived in the last two decades by the Chinese Communist Party (CCP), which now emphasises China's 'spiritual' culture against Western materialism (*wuzhi wenhua*). Current CCP theory holds that modernisation involves both material and spiritual aspects; without careful controls, the former will overwhelm the latter, leading to selfishness, a decline in morality, and a fragmented society.

For more information, see Meissner (2006).

Material heritage and its preservation in contemporary China are also complicated by Buddhist perspectives, particularly by the latter's emphasis on the transience of reality. Material preservation for historical or aesthetic reasons has never been a priority in China, as illustrated by a shared Buddhist and Confucian practice of temple renewal. This periodic renovation of monasteries and temples demonstrates how Chinese philosophy and religious practice do not emphasise material preservation or material authenticity (Mu, Li, Jian-Hong, Ji, Yan-Geng and Xiting, 2007). Moreover, the worlds of commerce and of culture have also never been strictly separated in either Chinese or broader Buddhist traditions. This has resulted in sacred space that is also social space, blurring the boundaries between sacred and profane, public and private, and religion and business.

The net result is the absence of any widespread cultural constraint on changes to material culture or on a privileging of material authenticity. That is to say, there is little evidence at Mount Wutai of any constituency that seeks to prevent heritage development in the name of authentic preservation. Instead, opponents to this plan see preservation as the problem.

Nevertheless, to achieve UNESCO recognition for sites such as Wutai and the cachet this credential carries in the marketing of heritage as a development resource, heritage planners must meet the expectations of the dominant transnational heritage protection model: preservation through spatial segregation. The result has been the displacement of local residents at places such as Wutai, not only in the name of economic development, as is so often the case in urban China, but also in the cause of heritage preservation.

Making do: Life as a heritage subject

The question of how less-powerful or powerless individuals respond to powerful forces has been at the heart of political debates for centuries. The seventeenth century English political philosopher John Locke asserted that individuals enter into a social contract with each other and the state, while in the nineteenth century John Stuart Mill cautioned against the monolithic power of existing social norms, and Karl Marx argued that economic forces limit an individual's capacity to achieve a meaningful life. Building on Marx's ideas, Italian theorist Antonio Gramsci (1891-1937) argued for the importance of cultural hegemony in explaining how a dominant class maintains control of a given society. According to Gramsci, power rests in coercive techniques that in their most developed form do not require explicit violence: the powerless acquiesce to their marginal positions.

This perspective remains quite influential in academic fields such as labour studies and cultural studies as a means of explaining the apparent acceptance shown by marginal groups to their oppression. This apparent passivity has, however, been challenged. James Scott, in his ethnographic work on peasant responses to development projects in Malaysia (Scott, 1985), which emphasised the non-violent and non-confrontational responses used to counter hegemonic social interventions, including techniques such as gossip, absenteeism, slack work efforts, and petty theft. Because power holders and elites typically do not associate such acts with resistance, they usually are dismissed as evidence of peasant backwardness or a lack of education. French theorist Michel de Certeau, writing not about peasants but modern consumers, took a similar approach to Scott on this issue of the self's place vis-à-vis power (de Certeau, 1984). In a consumer society, he asked, how do people respond to hegemonic institutions and forces that limit individual agency? People's usual actions in such situations, he suggested, are analogous to the relationship between speech and formal language rules. Like speech, people perform in response to (rather than mimic, replicate, or completely reject) formal rules and regulations, thus making their lives. In other words, both Scott and de Certeau have argued that when confronted with inequity and dominant forces, most people neither fully comply nor completely rebel: instead, they recognise their marginal status and seek to take what action is available. Meanwhile, de Certeau contrasts the technical, scripted, and decontextualised strategies of bureaucratic and corporate institutions with the tactics used by the targets of these strategies. Strategies, according to de Certeau (1984: 30), 'produce, tabulate, and impose on' space, while tactics 'use, manipulate, and divert' these projects. In other words, people seek to find a means to act in the shadow of power, what Certeau, echoing Scott, refers to as the 'art of the weak' (de Certeau, 1984: 37).

How might this relate to heritage in China? State strategies in China aim to produce heritage space. However, what these projects also aim to produce is a new type of person, a civilised (*wenming*) subject. The latter is dependent on the former; in the production of heritage space, the actor (in this case the central government's Ministry of Culture and State Administration for Cultural Heritage) aims to transform local residents into modern citizen-consumers. Signboards in and around the town of Taihuai urge residents to not only respect and protect the environment and temples, but also to refrain from spitting, swearing, vending, urinating in public, gambling, and engaging in superstitious practices. Through becoming guardians of Chinese culture (*wenhua*), local residents are supposed to become civilised Chinese, albeit displaced.

The Wutai case is not unique. Projects that seek to create protected zones for natural and material heritage often require the relocation of residents and businesses. And, as this example shows, local communities usually have little input into heritage plans, despite the fact that local residents are the people most directly affected by these projects and are spoken of as stakeholders. This illustrates the ways in which the socially constructed category of 'community' masks existing structural inequities based on age, gender, socio-economic class, and one's position in respect of power holders. At Mount Wutai, local residents are divided over compensation rates and the question of who actually is local and thus should receive resettlement funds, while business owners must grapple with being relocated to the outer fringes of the Park area in a place where few tourists currently venture. Meanwhile, monks, nuns and monastic officials have gained many benefits from becoming heritage subjects. First of all, the official 'Conservation and Management Plan for the Nominated World Heritage Site of Mount Wutai' does not require the displacement of registered monastic personnel. Second, after the demolition of all private hotels and hostels in the core zone, only monasteries will be allowed to host pilgrims and other visitors within this space. Not surprisingly, most of the major monasteries in and around Taihuai are currently building dormitories and guest quarters, despite the fact that the Master Plan explicitly prohibits new construction at temple sites. For example, the Plan states that "new construction, expansion and renovation are prohibited [...] there shall be no reconstruction of disappeared heritage in principle [and] new construction or expansion to the temples is strictly controlled" (GOC, 2008b: 239, 294). Yet the Plan, which was designed to strictly enforce material preservation by eliminating commercial enterprises, has led not just to preservation but also to widespread destruction (of existing homes and businesses) and new construction (of dormitories and temples). It has also enriched religious institutions by effectively providing them with a monopoly on heritage business, and violated the property rights of secular residents.

Residents have responded to their displacement with tactics that mirror other popular protests in China. Like state workers who have lost their jobs, migrant labourers who have been abused or cheated by unscrupulous factory owners, or urban residents evicted from their apartments, they have focused their anger at local officials, not the national government or ruling party (cf. Lee 2007). For example, shortly after local authorities began the demolition of homes in Taihuai in 2008, residents sent a delegation to Beijing with a petition. This letter summarised the history of the local community and its importance for Wutai's monasteries as a supplier of craftsmen, artisans, traders, and labourers. It also pointedly noted that it was "the masses of Wutai mountain who risked their lives to battle the Red Guards" during the Cultural Revolution, thus protecting monasteries and temples from (government-supported) attempts to destroy these and making it possible for the same government to now support their preservation as examples of world heritage (Anon., 2008: n.p.). Evoking the language of the Communist Party, petitioners argued that forcibly displacing them contradicted China's "scientific development" and would turn Taihuai into a "depopulated wasteland" (Anon., 2008: n.p.).

Despite this direct appeal to national authorities, by the summer of 2011 more than half of Taihuai's built space had been demolished (see Figure 2) and people not yet displaced had turned to worrying about receiving adequate compensation for their property. A shopkeeper in Taihuai summarised the situation in the summer of 2011 as a question of money. "Who should be paid, how much, and by whom?" she asked. "If there is no money, then there won't be any more demolition ... nobody is sure what will happen".

However, construction has slowed since that time. In fact, despite what is stated in the Master Plan, which was crafted with the help of UNESCO, as of the summer of 2012 Taihuai has not yet become a heritage park. Rather than a core zone where strict preservation rules exist, much of the area resembles a massive construction site. In addition to temple renovation projects that fall within the scope of the Master Plan, a wide range of other construction projects are either underway or recently finished, ranging from home and business renovation and expansion to dormitory construction at monasteries (see Figure 3) and, in at least one case, the construction of a completely new temple complex (Figure 4). This is in addition to official construction projects associated with the Plan, such as a new visitor centre and exhibition hall, a five star luxury resort, and a widened road through the valley.

Figure 2: Taihuai, Mount Wutai., July, 2011. The green space in the foreground has replaced neighboring homes, shops and fields. Photo credit: Robert Shepherd

Figure 3: Dormitory renovations, Tayuan Temple, Mount Wutai, July 2011. Photo credit: Robert Shepherd

Figure 4: The recently completed Wenshu (Manjusri) Temple, Taihuai, Mount Wutai, June 2012. Photo credit: Robert Shepherd

This building boom of commercial and religious space raises two pointed questions. First, of course, is the economic question. Why would someone renovate and expand their home or business knowing full well that it will likely be demolished in the very near future? The second is a managerial question: how and why are monasteries and temples that have been classified by the national government and UNESCO as World Heritage Sites being not just restored but expanded? How is this flouting of preservation guidelines possible, particularly in a country in which one party has controlled the state since 1949?

The answer to the first question lies in the strategic options open to property owners. Those who invest in a building that will be demolished are following a strategy known in Chinese as *qiangjian*, which translates as 'snatching or stealing' (*qiang*) and 'constructing' (*jian*). This term describes a process in which people strategically invest in renovations when they know they will be forcibly displaced. By investing in a property that is certain to be demolished, owners increase their compensation rates by taking advantage of increasingly complex national displacement regulations. For example, in an attempt to transform compensation into a purely objective and thus scientifically fair system, the State Council issued new regulations in early 2011 and tasked the Ministry of Construction with their implementation. These require developers (in the case of commercial projects) or local authorities (in the case of public projects such as this) to compensate owners for all aspects of a built structure, not just a fixed amount per square metre. This includes the quality of building materials, location, use, utilities, and even fixtures (GOC, 2011; Xinhua, 2011).

This state attempt to measure the value of built space objectively has not led the public to view the displacement process as more transparent or fair. Instead, it has encouraged short-term renovation projects designed to increase compensation rates: a profoundly different type of creative destruction than what had been imagined by political economists such as Joseph Schumpeter or Karl Marx. It is also a process that further contributes to a local atmosphere of distrust because what is designed to be a more transparent and hence fairer compensation process is widely perceived as an increasing complex system that enables unequal outcomes.

In and around Taihuai, people who are to be relocated or believe they will be in the future have added new rooms, fixtures, doors, windows and in some cases entire new floors to their homes and shops. The district government responded to this by arbitrarily decreeing height limits on all buildings. This decree has had little noticeable effect, primarily because a threat of demolition for buildings out of compliance carries little weight when these same buildings are already scheduled for removal. Indeed, within months of issuing this decree in 2011, local officials backtracked, revising the new regulations to allow renovations on existing buildings if owners removed newly built third floors.

State investments in the Wutai Shan project are concentrated in two adjacent sites near the village of Jingangku, 23km south of Taihuai and a few kilometres outside the south gate of the new park. A 'national park and world heritage centre' is under construction (Figure 5), consisting of a visitor centre and museum, an exhibition hall, a shopping complex, and an international resort, while on the edge of the village a satellite housing community has been completed that in theory should house displaced residents (Figure 6).

As of June 2012, the service complex and parking facilities had been finished, while resort construction had been started. Meanwhile, the new housing complex at Jingkangku intended for displaced Taihuai residents remained mostly empty, although the complex had been completed in the spring of 2010. Why a complex designed to house 1,857 households and 6,500 people remain mostly empty two years after being completed, especially in a country that faces an ongoing housing crisis, is puzzling. Local residents suggest a variety of possible reasons.

Figure 5: Construction workers at Mount Wutai Tourist Reception Centre, June 2011. Photo credit: Robert Shepherd

Figure 6: Jingangku Resettlement Village, June 2012. Photo credit: Robert Shepherd

♦   "Those houses haven't been allocated yet", an elderly man said. "The authorities still have to determine who qualifies".

♦   "They cost too much", a woman asserted. "When you multiple the price per square metre by the size no one has that kind of money".

♦   "The people who lost their land don't want to move so far away", said another woman. "How will they get back and forth to Taihuai?"

♦   "It's a money problem," explained a man who drove an unlicensed cab. "The government doesn't have the money to pay the builder, so he won't turn over the keys".

♦   "It's a land problem," asserted another man. "The people who should live there are peasants. They lost their land, and these new places don't give owners land rights".

Meanwhile, one local official estimated the district government had already borrowed approximately one billion Yuan (equivalent to $153 million or £94.7 million) by 2010 for the heritage project. The overall cost of the 20-year project is estimated to be 5.3 billion Yuan (approximately $830 million or £513.5 million) by 2025. An October 2010 press release by the Wutai County government lauded the county's Communist Party secretary for his development plans, estimated annual tourist revenues as 2.06 Yuan ($326 million or £217 million), and confidently projected total revenues to rise to 6 billion Yuan ($950 million or £631.7 million) by 2015 (Shanxi Audio-Visual Department, 2011). These loans are supposed to pay for land acquisition, infrastructure improvements, and new tourist facilities, including a 200 million Yuan performing arts and 20,000 person exhibition hall. They are also supposed to pay all compensation costs for displacement, including the costs associated with acquiring land near Jingangku and the construction of the new housing complex. The district government is responsible for paying these loans, but the officials who arranged the loans in the first place will be gone from their positions when payment is due. This is because job performance at the district level in China is primarily evaluated on economic development criteria and social stability. If officials can demonstrate that they have achieved 'development' with a minimum of public protests, they will be promoted. Thus, one unintended result of a state policy aimed at more accurately evaluating the effectiveness of local officials is to encourage such officials to take on burdensome bank loans for which they themselves will not be responsible.

The main issue is not whether local residents will be displaced as part of this heritage plan: people accept this as self-evident. Indeed, since petitioning the central authorities in 2008 there has been little visible opposition to these development plans. The key issue now is compensation. Those residents not yet displaced estimate that they should receive as much as 9,000 Yuan per square meter, at least seven times what had been paid to the farmers first displaced in 2008. For someone with a shop or guesthouse of 100m², this translates into a compensation package of approximately $140,000 (or £86,630), a sum most residents would have found unimaginable a decade ago.

Many local owners, in addition to making strategic improvements to their properties, have begun renting space to outsiders, especially Tibetan entrepreneurs from as far away as Lhasa. Taking advantage of popular interest in Tibetan religion and culture among urban Chinese professionals (who comprise most visitors to Wutai), these entrepreneurs sell jewelry, art, and religious articles such as statues, Buddhist rosaries, and incense. Between the summers of 2011 and 2012, six Tibetan thanka (Buddhist painting) shops opened in Thaihuai. Property owners, meanwhile, have shifted from complaining about their looming displacement to worrying about the local government's ability to pay them market value for their properties. Indeed, the potential total cost of displacement, especially if the new national compensation law is effectively enforced and local strategies of qiangjian succeed, are staggering.

The UNESCO response to the political, social, and economic reasons behind heritage projects in China such as this is to emphasise the preservation and conservation of cultural and natural sites, separated from contemporary social action (Li and Sofield, 2009). For example, the UNESCO summary recommendation report on Wutai Shan briefly notes that the movement of residents had provoked local anger, yet adds that "most of the people are willing to cooperate" (UNESCO, 2009: 6) and asserts that by 2020, Jingangku Township will host parking, service, and tourist facilities, thus suggesting that in the long-term local residents will benefit from this heritage project.

What this report fails to note is not just divisions among residents affected by this project but also bureaucratic tensions among different parts of the state based on their own particular interests. Overall management of the Park is divided between the Ministry of Housing and Urban-Rural Development and the Construction Authority of Shanxi Province. However, within the Park, forest reserves are overseen by the State Forestry Administration, temple sites by the State Administration of Cultural Heritage, religious practice at temples and monasteries by the State Administration for Religious Affairs, geological sites by the Ministry of Geology, fossils by the Ministry of Land and Resources, and tourism by the National Tourism Administration. These vertical ties clash at times not only with each other but also with a different set of state actors emanating from the Shanxi provincial government down to local county authorities, who are responsible for funding most of the infrastructure costs.

Finally, 29 different international, national, and provincial conventions, laws, and decrees impact the site. These range from the 1972 Convention on World Heritage and various State Council decrees on heritage protection to national laws regulating geological heritage (1995), forests (1998), fossils (2002), cultural relics (2003), religious practice (2004), and scenic areas (2006).

The net result is a widely diffused set of interests among stakeholders. Forestry officials have little interest in state efforts to improve access to the Wutai valley, just as officials who oversee religious practices are most likely not enthused about the spike in religious visitors, not to mention the thousands of Tibetan and Mongolian monks who now spend summer months in the Park area. At the local level, however, most officials are content to see as many tourist arrivals as possible, since each admission ticket adds revenue to their budgets and most will not be in positions of local responsibility when loans come due.

Conclusions

UNESCO's emphasis on the technical questions of material preservation and the bureaucratic issues of conservation management within a spatial framework of functional segregation ignores, at least in this case, the actual impact heritage designation has had on residents of the area. Although the Master Plan alludes to local partnerships and multiple stakeholders, this does not necessarily mean that local residents are included in conversations. Indeed, it would be difficult to do so precisely because local residents are *subjects* of this plan, targeted for transformation into modern citizens. Thus, 'stakeholder' in the context of this project alludes to bureaucratic interests, while 'collaboration' is aimed at different levels of government, not between 'the state' and local residents. Community partnership is presented as an unqualified good which will result in a local population that is simultaneously modern, conservation-conscious, and supportive of heritage. In reality, and quite predictably, local residents demonstrate little concern about heritage preservation. They instead focus on how this particular state project impacts their own lives.

The Master Plan for Mount Wutai has two goals. First, it aims to replace local residents and their small businesses with a National Park filled not with people but heritage, meeting UNESCO's expectations of how a core zone at a World Heritage Site should look. This plan also seeks to re-make residents into more fully civilised citizens. This will occur through the promotion of 'scientific tourism' (GOC, 2008b). Unlike uncontrolled tourism, scientific tourism will, from this perspective, generate revenue and provide the public with 'opportunities for training and education', a better appreciation of world heritage, and, crucially, a model in how to be modern (GOC, 2008b: 198).

This civilisational project underscores the different objectives of UNESCO and Chinese authorities. For the former, preservation is the paramount goal and uncontrolled tourism is by implication a potential threat. However, for the latter, the increased number of visitors generated by this project contributes to the promotion and cultivation of a civilised consciousness and lifestyle among local residents. In this sense, this project is aimed not at preserving the past but at shaping the present. Given this, the tactics used by local residents in the face of a development campaign that seeks to remake both local space and local people are understandable: not resistance, since to resist heritage is to be labeled as anti-modern, but, to borrow from Michel de Certeau, a series of 'guileful ruses' in the shadow of this Master Plan.

References

Anon. 2008. Moving residents betrays history. Reprinted in *The Manchester Guardian,* March 13, 2008. http://www.guardian.co.uk/world/2008/mar/13/china?commentpage=1

de Certeau M. 1984. *The practice of Everyday Life.* Berkeley: University of California Press.

Chen S, Chen H. 2010. Cultural heritage management in China: Current practices and problems. In Messenger P, Smith G. (eds) *Cultural Heritage Management: Global Perspective.* Gainsville: University of Florida Press; 70-81.

China National Tourism Administration (CNTA), 2011. *Major Statistics of China Tourism, January-December 2010.* http://www.cnta.gov.cn/html/2011-1/2011-1-19-8-51-57548.html

China National Tourism Administration (CNTA), 2009. *Major Statistics of Chinese Domestic Tourism 2007.* http://en.cnta.gov.cn/html/2008-11/2008-11-9-21-42-63473.html

Denton K. 2005. Museums, memorial sites, and exhibitionary culture in the People's Republic of China. *The China Quarterly* **183**: 565-586.

Gaetano A, Jacka T. 2004. *On the Move: Women and Rural-to-Urban Migration in Contemporary China.* New York: Columbia University Press.

Gau M. 2008 *The Battle for China's Past: Mao and the Cultural Revolution.* London: Pluto Press.

Gimello R. 1992. Chang Shang-Ying on Wutai Shan. In Naquin S, Fang-Yu C. (eds) *Pilgrims and Sacred Sites in China.* Berkeley: University of California Press; 89-149.

Gladney D. 2004. *Dislocating China: Muslims, Minorities, and Other Subaltern Subjects.* Chicago: University of Chicago Press.

Government of China (GOC). 2008a. *Nomination Report for Mount Wutai.* Beijing: Ministry of the State Administration of Cultural Heritage.

Government of China (GOC). 2008b. *Conservation and Management Plan for the Nominated World Heritage Site of Mount Wutai.* Beijing: Ministry of the State Administration of Cultural Heritage.

Government of China (GOC). 2011. *State-owned Land and Compensation Ordinance [Public Law 590]*. Beijing: State Council.

Hevia J, 2001. World heritage, national culture, and the restoration of Chengde. *Positions* **9** (1): 219-243.

Ho DD, 2006. To protect and preserve: Resisting the destroy the Four Olds Campaign, 1966-1967. In Esherick J, Pickowicz P, Walder A, George A. (eds) *The Chinese Cultural Revolution as History*. Palo Alto: Stanford University Press.

Lee CK. 2007. *Against the Law: Labor Protests in China's Sunbelt and Rustbelt*. Berkeley, University of California Press.

Li FM, Sofield T. 2009. Huangshan (Yellow Mountain), China: The meaning of harmonious relationships. In Ryan C, Huimin G. (eds) *Tourism in China: Destinations, Cultures, and Communities*. London: Routledge; 157-167.

Meissner W. 2006. China's search for cultural and national identity from the nineteenth century to the present. *China Perspectives* **68** (November-December 2006): 41-54.

Mu Z, Li H, Jian-Hong W, Ji L, Yan-Geng J, Xiting, L, 2007. Religious tourism and cultural pilgrimage: A Chinese perspective. In Raj R, Morpeth ND (eds) *Religious Tourism and Pilgrimage Management: An Alternative Perspective*, Cambridge, MA: CABI Publishing; 98-112.

Nyíri P. 2006. *Scenic spots: Tourism, the state, and cultural authority*. Seattle: University of Washington Press.

Patin V. 2002. Will market forces rule? In Dutt S. (ed.) *UNESCO and a Just World Order*. New York: NOVA Science Publishing; 138-140.

Scott JC. 1985. *Weapons of the Weak: Everyday Forms of Peasant Resistance*. New Haven: Yale University Press.

Scott JC. 1998. *Seeing like a State: How Certain Schemes to Improve the Human Condition have Failed*. New Haven: Yale University Press.

Shanxi (China) Audio-Visual Department. Wutai County's attempt to achieve the five Wutai Shan targets, November 22, 2010. http://www.chinawts.com/list/budnews2/173117366.htm

Shapiro J. 2001. *Mao's War against Nature: Politics and the Environment in Revolutionary China*. New York and Cambridge: Cambridge University Press.

Shepherd R. 2012. *Faith in Heritage: Displacement, Development, and Tourism in Contemporary China*. Thousand Oaks: Left Coast Press.

UNESCO. 2008. *Tentative World Heritage List: Mount Wutai Administrative Bureau*. Accessed October 22, 2012. http://www.whc.unesco.org/en/tentativelists/1621/

UNESCO, 2009. *Evaluation Report: Mount Wutai (China), No. 1279*. Paris: ICOMOS, March 10, 2009.

United Nations World Tourism Organization (UNWTO). 2012. *Compendium of Tourism Statistics, 2012*. Madrid: United Nations World Tourism Organization, June 6, 2012.

WCCD (1995). *Our Creative Diversity: Report of the World Commission on Culture and Development*. Paris: UNESCO Publishing House.

Wright AE. 1959. *Buddhism in Chinese History*. Palo Alto: Stanford University Press.

Xinhua, January 22, 2011. *China Issues New Regulations on House Expropriation*. http://www.chinadaily.com.cn/china/2011-01/22/content_11900647.htm

Ancillary Student Material

Further reading

McLaren A. 2011. Environment and cultural heritage in China: Introduction. *Asian Studies Review* **35** (December 2011): 429-437.

Ryan C, Gu H. 2009. Constructionism and culture in research: Understandings of the fourth Buddhist festival, Wutaishan, China. *Tourism Management* **31** (2): 167-178.

Shepherd R. 2009. Historicity, fieldwork, and the allure of the post-modern: A reply to Ryan and Gu. *Tourism Management* **32** (1): 187-190.

Shepherd R. 2012. *Faith in Heritage: Displacement, Development, and Tourism in Contemporary China*. Walnut Grove: Left Coast Press.

Svensson M. 2006. *In the Ancestor's Shadow: Cultural Heritage Contestations in Chinese Villages*. Stockholm, Sweden: Working Paper #16, Centre for East and Southeast Asian Studies, Lund University http://www.ace.lu.se/images/Syd_och_sydostasienstudier/working_papers/M_Svensson.pdf

UNESCO, 2009. Mixed properties - New Nominations - Mount Wutai (China). 33rd Session of the World Heritage Committee, Seville Spain, July 20, 2009. http://whc.unesco.org/en/decisions/2225

Yu L, Shepherd R, Gu H. 2012. Tourism, heritage and sacred space: The case of Wutai Shan, China. *Journal of Heritage Tourism* **7** (2): 145-161.

Related websites

Anonymous, 2008. Moving residents betrays history. *The Manchester Guardian,* March 13, 2008: http://www.guardian.co.uk/world/2008/mar/13/china?commentpage=1

Beijing Cultural Heritage Protection Center (CHP). "About CHP", http://en.bjchp.org/?page_id=1392

UNESCO, 2008. *Tentative World Heritage List: Mount Wutai Administrative Bureau*.
    http://www.whc.unesco.org/en/tentativelists/1621/

UNESCO, 2009. *Mount Wutai* (description and supporting documentation): http://
    whc.unesco.org/en/list/1279/documents/

Self-test questions

Try to answer the following questions to test your knowledge and understanding. If you are not sure of the answers, please re-read the case study
and refer to the suggested references and further reading sources.

1   What are the official goals of the Mount Wutai heritage management
     project?

2   How have local residents of the Wutai area responded to this World
     Heritage project?

3   Describe the clash of interests within and among both the local
     community and Chinese state bureaucracy over the Mount Wutai
     heritage management project.

4   Describe and contrast the different development goals of this project.
     Who and what are targeted for development?

5   To what extent might there be a clash of interests among various state
     entities in China and UNESCO when it comes to the relationship
     between cultural heritage preservation and tourism?

Key themes and theories

The key themes raised in this case study relate to the following:

♦   Impact of world heritage projects on existing communities:
     ♦   Financial impact on local residents
     ♦   Economic impact on local businesses
     ♦   Commercial impact on religious institutions at heritage sites
♦   The use of tourism at heritage sites as a development tool:
     ♦   Balancing visitor experiences and the carrying capacity of heritage
          sites
     ♦   Trade-offs between environmental protection, heritage
          preservation, visitor expectations, and local community needs

♦ The effects of governmental decentralisation on heritage preservation in China:

    ♦ Heritage as a revenue generating tool for local authorities

    ♦ Fragmentation of central government interests in heritage sites

    ♦ Local responses to displacement

♦ UNESCO and Chinese perspectives on the organisation of world heritage space:

    ♦ Universalist concepts of spatial segregation for preservation.

    ♦ Buddhist concepts of the relationship between sacred and profane space.

The key theories relate to:

♦ Strategies and tactics for resisting displacement in China

♦ Chinese views of the relationship between nature and culture

♦ Buddhism, material preservation, and cultural heritage

♦ Modernisation in China under Mao Zedong and Deng Xiaoping

♦ Subaltern responses to state development campaigns

For additional information on any of the above themes and theories use these headings as key words to search for materials and case studies.

BRINGING HERITAGE TO LIFE

10

The Causeway Coastal Route and Saint Patrick's Trail

Heritage Tourism Route Development in Northern Ireland

Stephen Boyd

Introduction

Tourist attractions can be grouped into three categories: points (e.g. individual tourist sites), lines (e.g. routes and trails) and areas (e.g. resorts, other defined spaces). There has been a tendency, however, for the literature to focus on the former and the latter categories, with relatively limited attention being paid to linear tourism spaces and opportunities. This is rather surprising, as national visitor surveys often list general sightseeing as the number one attraction to visitors. This will often involve following a specific itinerary, possibly a specified route or trail as set out by internationally recognised brown road signs. Destinations that use a distinctive food or drink products in their marketing often follow this up by offering visitors the opportunity to take in the total experience of that region's offering by following a food or drink trail. Those with an interest in culture, heritage or religion often experience it by travelling a recognised trail, for example by walking a pilgrimage route.

Fundamental to tourism is the requirement of actually travelling and being mobile. This always takes place in a linear fashion. Leiper (1990) in his famous model, 'the tourism system', conceptualised this mobility as occurring between two poles, the generating and destination regions, with movement through what he referred to as the transit zone. Attractions are said to be found in the destination zone, as well as in the generating zone when it becomes the destination of inbound visitors. The transit zone is not often considered to be part of the attraction mix. In fact, the majority of research has focused on the destination region and the attractions within and these are usually either site/point specific (e.g. theme parks, resorts) or are presented as spaces/areas (e.g. regional and national parks) as opposed to linear/routes. This is not to suggest there are no routes or trails within destinations, for there clearly are. An early recognition of this was the work of Lue, Crompton and Fesenmaier (1993) in their study of destination-zone types. This identifies a number of different spatial configurations that include the possibility of linear groupings becoming attractions. These include 'en-route' attractions, where one or more attraction is visited en-route to a target destination; the 'regional tour', where several attractions are visited while in a target destination; and 'trip chaining', where tourists travel around a touring circuit of several destinations. The ideas of Lue et al. (1993) build on the earlier conceptualisation of destination planning by Gunn (1972), which introduces the idea of a 'circulation corridor' as the means of connecting individual destination zones within a wider destination region. Gunn does not, however, view the circulation corridor as a linear attraction in itself: rather, he notes that routes and trails may exist as a part of tourism supply within individual attraction clusters in specific destination zones. Hall (2008), meanwhile, builds on the early thinking of Gunn when he stresses the importance of connectivity within destination clusters and tourist businesses.

While the idea of linear space is fundamental to tourism and mobility studies, the extent to which research has been undertaken on tourism routes and or trails remains relatively scant. A cursory search for scholarly research on tourism 'and' trails, using the CAB Direct abstract index, reveals only 619 matches. This is a relatively small number compared to research on any other theme; nature-based tourism, for example is identified in the same index as having 14,095 hits. So why is there this paucity of research? A number of reasons may be put forward. First, it has not been a topic of interest to scholars; second, any research on trails is problematic because it requires collecting data at multiple sites, involving a mix of ownership and often a diverse range of stakeholders; and third, there is often a paucity of existing research on which to build.

The following presents a comparative case study of two routes within Northern Ireland, examining them as part of the overall tourism offering. One case is a touring heritage trail (the Causeway Coastal Route), while the other is a thematic touring trail (Saint Patrick's Trail). The cases differ in terms of how they were developed, their tourist appeal, and the challenges authorities face in how they are managed. Prior to presenting the "stories" behind the trails, it is useful to examine trails/routes from a wider conceptual typology perspective in order to situate our two case studies.

Trails/routes typology and conceptualisation

A useful starting point in studying trails and routes is to recognise that they exist at various scales and vary in their purpose. At one end of a spatial spectrum are mega-trails/routes. An example is the Silk Road, the recreation of Marco Polo's route connecting the spice world of the East to the markets of the West. This 12,000km route between Asia and Europe allows for exchange of cultures, crafts, ideas, technology, beliefs and people and forms an on-going project of the United Nations Word Tourism Organization since 1994. Currently, 24 countries are involved in marketing the route, with three identifiable circles of involvement: the Turkestan countries that are just opening their borders to tourism; those countries already open to tourism (i.e. China, Pakistan and Iran); and those at the start and end of the route (i.e. Japan, South Korea, and the members of the Association of Southeast Asian Nations and the countries the European Union). While each country markets and plans its respective section, the Silk Road offers the allocentric traveller (Heitmann, 2011) the opportunity to experience the whole route, as opposed to visiting parts of the route. Other mega-scale routes include La Ruta Maya through Central and Southern America, and the Slave Route in Western Africa.

At the intermediate-scale, trails and routes of interest to tourists exist within countries. These take the form of long-distance walking/touring trails. Examples include the Pennine Way in England (Mattingly, 2005; Morrow, 2005), the Southern Upland Way in Scotland (Bold and Gillespie, 2009), national historic trails such as the Mormon Trail and Oregon Trail in the United States, pilgrimage routes such as Camino de Santiago in Spain (Murray and Graham, 1997), and food and wine trails such as winery/beer/ale routes in Ontario, Canada (Plummer et al., 2005). The majority these routes and trails cross a predominantly rural landscape.

Small-scale trails and routes, meanwhile, exist mostly within an urban setting, talking the form of walking tours of historic districts. Examples include the Boston Freedom Trail, Gamla Stan in Stockholm, and Hong Kong (Cheung, 1999). Within the urban setting, trails have often been used as the means of repackaging existing attractions. An example of this is in Budapest (see Ratz, Smith and Michalko, 2008).

In addition to scale, it is possible to subdivide routes and trails according to their purpose. The principal divide is between general and thematic. For example, mega-trails tend to be more general than thematic, as they form past migration and trade routes. Intermediate-scale trails, in contrast, tend to have a natural environment theme. Examples include greenways (Mundet and Coenders, 2010) and hiking trails (McNamara and Prideaux, 2011). Others have a past and current pilgrimage rationale. Small-scale trails, meanwhile, tend to be theme-driven, for example industrial, cultural or historic (Casbeard, 2010), literary (MacLeod, Hayes and Slater, 2008) or peace-related (Lash, Smith and Smith, 2010).

In terms of development of a conceptual model of trail/route experience, it is possible to suggest the following categorisation. Scenario A exists where the traveller chooses to experience the entire route, including the intervening attraction nodes within (individual tourist attractions). Scenario B is where only certain nodes (visitor attractions) are visited along the route, while not taking the route itself. A third scenario (C) is where a section of the route is visited (including any intervening nodes along that chosen section). Scenario D is where visitors use the route as a spine from which to deviate and visit other places connected to existing nodes along a section of the route. It is important to recognise that all four scenarios take place within an operating environment of policy, planning, management, as well as institutional arrangements and stakeholders. A schema of the above conceptualisation of possible route experience is shown as Figure 1.

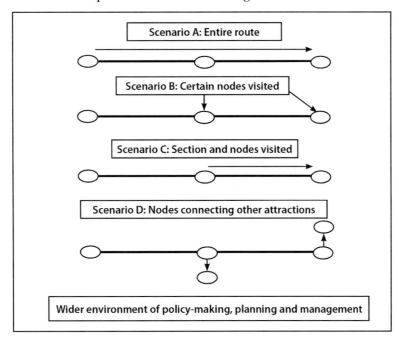

Figure 1: Schema of the possible route experience

A useful example of a route that encapsulates all of the above scenarios is the Camino de Santiago pilgrimage route in Northern Spain (Graham and Murray, 1997). Scenario A is represented by those who chose to experience the whole trail. In this case, the traditions and history become the attraction to travellers, who view travelling the route as undertaking a pilgrimage. Scenario B is represented by those visitors interested in the history and heritage of the various tourist-historic cities (the nodes) along the route such as Leon and Santiago de Compostela. Scenario C would relate to those travellers interested in experiencing only the eastern side of the route (from Pamplona to Burgos). Scenario D exists when travellers chose to deviate off the route from one of the principal nodes to visit other related pilgrimage and heritage attractions, such as the monastery of Santo Domingo de Silos. This conceptual model is applied later to the cases of the two routes in Northern Ireland. Prior to this, it is necessary to situate the two case studies within the wider context of the history of tourism development in Northern Ireland.

Tourism in Northern Ireland and trail/route development

Northern Ireland has had a difficult history with regard to tourism. It is a region that has experienced varying degrees of violence, civil unrest and overt terrorism. In extreme cases, some sections of the community relate the struggle as a war against the British government and its political apparatus. Boyd (2013) provides a concise history of tourism for the region, dividing time into three periods.

The first period relates to the pre-violence years prior to 1969, where a normal tourism environment existed in which the destination was visited by mainly UK tourists, looking to experience a 'bucket-and-spade' holiday at the Edwardian and Victorian seaside resorts located along its eastern and northern coastline. The Northern Ireland Tourist Board (NITB) was set up under the 1948 Tourist Act as the national governing body for the industry to provide leadership as well as to market the region. It is significant that this development preceded any legislation on tourism within the rest of the United Kingdom.

The second period covers the overt violence (i.e. terrorism) by the Irish Republican Army (IRA) between 1969 and 1994, or what many Catholic residents (i.e. nationalists) would characterise as the struggle for their rights and views to be recognised. These were 'lost years' of development and growth compared to that which the rest of northern Europe enjoyed. The negative image and perception of Northern Ireland, coupled with a lack of suitable infrastructure, the weakness of the NITB in not promoting the region and encouraging tourist development, and the inability to react to changing holiday trends away from domestic holidays, meant that the region failed to develop its full tourism potential. It was not until the early 1990s that visitor numbers returned to pre-violence levels, when dialogue began between the British and Irish governments and the political wing of the IRA (Sinn Fein), resulting in a 'ceasefire' of terrorist activity in August 1994. Tourist numbers increased by 20% in 1995, but inherent weaknesses remained within the industry that over the past quarter of a century had been severely stifled in terms of product development, and had seen little or no challenge in terms of the quality enhancement of existing products.

The third and final period covers the post-violence years to the present day (1994 onwards). Boyd (2013) notes that over the past two decades attention has shifted to include reviewing existing accommodation provision, attracting new investment (such as branded, major chain hotels), setting (generally unrealistic) goals of increased visitor numbers (particularly holiday visitors) and tourist spend, and developing new products and a stronger attractions base. Boyd (2000) has highlighted that prior to 2000, the product base was heavily reliant on heritage and culture, with the remaining top attractions being beaches and fun parks associated with what were by then declining Victorian and Edwardian resorts. It was during the 2000s that the Northern Ireland Assembly (devolved government had resulted from the signing of the Good Friday Agreement in 1998) embarked on an ambitious programme of new product development that represented distinct and unique aspects of Northern Ireland's landscape, culture and heritage in order to compete in an international market place. These are known as 'signature projects', in that they were designed to offer the best opportunities for tourism growth, to create attractions and attraction space that were deemed 'world class' and to create international standout for the region. It was within this wider context of signature projects that routes of the kind considered here developed, either as part of a signature project or connecting a number of such projects together.

In summary, the signature projects included (Boyd, 2013):

♦ **Titanic & Maritime Belfast** – the building of a 'world-class' visitor attraction to showcase the story of the Titanic, conceived, designed and built in Belfast, as well as focus on shipbuilding and seafaring in Belfast (the visitor attraction opened on the one hundredth anniversary of the maiden voyage and sinking of RMS Titanic, April 2012).

♦ **Giant's Causeway, Antrim & Causeway Coast Area** – the building of a new visitor centre at the Giant's Causeway (the previous centre was destroyed in a fire in 2000), a signed coastal driving route (the Causeway Coastal Route), as well as number of stops with infrastructural improvement and interpretation along the route.

♦   **Walled City of Derry** – the only complete walled city in Ireland, the Walled City of Derry project includes improved public realm, refurbishment and redevelopment of a number of key attractions (those being a museum, several churches and a theatre).

♦   **Saint Patrick and Christian Heritage** – a driving route focused on key sites that have a connection to Saint Patrick's life, legacy and landscape.

♦   **Mournes National Park Area** – amended following local resistance to become a coastal route; a signed driving route along the coast and the Mourne mountains.

It is clear from the above list of the signature projects that the two routes that are the subjects of the present cases are key elements of a wider strategy to growing the supply side of tourism across the region. It should also be pointed out that the Causeway Coastal Route acts to link together three of the five signature projects and their respective regions. At one end of the route is the Walled City in Derry/Londonderry[1], while at the other end is the Titanic and Maritime product offering in the capital city of Belfast. The new visitor centre at the Giant's Causeway, meanwhile, is a key node and major attraction midway along the route. The signature projects have been in the cost of £75 million, with the majority of funding coming from the public sector through a Programme for Government between 2008 and 2011.

Northern Ireland today is a safe, accessible and attractive destination, where tourism generates £510 million in direct spending a year. It has enjoyed approximately 2 million international visitors for the past few years, as well as 1.4 million domestic visitors. While tourism contributes 2.9% of region's gross domestic product, it remains well below that of its local competitors (in the Republic of Ireland the figure is 4.4%, in Scotland it is 5% and in Wales it is 7% of gross value added). Despite this, tourism directly supports 30,000 full-time-equivalent jobs. The recently released 2020 tourism strategy estimates the potential of the industry to support 50,000 jobs, attract 4.5 million visitors and generate £1 billion for the Northern Ireland economy every year. Alan Clarke, the Chief Executive of the NITB, views the signature projects as "offering visitors the reason to choose Northern Ireland, the reason to stay longer and the reason to spend more" (NITB, 2012: 2). They collectively act as leverage to build on existing demand, offer the 'wow factor' that is necessary to appeal to international visitors, and help establish the region's

---

1   The preferred name of the city is Londonderry by unionists and Derry by nationalists.

unique selling points. Route development is part of that new tourism offering. The 'stories' behind the two case studies are now considered, addressing issues of planning, development and stakeholder assessments of how they are managed.

The Causeway Coastal Route

Planning and development

Early tourism planning identified a distinct 'zonal' arrangement (Inskeep, 1994), whereby opportunities and attractions were clustered along a section of the north coast of the region. Boyd (2000) extended that thinking in his research on heritage tourism, where he added clusters for the key cities of Belfast, Armagh (to be discussed in more detail in the Saint Patrick's Trail) and Derry/Londonder, where the strength of that cluster arrangement was dependent on whether attractions were free or fee-paying. With the physical development of the Causeway Coastal Route (CCR), visitors can make a formal connection between the attractions in Belfast, Derry/Londonderry and those that are located in between. The latter may be viewed in terms of the law of intervening opportunity, where visitors can choose the number of places they stop at and the length of time they spend at each. Alternatively they may choose to traverse the whole route, taking in only the start and end depending on their point of entrance and egress. In so doing, visitors are choosing Scenario A as shown in Figure 1.

A deliberate strategy in the development of the route was not only to link the signature projects that have already been discussed but also to connect the visitor indirectly to the range of attractions offered in both city regions, recognising that midway along the route is the world renowned World Heritage Site (WHS) of the Giant's Causeway

The CCR is labelled a general sight-seeing touring trail, but it is also an opportunity to experience one of the most dramatic routes in the world. It is, according to the NITB, 'the essential Irish journey', where the 80-mile route offers panoramic views of windswept cliffs, spectacular scenery, relatively unspoilt beaches, historic castles, resort communities, coastal villages, churches, heritage centres and forts (see Figure 2). According to the travel section of the Independent newspaper in 2009, the CCR was regarded as the best coastal route in the UK, on a par with the Garden Route in South Africa and the Pebble Beach/Carmel Coastal Drive in California. The CCR was part of the Causeway Coast and Glens Masterplan (2004-13), and the route (including two additional inland routes) was developed in conjunction with 10 local authority regions that the route passes through (from Derry City Council in the northwest, to Newtownabbey Borough Council on the northern edge of Belfast). In total, there are 400 brown signs that received ministerial approval and sign-off in July 2007, at a combined cost of £700,000. As Figure 2 shows, there are nine scenic inland routes and three Areas of Outstanding Natural Beauty (AONBs). These can be reached from entry points along the route itself (reflecting Scenario D in Figure 1). There are also 15 highlight 'stops' identified along the route. These all have the potential to act as points of intervening opportunity, either as major or minor nodes/attractions.

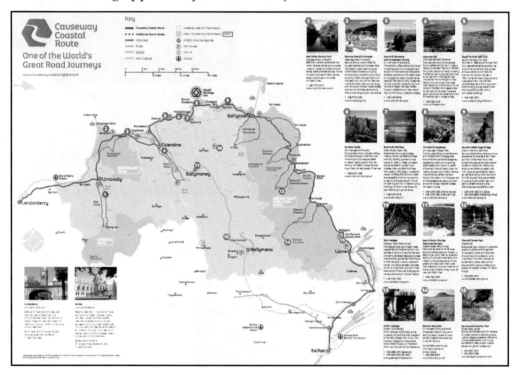

Figure 2: Causeway Coastal Route: Source: Tourist Brochure, NITB (2011). The smaller shaded areas represent Areas of Natural Beauty (AONBs) that can be accessed from the route. The larger shaded area represents the Causeway Coast and Heritage Glens Region that spans the 10 local authorities

The principal node/attraction found midway along the CCR is the Giant's Causeway, the only WHS in Northern Ireland. It received WHS inscription status in 1986, at the same time as Stonehenge in England. This represents Scenario B in Figure 1. Situated on the Province's north coast (see the UNESCO symbol in Figure 2), this marvel of 40,000 solidified basaltic hexagonal columns, formed from a lava flow of an extinct volcanic eruption in the region's geological past, protrudes out of a cliff face and forms a section of the seashore. It has held the fascination of visitors and early writers as far back as the mid 1700s. Some of these early visitors travelled to view this marvel of nature using Europe's first hydro-electric tram, that operated out from the coastal resort of Portrush to the Causeway from 1883 to 1949.

 The Giant's Causeway has been integral to how Northern Ireland has marketed itself for tourism. The hexagon is the logo of the Northern Ireland Tourist Board (the National Tourism Organisation, NTO), and the Giant's Causeway has been a popular image on promotional material over the years. Since early records began in the 1970s, when the NITB first collected statistics at visitor attractions, the Causeway has consistently been in the top three visitor attractions. Most years it has held the top spot.

There has been a long history of commercial activity at the Giants Causeway. Early pictures reveal souvenirs sold from small huts, as well as interpretation and guiding services being offered to elite visitors, all located on the service road that led down to the causeway itself. A modern visitor centre, built in the form of two adjoining Irish cottages, was partially destroyed in a fire in 2000, with the loss of the interpretation centre. Temporary facilities were erected pending a new centre being built; a wood-framed structure serving as a souvenir shop. Unfortunately, a protracted period of time ensued before government plans, which had been in place since 2003, were approved and a new visitor centre built. The new centre opened in the summer of 2012 at a cost of £18.5 million (see Figure 3). Visitors can choose to park at the centre itself or have the option of a park-and-ride scheme from the nearby village of Bushmills (which is also home to the world's oldest working whiskey distillery). Alternatively, visitors can take a nostalgic journey on a narrow-gauge heritage railway that runs from Bushmills to the Causeway: the station is only a few hundred metres away from the new visitor centre. Two 40-seater carriages are equipped with audio commentary facilities that offer visitors a history of the electric tramway and of places of interest along the short journey to the Causeway.

The Giant's Causeway has in the past been viewed as a stand-alone attraction: some organised tours chose to combine it with a visit to the nearby Old Bushmills Distillery (representing Scenario D in Figure 1: an attraction off the route itself), thereafter leaving the coastal region and returning to Belfast or even travelling further afield to places such as Dublin, using major inland arterial routes. Since its opening, the visitor centre, combined with the actual viewing of the Causeway itself, has the potential to act as the base from which visitors choose to explore all that the CCR has to offer, thereby bringing the law of intervening opportunity into play.

Figure 3: The new visitor centre at the Giant's Causeway. Photo credit: Stephen Boyd. Architecturally appealing, the centre is built into the landscape, creating the 'wow factor' for visitors, offering interpretation, exhibitions, retail, catering services and tourist information

These opportunity nodes include a number of heritage sites, in particular castles, which are unlikely to have sufficient pulling power on their own. For example, Carrickfergus Castle, on the shores of Belfast Lough, is famed as one of the few remaining Norman castles in the region. It is steeped in history from the time it was built by John de Courcy in 1177 as his base in Eastern Ulster. Today's visitor can take a tour of the castle, learn about its history in its interpretation centre and use it as a short stop as they travel along the CCR. Other key attractions/nodes on the route (along the north coast section) include the tourist centre of Ballycastle, known as the venue for Ireland's oldest open fair (traditional in the past as a horse-trading fair: a practice that still takes place but within strict ethical controls), which takes place in the last weekend of August. Another node/attraction, also along the north coast, is Dunluce Castle. This is a ruined medieval castle with an interesting history of occupation by several Irish families: first the McQuillan's (in the 13th to 15th centuries) and then the MacDonnell's (in the 16th to 17th centuries), before falling into disrepair. The castle is popular in imagery used to promote this region of Northern Ireland: it is often shown as the backdrop silhouetted against the night sky. Used as a setting in some scenes in Game of Thrones (a UK television series set in the time of King Arthur), the remains of the castle serve as another short stop, offering visitors the opportunity to walk through the ruins of the castle, as well as to learn about its history and certain stories in a recently renovated interpretation centre.

Other nodes along the north coast are the seaside resorts of Portrush, and Portstewart. Dating back to the Victorian and Edwardian periods, the lure of the sea and the rise of sea (cold-water) bathing culture, both resorts have suffered over the years and have become principally domestic holiday 'bucket-and-spade' destinations. Events as of late have seen something of a rejuvenation, whereby these resort destinations are host to a range of annual events that cover most of the peak summer season. Portrush hosted the Irish Golf Open in 2012, and the town is now marketed with a distinctly golfing label as it is home to two of the three major internationally renowned Northern Irish golfers. The last two examples of nodes (Dunluce Castle and the resorts of Portrush and Portstewart) are in relatively close proximity to the Giant's Causeway and its visitor centre, and so combined they illustrate Scenario C in Figure 1.

A significant amount of investment has gone into projects along the CCR. Tourism infrastructure improvements took place at 40 sites along the route, with the majority of these under local council ownership. According to an Audit Commission report on the signature projects, published in 2012, the combined cost of these improvements was £8.6 million, of which £4.1 million was supported by NITB grants facilitated through its Tourism Development Scheme (the monies committed by the NTO must be matched by the other party/owner). Table 1 itemises some of the projects that have received funding from the NITB along the CCR or its connected inland loops.

Table 1: Financially Assisted Projects for the Causeway Coastal Route (2008-11)

Projects Funded	Financial Assistance (£)
Ballycastle Town Environ and Rathlin Island	379,458
Causeway Coastal Route Alive (CCR Alive)	72,263
Causeway Coastal Route Interpretation Programme	244,846
Compelling a visit	23,794
County Antrim Yacht Club	126,009
Dunluce Castle	103,875
East Strand Physical Improvement & Interpretation Programme	501,231
Garron Point	26,250
Giant's Causeway Bushmills Railway	142,005
Giant's Causeway Visitor Experience	9,250,000
Glenarm Village and Carnfunnock Country Park	128,391
Jordanstown Loughshore Park, Newtownabbey	659,549
Limavady Tourist Information Centre	29,534
Portglenone Marina	225,849
Total Amount (£2,663,054 if Giant's Causeway Visitor Experience not included).	11,913,054

Source: NITB (2012)

Managing the Causeway Coastal Route

Partnerships have received a favourable press by scholars as a useful mechanism for effective management for settings that involve multiple stakeholders and cover a mix of setting and ownership (Bramwell and Lane, 1999, 2000; Boyd and Timothy, 2001). Defined by Bramwell and Lane (1999: 179) as "regular, cross-sectoral interactions between parties, based on at least some agreed rules or norms, intended to address a common issue or to achieve a specific policy goal or goals", they become almost standard practice within tourism management that involves some sort of partnership agreement or dialogue between different parties. Boyd and Timothy (2001), working in the context of WHSs (of which one example was the Giant's Causeway), argued that within partnerships there is the potential for three elements to exist: first is type (which can range from informal to formalised); second is the approach taken to the partnership (ranging from grassroots to agency-led); and third is the extent of cooperation that exists between partners (which can range from limited to full).

In the case of the CCR, a formalised, agency-led partnership was put in place between the NITB, the National Trust and all the local councils and heritage bodies (such as the three AONBs management bodies and the wider Causeway Coast and Glens Heritage Trust) whose jurisdiction covers the geographical area of the CCR (including its inland scenic loops). The extent of cooperation was more toward the full end of the spectrum as opposed to limited. Collectively the councils agreed to fund the route, in that they paid for brown road signs that fell within their jurisdiction. Agreement was also reached on the need for route enhancement. This saw a technical study (commissioned by the NITB), part-funded by the International Fund for Ireland, undertaken in June 2008. The study examined 71 individual sites and considered a myriad of issues including the strategic importance of the site, its existing condition, health and safety, economic benefit, access, visitor interest, value for money, cleanliness, ownership, visitor ownership, cleanliness, visitor amenities, retail, catering, landscape treatment, parking, public transport and disability access. Of the 71 sites, 17 were given Priority A status, 23 Priority B, 19 Priority C, with 12 considered to have limited potential. The combined cost of recommendations for all sites came to £6.5 million. This was followed in December 2009 by an interpretation study to develop storytelling at sites along the route to create a 'seamless story' of 'the essential Irish journey'. There was found to be an inconsistent message, with much variation in style and design at stops along the route. Through partnership work, by March 2011 physical improvement had taken place at 15 identified sites (see Figure 2). With respect to interpretation, the NITB and key partners developed and implemented interpretation resources at these key points, allowing visitors to uncover the region's rich cultural heritage (NITB, 2012). In place are panels, way-markers and bespoke benches that enhance the visitor offering and improve visitor orientation: all designed to encourage visitors to get off the route and explore its various nodes/attractions.

It was agreed that each council would maintain those sites that fall within their jurisdiction, and they can chose to manage the impacts adopting either supply-side or demand-driven techniques that have widely been written about in the academic literature (e.g. Garrod, 2008; Hall and Lew, 2009).

There remain a number of wider servicing issues that require buy-in from the private sector. These include putting in place more places to eat, more high-quality accommodation (four star and above), particularly along the north coast section. The lack of rooms results in visitors staying in Belfast. Back in 2009, a Portrush Regeneration Strategy invited tender bids for private-sector development of four-star hotel accommodation, including a conference centre. To date, however, no new quality accommodation stock has been added, with the only significant improvements being an enhancement of the public realm, which has been public-sector funded. Moreover, this was specifically prior to the Irish Open Golf tournament in Portrush in 2012.

As for the impact of the CCR on increased footfall, there is some anecdotal information to suggest that this has risen since the route was established. A visitor survey at the Giant's Causeway in June 2007, with a base of 575 respondents, noted that 78% had heard of the CCR and 63% had used the CCR to get to the Giant's Causeway, as opposed to the faster inland major arterial routeway (a positive outcome given that the route only got official signage earlier that year). More recently, in the Northern Ireland visitor attitude survey 2011 for the Causeway Coast and Glens destination, when asked what activities and attractions they visited, eight in 10 stated they had visited the Giants Causeway, seven in 10 had followed the CCR and one in four had visited a historic castle or house, suggesting that the CCR was the preferred way to access this region and take in its historic attractions. Although focused on the premier attraction along the route, the Giant's Causeway, a press release by the NITB in November 2012 announced that in the four months since it opened, the Giant's Causeway visitor experience had received 300,000 visitors from over 130 countries: considerably more than any other year for that short period. Looking forward, the Causeway Coast and Glens Tourism Partnership (a region that takes in six of the nine councils that are involved with the CCR) published its Tourism Area Plan for 2012-2017, in which it acknowledged the route as a premier touring route as part of its 2012 baseline for growth (Causeway Coast and Glens Tourism Partnership, 2011).

Saint Patrick's Trail

Planning and development

Religion has been intertwined with politics since Northern Ireland was formed by partition from Southern Ireland in 1921 under the terms of the Government of Ireland Act of 1920. However it has played a limited role where tourism is concerned. Northern Ireland is not on par with other religious tourism destinations like the Vatican City, Jerusalem, and Medjugorie in Bosnia-Herzegovina, and while it is not normally considered to be a pilgrimage/religious tourism destination, it does have a number of Christian heritage attractions (Simone-Charteris and Boyd, 2010). These are mostly sites connected to the patron saint of Ireland, Saint Patrick, and include what is believed to be his burial site, Downpatrick, the first church he founded at Saul, the two Saint Patrick's cathedrals in the city of Armagh, and Saint Patrick's Trian (a visitor centre which tells the story of Patrick at Armagh). These sites are connected through the Saint Patrick's Trail.

The Saint Patrick's & Christian Heritage signature project (within which the Trail is a significant element) was chosen by the NITB because of the market potential for Christian heritage, as well as the diversity, integrity and authenticity of the product base, and also the wealth of place association connected with Saint Patrick. The aim of the project was to create a literal and metaphorical series of journeys through landscape and culture, myth and reality that allowed the visitor to follow in the footsteps of Patrick's personal journey from ordinary man to saint. The aim was also to allow people to reflect on how his legacy has shaped the contemporary landscape, culture and Christian heritage of Ireland. The development of the route was primarily based on the urban centres of Armagh and Downpatrick, with Bangor and Newry as secondary clusters (see Figure 4). A three-year Action Plan was launched by the NITB in March 2005. This was developed around six priority themes: working in partnership; developing a Saint Patrick's Trail; creating a memorable experience; developing a coordinated events and festival programme; strong marketing and branding; and developing cross-border activities (Simone-Chatertis and Boyd, 2010).

The Action Plan involved an extensive mix of partners including public bodies comprising the NITB, Government departments (including the Department of Enterprise, Trade and Investment, the Northern Ireland Environment Agency, the Department of Regional Development, the Department of Social Development, and the Department of Agriculture and Rural Development), and local councils (e.g. Down District Council, Armagh City District Council, and Newry and Mourne District Council).

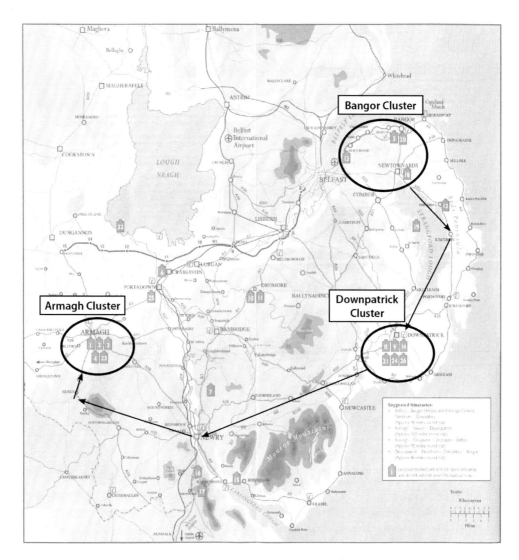

Key to attraction clusters

Downpatrick: six key attractions: Down Cathedral & St. Patrick's Grave, St. Patrick Centre, Down County Museum, Inch Abbey, and outlying attractions of Saul Church and Struell Wells

Armagh: five key attractions: Armagh Cathedral (Church of Ireland), Armagh Cathedral (Roman Catholic), Armagh County Museum, Armagh Public Library & St. Patrick's Trian

Bangor: Bangor Abbey, North Down Heritage Centre, and outlying attractions of Holywood Priory and Movilla Abbey

Figure 4: Saint Patrick and Christian Heritage Route with recognised attraction clusters. *Source:* Modified from Charteris and Boyd (2010). The Saint Patrick & Christian Heritage Route runs from Bangor to Downpatrick via the east side of Strangford Lough, and across to Armagh city via the city of Newry, or in reverse if starting point is in the city of Armagh

Also included were public-private tourist organisations such as visitor and convention bureaux and regional tourism partnerships (e.g. Armagh Down Tourism Partnership); and private tourist organisations including visitor attractions (e.g. the Saint Patrick Centre, Figure 5, and the Saint Patrick's Trian Visitor Complex), churches and cathedrals (e.g. Saint Patrick's Church of Ireland Cathedral and Saint Patrick's Roman Catholic Cathedral), tour companies (e.g. Armagh Guided Tours and Legendary Days Out), and community organisations (e.g. Saint Patrick's Trail Advisory Groups).

Figure 5: Saint Patrick Visitor Centre, Downpatrick. Photo Credit: Stephen Boyd

Figure 6: Saint Patrick's grave in the grounds of Down Cathedral, Downpatrick. Photo Credit: Stephen Boyd

Figure 7: Welcome sign to Downpatrick: a stylised representation of Saint Patrick. Photo credit: Stephen Boyd

Figure 8: Signage showing the bishop's mitre that designates the trail. Photo credit: Stephen Boyd

The Trail formed part of the wider signature project entitled 'Christian Heritage/Saint Patrick', as the eastern section of the trail takes in the city of Bangor and the Ards Peninsula: both areas were associated with another Saint (Columbanus, educated in Bangor, born in around AD 543, left to set up monasteries in France, Italy and Switzerland) and other religious locations (Grey Abbey, Inch Abbey and Nendrum Monastic Site). The combined trail represents a 92-mile signed driving route from Bangor to Armagh which ties together four key sites (associated with Columbanus) and 11 sites which have a strong link to Saint Patrick's life, legacy and landscape (NITB, 2010). There are a number of locations that are not on the route itself but can be easily accessed from it (representing Scenario D in Figure 1). These include Saul Church, the site where Saint Patrick did his first preaching in AD 432, and Slieve Patrick, a hill that is a genuine pilgrimage site, climbed once a year on the third Sunday of June, on top of which is erected the largest statue of Patrick looking out on Carlingford Lough, the place where it is believed he first set foot in Ireland.

Capital spending in the region of £8 million has gone into 20 projects along the route, including interpretative signs, and improved access to and interpretation of St. Patrick's grave (Figure 6 and 7). In keeping with a consistent look of the interpretation, bespoke panels called 'totem poles' have been erected at 14 sites on the Saint Patrick's Trail from Bangor Abbey to both Saint Patrick's cathedrals in Armagh, creating a certain brand (NITB, 2012).

Management

Unlike the CCR, Saint Patrick's Trail is just past the stage of project development, with all 20 projects completed by April 2012. As with the CCR, however, management is to be the responsibility of the various councils and government bodies involved. With enhanced public realm, and consistent brand in terms of interpretation, the NITB is confident that this signature project will help create major opportunities for community benefits (e.g. jobs, income and business growth), uplift the region's profile and appeal as a year-round destination, and contribute £30 million per annum towards the local economy. As with the CCR, the absence of a four-star hotel in Downpatrick remains a major deterrent to growing international tourism around the Saint Patrick brand. According to Tim Campbell, "six million people celebrate Saint Patrick around the world and that's the true impact and market potential" (Personal Correspondence, June 2011). At present, fewer than 150,000 visitors per annum pass through the visitors centre in Downpatrick. If the trail was to attract even a fraction of that potential, issues of how sites are managed will be critical in future. Currently, many attractions/nodes along the trail show negligible visitor impact: they either represent visitor centres, museums and places of worship. These locations have benefited from NITB-assisted funding with respect to signage (Figure 8), shop facilities, interpretation panels (totem poles) and ease of access for elderly and disabled visitors. Those that experience larger visitor numbers (such as the grave at Downpatrick), will need to be managed effectively now that access is to the grave has been improved. The outlying sites/attractions (Saul Church and Slieve Patrick) will probably not suffer from increased footfall given their location to the main attractions: they are off the main trail and are unlikely to be visited by tour parties/buses. The latter of the two sites is viewed as a site of 'pilgrimage', whereby local people climb to the top to the statue of St Patrick on the third Sunday of June each year. Any visitor choosing to complete this climb would require several hours and this would only be realistic if they were staying within the Downpatrick cluster region for several days. Given that it is marketed as a touring route, it unlikely that the physical impact and damage at this outlying stop will be of much concern.

Discussion and conclusions

This case considers the stories of two contrasting heritage routes in Northern Ireland. The CCR has received the most attention and investment (if the costs of the new visitor centre at the Giant's Causeway is factored in). It links the region's most-visited destinations and attractions (situated across the Causeway Coast and Glen region). Visitors in the past to Northern Ireland would have chosen to travel from the gateway of the capital Belfast to the attractions on the North coast of the Province via the coastal road. The scenery along the east and north coast of Northern Ireland has been well recognised as a tourist asset that has featured prominently in past marketing literature. The rugged landscape with the cliffs, inlets, castles and coastal communities have helped 'sell' the image of heritage, quaintness and rurality. What the actual development and setting out of the route (CCR) has achieved is the physical 'marking out' of the route and identifying specific sites or nodes of intervening opportunity to encourage visitors to stop and immerse themselves in this Irish journey.

A consistent 'message' is effectively being presented to visitors via the interpretation panels at each stop as these have a consistent brand: they provide detailed information about each stop (with its attractions) as well as illustrating via a map that this is part of the wider CCR, encouraging visitors to pre-select other stops on their onward journey. As noted earlier, the CCR provides visitors with a route that connects three of the key visitor attractions/nodes that offer the wow factor and international standout: Titanic Belfast at the start of the route in Belfast, the Giant's Causeway WHS (toward the middle of the route) and the walled city of Derry/Londonderry at the end of the route. What the actual setting out of the Route can achieve is greater dwell time at smaller nodes/attractions found between these three key attractions. This has yet to be measured through surveys; nor has there been any focus on measuring the economic benefit of the Route to business located directly on or in close proximity to it. It is this type of research that must now follow to illustrate the degree of effectiveness the setting out of a formalised route has had to local economies. If the outcome is that increased footfall and dwell time only occurs at the key attractions/nodes along the route (start, middle and end), then the route itself has only had the beneficial effect of 'joining up' certain attractions and places for visitors, and the routeway is effectively just that: a route to connect a few key attractions. In the development of the Signature Projects, the national tourism body (NITB) envisaged that once in place, real opportunity existed to create 'signature destinations'. It would be disappointing if those intervening spaces (along with their attraction mixes) along the route were ignored by potential and future actual visitors. What is promising to see is that this Route has completed a number of key stages: formalisation with brown signs, physical improvements at key locations, consistent interpretation and established brand. The next step is to ensure that the Route is effectively managed. This, as noted above, will require vision, creativity and joined-up thinking given the number of stakeholders involved in this responsibility.

In contrast, the Saint Patrick's Trail came 'late to the game', with the project development stage only recently having been completed. Marketed as another essential journey that visitors are encouraged to take, it is unclear if this will appeal across the broader visitor profile that Northern Ireland enjoys. The actual achieving of a marked trail however provides the opportunity for more visitors to 'see' Saint Patrick country if this only means a circuit route out of Belfast stopping at Downpatrick at the visitor centre, his grave and then travelling across to Armagh to visit its cathedrals and their connection to Patrick, returning to Belfast via the main transport corridor of major A-roads and motorway network. A consistent message and brand is in place along the Route through interpretation panels that show other smaller nodes/attractions outside or outlying from the three key centres of Downpatrick, Armagh and, to a certain extent, Bangor. The next steps that must follow are to effectively market the Route to the potential six million people that have some connection to the brand through celebrating St Patrick's Day to see if footfall and dwell time increase. It is unlikely in the case of this Route that signature destinations will develop: the absence of quality commercial accommodation raises a significant challenge to encourage visitors to stay in the region beyond those journeying through or engaging in day-trips to experience 'St. Patrick country'. Nevertheless, even if less anticipated footfall occurs, the management of the Route and its sites/nodes is essential and the challenge here is not that dissimilar to that of the CCR given that the

Route encompasses a number of jurisdictions and involves a range of stake-holders. Another challenge will be to see if the tourism businesses located within the clusters shown in Figure 4 can form effective networks to grow their businesses with clear and effective links and messages to those visitors interested in St Patrick and other religious sites, where growth is both linked to St. Patrick and separate of this brand.

The contrast between the two Routes is made strikingly clear in a recent Audit Commission (2012) report. Part of the report offered stakeholder assessment of each of the five signature projects. Thirty three stakeholders were interviewed across all five signature projects, and asked if any of the projects offered both 'international standout' and 'would deliver value for money'. The findings clearly demonstrate what Route will be the more significant for tourism in Northern Ireland: 24 stakeholders saw the CCR as offering international standout, with the WHS at the Giant's Causeway being the key attraction, although only 17 said it would deliver value for money. In contrast, few stated that Saint Patrick's SP (which includes the Route) would achieve international standout, with only 13 having the view that it would deliver value for money. Despite this negative assessment of the latter, the two routes/trails have the potential to appeal to particular niches, and to form part of a wider diverse portfolio of opportunities being created for today's visitor to Northern Ireland.

References

Bold V, Gillespie S. 2009.The Southern Upland Way: Exploring landscape and culture. *International Journal of Heritage Studies* **15** (2/3): 245-257.

Boyd SW. 2000, Heritage tourism in Northern Ireland: Opportunities under peace. *Current Issues in Tourism* **3** (2): 150-174.

Boyd SW. 2013. Tourism in Northern Ireland: Before violence, during and post violence. In Butler RW, Suntikul W. (eds) *Tourism and War*. London: Routledge; 176-192.

Boyd SW, Timothy DJ. 2001. Developing partnerships: tools for interpretation and management of World Heritage Sites. *Tourism Recreation Research* **26** (1): 47-53.

Bramwell B, Lane B. 1999. Collaboration and partnerships for sustainable tourism. *Journal of Sustainable Tourism* **7** (3/4): 179-181.

Bramwell B, Lane B. (eds) 2000. *Tourism Collaboration and Partnerships: Politics, Practice and Sustainability*. Clevedon: Channel View.

Casbeard R. 2010. Slavery heritage in Bristol: History, memory and forgetting. *Annals of Leisure Research* **13** (1/2): 143-166.

Causeway Coast and Glens Tourism Partnership. 2011. *Tourism Area Plan 2012-2017; Growing Tourism Together*. Edinburgh: BTS Solutions.

Cheung SCH. 1999. The meaning of a heritage trail in Hong Kong. *Annals of Tourism Research* **26** (3): 570-588.

Garrod B. 2008. Managing visitor impacts. In Fyall A, Garrod B, Leask A, Wanhill S. (eds) *Managing Visitor Attractions: New Directions*, 2nd Edition, Oxford: Butterworth-Heinemann.

Graham B, Murray M. 1997. The spiritual and the profane: The pilgrimage to Santiago de Compostela. *Ecumene*, **4** (4) 389-409

Gunn CA. 1972. *Vacationscape: Designing Tourist Regions*. Austin, TX: Bureau of Business Research, University of Texas.

Gunn CA. 1994. *Tourism Planning: Basics, Concepts, Cases*. Philadelphia: Taylor and Francis.

Hall CM. 2008. *Tourism Planning: Policies, Processes and Relationships*. Harlow: Prentice Hall.

Hall CM, Lew AA. 2009. *Understanding and Managing Tourism Impacts: An Integrated Approach*. London: Routledge.

Heitmann S. 2011. Tourist behaviour and tourism motivations. In Robinson P, Heitmann S, Dieke P (eds) *Research Themes for Tourism*, Wallingford: CABI; 31-44.

Lash GY, Smith AK, Smith C. 2010. Domestic tourism and peace: The Atlanta peace trails experience. In Moufakkir O, Kelly I. (eds) *Tourism, Progress and Peace*, Wallingford: CABI; 118-133.

Leiper N. 1990. *Tourism Systems: An Interdisciplinary Perspective*. Palmerston North, New Zealand: Department of Management Systems. Occasional Paper 2, Massey University.

Lue CC, Crompton JL, Fesenmaier DR. 1993. Conceptualization of multi-destination pleasure trips. *Annals of Tourism Research* **20** (2): 289-301

MacLeod N, Hayes D, Slater A. 2009. Reading the landscape: The development of a typology of literary trails that incorporate an experiential design perspective. *Journal of Hospitality Marketing and Management* **18** (2/3): 154-172.

Mattingly A. 2005. Pennine Way and the dawn of the long-distance footpaths. *Walk*, **6** (1), 24-29.

McNamara KE, Prideaux B. 2011. Planning nature-based hiking trails in a tropical rainforest setting. *Asia Pacific Journal of Tourism Research* **16** (3): 289-305.

Morrow S. 2005. Continuity and change: The planning and management of long distance walking routes in Scotland. *Managing Leisure* **10**: 237-250.

Mundet L, Coenders G. 2010. Greenways: A sustainable leisure experience concept for both communities and tourists. *Journal of Sustainable Tourism* **18** (5): 657-674.

Murray M, Graham B. 1997. Exploring the dialectics of route-based tourism: The Camino de Santiago. *Tourism Management* **18** (8): 513-524.

Northern Ireland Tourist Board. 2012. *Financially Assisted Projects 2008-11*; Chief Executive's Foreword. NITB.

Northern Ireland Tourist Board. 2010. Annual Report 2009/10. NITB.

Plummer R, Telfer D, Hashimoto A, Summers R. 2005. Beer tourism in Canada along the Waterloo-Wellington Ale Trail. *Tourism Management* **26** (3): 447-458.

Ratz T, Smith M, Michalko G. 2008. New places in old spaces: Mapping tourism and regeneration in Budapest. *Tourism Geographies* **10** (4): 429-451.

Simone-Charteris M, Boyd SW. 2010. The development of religious heritage tourism in Northern Ireland: Opportunities, benefits and obstacles. *Tourism* **58** (3), 229-58.

Ancillary Student Material

Further reading

Fyall A, Garrod B, Leask A, Wanhill S. 2008. *Managing Visitor Attractions: New Directions*, 2nd Edition, Oxford: Butterworth-Heinemann.

Leask A, Fyall A. (eds) 2006. *Managing World Heritage Sites*. Oxford: Elsevier.

Olsen DH. 2006. Management issues for religious heritage attractions. In Timothy DJ, Olsen DH. (eds) *Tourism, Religion and Spiritual Journeys*, Oxford: Routledge; 104-118.

Timothy DJ, Boyd SW. 2006. Heritage tourism in the 21st century: Valued traditions and new perspectives. *Journal of Heritage Tourism* **1** (1), 1-16.

Timothy DJ, Olsen DH. (eds) 2006. *Tourism, Religion and Spiritual Journeys*. Oxford: Routledge.

Related websites

The following websites offer detailed information on the signature projects developed in Northern Ireland and the Giants Causeway World Heritage Site in particular:

Causeway Coastal Route: http://www.causewaycoastalroute.com/

Northern Ireland Tourist Board: www.nitb.com

Saint Patrick's Trail: http://www.discovernorthernireland.com/stpatrick/Saint-Patricks-Trail-Key-Sites-A2502

UNESCO: http://whc.unesco.org/

Self-test questions

Try to answer the following questions to test your knowledge and understanding. If you are not sure of the answers then please refer to the suggested references and further reading sources.

1   Who are the key partners in the management of the Causeway Coastal Route and Saint Patrick's Trail?

2   What are the five signature projects developed in Northern Ireland? Why were they developed?

3   What action was taken to ensure a consistent message or story is told for both the Causeway Coastal Route and Saint Patrick's Trail?

4   What are the key management challenges for both routes/trails?

Key themes and theories

The key themes that are raised in the cases studies relate to the following areas:

◆   Partnerships in visitor attraction development
◆   Trail/route design and development
◆   Trail typology
◆   Trails/routes as part of wider tourism supply

The key theories relate to:

◆   Tourism planning
◆   Tourism development
◆   Destination marketing
◆   Linear tourist attraction
◆   Route/trail experience scenarios

If you need further information on any of the above themes and theories, then these headings could be used as key words to search for materials and case studies.

11

Big Pit and Cape Breton

Finding Meaning in Constructs of Industrial Heritage

Mary Beth Gouthro

Post-industrial sites as heritage attractions

Mining and manufacturing were once the major employers of the labour force in developed nations. Remnants of economies driven by industrial and manufacturing activity[1] have since given way to predominately service-based economies. Advances in technology have also played a role in transitioning society from a manufacturing environment to a service environment (Harris, 1989; Prentice, 1993).

Coal mining was a chief factor contributing to the development of modern industry, and the beginning of the Industrial Revolution. Even though Britain as a nation is synonymous with the Industrial Revolution[2], other areas of the world, including British colonies, followed suit and made their own contribution to the industrial era. Commentators have since reflected on the social and economic impacts of the rise of the mining industry. Newton (1992) states that the development of productive and viable mining industries during the era was associated with growing economic wealth and the establishment of thriving communities. Pretes (2002), in contrast, argues that the industrial era gave rise to the notion of globalised capitalism, whereby human and natural resources were exploited for the benefit of a few.

---

[1]   This perspective does not overlook that currently in other areas of the world, industrial activity such as manufacturing and mining are growing areas of economic activity, especially in countries with high rates of economic growth such as China. Furthermore, the coal mining industry is still active in other areas of the developed world, including United States and Australia.

[2]   Within Great Britain, a number of different areas claim to be the 'heartland' of the Industrial Revolution: Ironbridge Gorge is one of them (McIntosh, 1997). Although the 'home' of the first iron bridge in the world, other areas in Great Britain that saw the rise of industry through the 18th century. The coal fields in the northeast of England and the iron and coal production areas of the South Wales region are other areas in the UK that lay claim to being 'the cradle' of the Industrial Revolution.

This case study considers the transition of two former coal mines into industrial museums. The two cases focus particularly on the meaning that is left behind for their visitors of such industrial heritage sites. The first of these sites is the Big Pit National Coal Museum in Blaenafon, South Wales (see Figure 1). The second is the Cape Breton Miners' Museum, a site that focuses on the rise of the coal mining industry on Cape Breton Island in Nova Scotia, Canada. The Big Pit Museum covers the history of over 200 years of extensive mining in South Wales and its role in the Industrial Revolution (Barber, 2002). The Cape Breton Miners' Museum, meanwhile, presents the history of the region's mining past and tells the story of how the industry grew on this small island located on the Atlantic coast of Canada. By the turn of the 20th century, Cape Breton's growing mining industry was supplying half of Canada's energy supply (Frank, 1980). Each museum tells the story of the meagre beginnings, subsequent growth, and eventual decline of the region's coal mining industry as it occurred in their respective post-industrial communities, and relative to their time and place historically.

Figure 1: The winding engine wheel at Big Pit Museum. Photo credit: Mary Beth Gouthro

What is it then, about these derelict sites, rusting and decomposing machinery, and stories depicting labour unrest and personal hardship that draws visitors to industrial heritage sites? How do they enable us to identify or sympathise with these ancestors? What, if anything, do such sites say about humanity more widely?

Mines and heritage tourism

The links between mining sites and heritage tourism have been studied from various perspectives (Light and Prentice, 1994; Edwards and Llurdés i Coit, 1996; Rudd and Davis, 1998; Prentice, Witt and Hamer, 1998; Wanhill, 2000; Pretes, 2002; Cole, 2004). The features of mining attractions are unique, in that they are not typical of other tourist attractions such as theme parks. Coal-mines-turned-museums are themselves former production spaces, transitioned into places for tourism consumption (Richards, 1996). In the case of the Big Pit Museum, it was felt that while the scars of the Industrial Revolution may not hold appeal to tourism, the landscape, society and culture of the mining communities should be documented and conserved before they are lost or forgotten (Wanhill, 2000). The uniqueness of former mining sites that have been turned into attractions is that they tell the history of a time when exploiting a region's resources was commonplace (Edwards and Llurdés i Coit, 1996). An exception to this is the Potosí silver mines in Bolivia (Pretes, 2002), where underground tours take place alongside the actual mining of silver, allowing visitors to observe current mining practices. However, even though the Potosí silver mines are still in operation, those visiting the Potosí silver mines come to hear the story of struggle, success, hardship and decline of an industry and its people, in much the same way as visitors are drawn to Welsh mines (Wanhill, 2000).

Many mining attractions offer a tour of the underground environment and for many people this is the highlight of the visit: at the Big Pit Museum, for example, visitors drop 90m in a cage down a deep shaft (see Figures 2 and 3) into the darkness (Wanhill, 2000). While underground, visitors are able to observe conditions of miners who worked in such conditions (Edwards and Llurdés i Coit, 1996). In the mines-turned-tourist-attractions discussed here, the underground tours are given by former or current miners themselves, thus providing first-hand accounts to visitors about what it is like to work underground. Being underground means being in a potentially dangerous environment: accidents, sometimes fatal, have always been a feature of mines (Bulmer, 1975). Moreover, present-day mining disasters are not uncommon, and often make the world's headlines: those in Turkey, Chile and Gleision

(Wales) are examples from the last few years alone. This feature adds to their appeal to visitors. Pretes' (2002: 452) study of the Potosí silver mines reflects this, as visitors "seem to relish narrating their tales of survival in apparently dangerous situations".

Figure 2: Group at the pit head waiting to descend. Photo credit: Mary Beth Gouthro

Figure 3: School group waits to descend into the Big Pit. Photo credit: Mary Beth Gouthro

Mining museums as industrial heritage sites

This section provides descriptions of the industrial history and tourism context of each of the sites under consideration in this case: the Cape Breton Miners' Museum and the Big Pit National Coal Museum in Wales. Each museum presents its story of how the coal mining industry rose and fell over time, along with the social and economic implications for the people involved. This section also presents some of the similarities and differences between the two sites. We see that although the two sites are located in different countries, their respective histories and what they currently 'share' as their industrial heritage exhibits more similarities than differences.

The Big Pit National Coal Museum

The Big Pit Museum is under the direction of the National Museum Wales, run by the Welsh Government. It lies at the north-eastern tip of the South Wales coalfield and falls within the Blaenavon[3] UNESCO World Heritage Site. This status is due to the museum's close proximity and geographical association with surrounding regional features left over from the Industrial Revolution, including the 200-year-old Blaenafon Ironworks[4].

The Big Pit Museum is made up of both above-ground and underground assets associated with what was once a fully functional colliery (see Figure 4). The above-ground features include the winding house, sawmill and mortar mill, tram circuit, pit head, fan house, pithead baths and exhibitions, original canteen, explosives magazine, blacksmith's shop and simulated mining galleries that demonstrate more modern mining techniques. These features of the museum allow visitors to see what other activities besides working underground took place. This includes the work of engineers, carpenters and blacksmiths, all of whom were instrumental in the process of mining coal in the mine's long history. At its peak of mining activity, the blacksmiths' shop alone had nine forges, where tools and equipment needed for miners and the horses were produced and repaired.

The Big Pit Museum also includes a tour of the underground coal mine. Visitors are taken to the pit bottom, 90m underground, in the shaft's cage. From there they accompany a guide to see the inner workings of the mine, including the coalface itself and its machinery, and learn more about the nature of the work the miners did underground.

The underground workings are 90m underground, dropping to 135m in places. The inner workings of the mine are a collection of old tunnels that have been dug out and interconnected as a result of centuries of mining in the area. The visitors with their guide tour the inner workings for an hour, viewing the construction of mine supports, coal and machinery, including haulage engines that are currently out of commission yet remain underground. The haulage engines were used to lift men and coal up and down the

---

3   UNESCO uses the name Blaenavon as opposed to the Welsh name, Blaenafon.

4   Blaenafon Ironworks is managed by Cadw, the official guardian for the built heritage of Wales, operated on behalf of the Welsh Government.

mine shaft. Another popular feature of the underground mine is the horses' stables. For many years, horses were cared for and remained underground in their role as 'work' horses for hauling coal and equipment. The cage (i.e. lift) that carries guides and visitors up and down the mine shaft is also a key feature of the underground experience. Visitors are also required to wear a helmet with lamp, battery pack and 'self-rescuer' for ventilation emergencies. The guides describe the various mining methods used underground, while also sharing their own experiences of working as a coal miner.

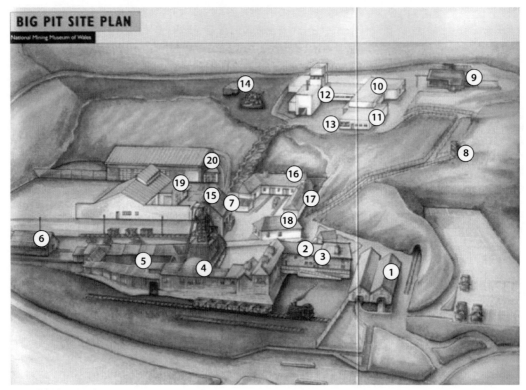

BIG PIT SITE PLAN
National Mining Museum of Wales

Plan legend:

1. Reception and Gift Shop
2. Waiting Rooms
3. Toilets
4. Underground Tour/Pit Head
5. Tram Circuit/Lamproom
6. Saw Mill and Mortar Mill
7. Winding House
8. Mining Galleries
9. Fan House
10. Pithead Baths and Exhibitions
11. Canteen
12. Toilets
13. View Point
14. Explosives Magazine
15. Toilets
16. Blacksmiths Shop
17. Education Room
18. Café
19. Operations and Resource Building
20. Conservation Workshop and Stores

Figure 4: Big Pit site plan. Source: National Museum Wales (2005)

The miners' baths, or the pithead baths as they are more commonly known, date from the Second World War, and still possess the fittings original to the building being opened in 1939. The original hot-air lockers for drying clothes, shower cubicles, automatic boot brushers and a fully equipped medical room (see Figures 5 and 6) are left as they were from years gone by. As such, it remains the best-preserved example of its kind in all of Wales.

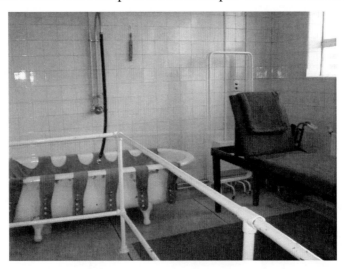

Figure 5: Miners' medical room at the Big Pit. Photo credit: Mary Beth Gouthro

Figure 6: Miners' medical room at the Big Pit. Photo credit: Mary Beth Gouthro

The main exhibit area of the museum is also located within this building, along with the original canteen that now sells refreshments to visitors instead of miners. Also found on the surface of the Big Pit Museum is a gallery that has been converted into an exhibition area to resemble a drift mine, and the mining galleries (described further below). This exhibition shows simulations of more modern mechanised mining techniques used in the latter part of the 20th century. There is a mixture of interpretation elements throughout the site grounds (see Figure 7).

Figure 7: Visitors peer into miner lockers turned into display units with miner kit and supplies on view

The industrial history of the Big Pit Colliery

Although there are signs of some form of coal mining as early as the late 13th century in the South Wales coalfields (Egan, 1987), parts of Wales were beginning to realise the full thrust of the industrial revolution as early as the late 17th century (Edwards and Llurdés i Coit, 1996; Wanhill 2000). The Big Pit colliery possesses a number of natural and human-made elements that contribute to the uniqueness of its mining past. Due to its location on the north-eastern tip of the South Wales coalfield, its unique geology allows for natural drainage of water through and out of the mine, typically a high maintenance cost of other collieries. The Big Pit is also the oldest deep mine in the South Wales coalfield: its current shaft being sunk in 1860 (Edwards and Llurdés i Coit, 1996). The uniqueness of the Big Pit was in fact that its shaft was uncommonly wide when it was first sunk. At 6m across, it allowed for two drams[5] of coal to be lifted in and out of the mine at the same time (Barber, 2002). Most shafts that had been sunk up to that time were only half this size, with only one cage. The Big Pit is actually a collection of several separate mines interconnected underground during its 200-year history.

---

5   Dram (or tram) as it is sometimes referred is the Welsh term for a small truck used to carry coal or supplies.

Mining started on the site as early as 1812, at the time supplying coal and iron ore (ironstone) to the nearby Blaenafon Ironworks (National Museum Wales, 2005).

The workforce at the Big Pit rose and fell over time. At the end of the 19th century, 528 men working at Big Pit and this number rose to 1,154 men by 1914 (National Museum Wales, 2005). Workforce numbers slowly dropped over time, so that by 1979 the number had dwindled to 250 men producing 72,000 tons of coal a year (Barber, 2002). This output is dwarfed by the five million tons produced in the whole Blaenavon region at the start of the 20th century. Coal mining ceased at the Big Pit colliery in November 1979 and by February 1980 the mine had closed due to the exhaustion of workable reserves (National Museum Wales, 2005). The transition from operating coal mine to mining museum occurred in April 1983, when the Big Pit colliery became the Big Pit Mining Museum (see Figure 8). This marked the first time in the Big Pit's mining history that tourists instead of miners were taken underground to the pit bottom.

Figure 8: Big Pit winding engine wheel in the foreground of Blaenavon industrial landscape. Photo credit: Mary Beth Gouthro

The Blaenavon industrial landscape

The Big Pit Mining museum is encompassed within a wider area of industrial ruins in Blaenavon, which includes the remains of a 200-year-old ironworks. The Big Pit is framed by its close presence to the remains of the Blaenavon Ironworks which makes up the second pillar of Blaenavon's World Heritage status alongside the Big Pit Museum. It too is a dominant feature of the area's industrial landscape and is often visited by those that come to see the Big Pit Museum. In November 2000, the World Heritage Committee of UNESCO inscribed the 'Blaenavon Industrial Landscape' on the list of World Heritage Sites.

The World Heritage Committee stated that:

> The area around Blaenavon bears eloquent and exceptional testimony to the preeminence of South Wales as the World's major producer of iron and coal in the 19th century. All the necessary elements can be seen in-situ, coal and ore mines, quarries, a primitive railway system, furnaces, the houses of the workers, and the social infrastructure of their community (Barber, 2002: 13).

The existence of the ironworks is due to the area's rich deposits of iron ore, limestone and coal, all elements required in the iron-making process. It first started with three blast furnaces and from the late 18th century to the early 20th century was one of the largest ironworks[6] in the world (Barber, 2002). There are substantial remnants of surviving structures still left on site, making it one of the best-preserved blast furnaces of its period anywhere in the world (Barber, 2002). Remains of other ironworks in the UK may be found in Shropshire, Leicestershire, Cumbria and Argyll, yet none have survived as well as Blaenavon. The history of coal mining and iron-making in the Blaenavon area demonstrate the area's significance in its contribution to the rise of the Industrial Revolution.

The Cape Breton Miners' Museum, Glace Bay, Nova Scotia

The Cape Breton Miners' Museum is located in Glace Bay on Cape Breton Island, Nova Scotia, Canada (Figure 9). The museum opened in 1967 as a result of a community effort to preserve the story of the region's industrial past. It is made up of a number of different features and attributes. The museum complex is made up of a main exhibition area, underground tours of a coal

---

6   As early as 1796, the Blaenavon Ironworks was producing 5,400 tons (5,486 tonnes) of iron a year, compared to a peak of 14,000 tons (14,224 tonnes) of iron produced by five fully operational blast furnaces in 1812 (Torfaen Borough Council et al., 1999).

mine (Figures 10 and 11), and a small miners' village that display replicas of period buildings and possessions from the mid-1850s onwards (Figure 12).

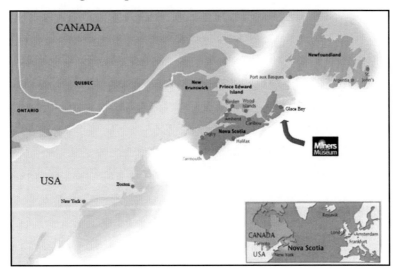

Figure 9: Map of Cape Breton. Source: Mary Beth Gouthro

Figure 10: Visitors to Cape Breton Miners' Museum gather around underground garden. Photo credit: Mary Beth Gouthro

The main exhibition area displays winding engine wheels found at pitheads that would lift and lower miners and coal in and out of the mine. It also displays other items including a hydraulic roof support used underground, an underground ambulance rail car, collections of period lamps and lanterns used underground, pit clothing, and various tools commonly used underground. Period photos spanning 150 years of the area's history are also on display and include images of the mining communities and the miners working underground over the years.

Figure 11: Group lead by retired miner Wishie Donovan at Cape Breton Miners' Museum underground. Photo credit: Mary Beth Gouthro

Figure 12: Visitors observing mining machinery at outside of Cape Breton Miners' Museum. Photo credit: Mary Beth Gouthro

History of Cape Breton's mining industry

Cape Breton is a small island that lies at the north-eastern tip of the Canadian province of Nova Scotia. In terms of land mass, Nova Scotia is slightly smaller than Northern Ireland and in terms of size just over 55,000km^2, yet its coal production rivalled some of the collieries in operation in South Wales during their peak production periods in the late 1800s and early 1900s. Cape Breton's coal mines provided half of Canada's energy demands at the turn of the 20th century. It differed from the of sort of mining common in South Wales in that it was submarine mining, where the seams of coal were layered in underground strata that stretched for miles beneath the sea bed. The ability of the Cape Breton coal fields to contribute to the wider efforts of UK colonies in the Industrial Revolution more generally is illustrated below by English mining engineer Richard Brown[7]. The following passage was written during the latter half of the 19th century and reflects his thoughts on the potential growth of the coal trade on Cape Breton Island during this time:

> I trust also that ship owners and commercial men generally will be glad to learn from these pages that Cape Breton, which, from its geographical position has been aptly styled "The Long Wharf of America", possesses abundant supplies of excellent steam fuel, commodious harbours, and, in fact, every necessary qualification for becoming the great coaling station of the innumerable steamers which are rapidly superseding sailing vessels in the navigation of the Atlantic (Brown, 1871: iii-iv).

Cape Breton Island lies on the eastern seaboard of North America and is geographically positioned just above the north-eastern United States. This makes the island's location a practical shipping point of departure for sailing vessels and steamers bound for other parts of the United States and Europe. Cape Breton's early demand for coal was fed primarily by a domestic market[8] and throughout the 19th century its biggest trading partner was the United States[9] where a steady demand for coal was fed by US Civil War.

During this time, however, some local business advocates in the Cape Breton mining region grew weary of the restrictive growth opportunities imposed by the General Mining Association (GMA) after 1826. As a result, they pursued a campaign to endorse more control and input into colonial economic development. By 1858 they succeeded in restricting the GMA's rights over the minerals and control was passed over to the colony of Nova Scotia, thus beginning the expansion of smaller mining companies (Frank, 1980). As the mining industry evolved and became more organised in Cape Breton, in 1893 the Dominion Coal Company was in formed, thereafter managing most of the region's collieries.

---

7   An English engineer employed by the GMA (the General Mining Association) in the latter half of the 19th century.

8   The domestic market was made up of the other colonies of British North America until they combined in 1867 to become the Confederation of Canada. This meant the coming together of three colonies in British North America into four Canadian provinces: Ontario, Quebec, Nova Scotia and New Brunswick.

9   A Reciprocity Treaty between the US and the British North American colonies allowed duty-free trade with the US until 1865. This fed a steady market for Cape Breton coal to US Markets (Frank, 1980). After 1865, however, the Treaty expired, ending a boom of supply to US markets.

Table 1: Cape Breton Coal Mines Colliery Production from 1833-2001

Colliery	Location	Seam	Average Height	Year Opened	Year Closed	Total Output (Short Tons)
1A	Dominion	Phalen	7'3"	1893	1927	14,786,710
18	Glace Bay	Phalen	7'3"	1924	1955	19,065,716
2	Glace Bay	Phalen	7'2"	1899	1945	29,760,554
3	Glace Bay	Phalen	7'0"	1887	1915	4,453,893
4	Glace Bay	Phalen	6'7"	1866	1961	32,063,317
5	Reserve	Phalen	7'8"	1872	1938	14,441,284
6	Donkin	Phalen	6'6"	1904	1933	4,288,321
7	Glace Bay	Hub	9'6"	*1861	1918	2,435,820
8	Glace Bay	Harbour	6'0"	1858	1914	5,890,212
Princess	Sydney Mines	Harbour	5'6"	1876	1976	30,389,710
9	Glace Bay	Harbour	6'9"	1899	1924	7,133,585
Florence	Florence	Harbour	5'0"	1902	1961	19,096,707
10	Reserve	Emery	3'8"	1905	1942	7,533,557
11	Glace Bay	Emery	4'7"	1899	1949	8,464,458
12	New Waterford	Harbour	6'11"	1908	1973	33,504,399
14	New Waterford	Harbour	6'6"	1908	1932	6,583,361
15	New Waterford	Phalen	5'9"	1910	1925	1,579,187
16	New Waterford	Phalen	4'6"	1911	1962	20,217,008
17	New Victoria	Harbour	7'0"	*1833	1921	2,055,799
18	New Victoria	Har/Pha	6'0"	1938	1966	5,727,933
20	Glace Bay	Harbour	6'0"	1939	1971	17,755,108
21	Birch Grove	Gowrie	5'3"	1910	1925	1,969,905
22	Birch Grove	Gowrie	5'7"	1912	1930	3,158,254
23	Dominion	Gardiner	u/k	never worked		
24	Glace Bay	Emery	4'11"	1919	1953	6,248,248
25	Gardiner Mines	Gardiner	4'0"	1941	1959	2,320,236
26	Glace Bay	Harbour	7'0"	1943	1984	24,601,435
Lingan	New Waterford	Harbour	u/k	1970	1992	24,621,094
Prince	Point Aconi	Hub	u/k	1975		**19,500,896
Phalen	New Waterford	Phalen	u/k	1984		**14,486,057

    ** Indicates multiple openings and closings

    ** As of 31 December 1996

Source: Cape Breton Miners' Museum Library Archives (2006)

The price of coal dropped after the First World War, spurring an economic crisis in Cape Breton's mining industry that led to more change in the running of the collieries in the region. In 1921, the British Empire Steel Corporation (BESCO) assumed all control over the coal and steel industries in Nova Scotia. By 1928, BESCO was grouped into a new holding and operating company called the Dominion Steel Company. Over time this company continued to come under different ownership until the federal government of Canada took over the full operation of Cape Breton coal mines in 1968.

Coal production in Cape Breton reached its peak production after the Second World War, with 25,000 miners working in 13 mines (see Table 1). From the early 1800s through to the closure of the last mine[10] in 2001, almost 30 mines opened and closed in Cape Breton, with varying levels of production output and life spans during that time.

South Wales and Cape Breton: Where is the common ground?

Both Cape Breton and Blaenavon saw the growth of coal mining due to their geological assets (i.e. coal) and their ideal locations for shipping (being at or close to water ports enabling global trade and shipping of minerals). These assets made each location a prime candidate for industrial growth. Each also had convenient access to iron ore and limestone, thus making the production of iron and steel sister industries to coal mining. As these industries grew and prospered, and the economic benefits that went with it were passed on to the mining communities; even though most of the wealth was realised by the coal owners. Contrary to common perception, however, the coal owners did not in fact own the coal. In the Welsh context, the coal owners did own the equipment and the buildings needed to mine the coal, yet the land was typically leased to them from landowners, who were not interested in mining of coal themselves (Egan, 1987). In Cape Breton, commercial mining began in 1826 under a GMA royal charter, giving London industrialists exclusive control over the mineral deposits in Nova Scotia (Frank, 1980). It is believed that the GMA was formed after the King George IV's brother, the Duke of York, was forced to sell leases to help pay for the extravagant expenses incurred by his mistresses (Newton, 1992).

Another feature shared by each location is that both the Blaenavon and Cape Breton mined bituminous coal. This was no rival for the anthracite coal typically mined in other parts of South Wales and in the US coal fields of Pennsylvania – anthracite was favoured for its smokeless properties, whereas

---

10   Phalen colliery in New Waterford was the last coal mine to close in Cape Breton, in 2001.

bituminous coal was used for other industrial uses such as commercial and household heating – however production also rose steadily in both locations as the turn of the 20th century approached. Over five million tons of coal was mined in the Blaenafon collieries in 1908 and Cape Breton Island reached seven million tons by 1917[11]. However, throughout the remainder of the 20th century changing market conditions and a corresponding decline in the workforce plagued both areas, resulting in reduced productivity.

In 1947, an attempt to resurrect the coal industry in the UK was initiated with the creation of the National Coal Board. This meant a change of hands in ownership from the coal owners to the public hands of government. The nationalisation of the coal industry was welcomed by the collieries. In the Canadian context, a similar change occurred: Canada's federal government took ownership of the mines from existing coal companies by 1968. By that time, the coal industry in both countries had been through decades of decline and pit closures were common. This was part of an effort on the part of the governments in both countries to manage more effectively the trade of coal in domestic and foreign markets. Yet rising operational costs and changing market forces persisted, continuing to plague the industry on both sides of the Atlantic. Presently there are no mines operating in Cape Breton and the last operating mine in Wales, Tower Colliery in Glamorgan, ceased operations in January 2008.

Trade unions and labour unrest

During the rise of the coal industry in both Cape Breton and South Wales, the development of labour support organisations among the miners took place in different ways, resulting in a variety of outcomes. One implication of this was that the mining industry in both countries was beset with strike action and labour unrest, at different intervals in time and varying levels of intensity. Up to 1830, trade unions in the South Wales valleys looked very much like organisations made up of individuals with similar views on their own welfare, often referred to as 'clubs' or 'friendly societies' (Egan, 1987). After this time, trade unions in South Wales evolved and became aligned with other trade organisations in the north-west of England, such as the National Association for the Protection of Labour.

Trade unionism was generally slower to develop in the Welsh valleys than it was in other areas of the UK, yet by the 1870s the Lancashire-based Amalgamated Association of Miners had built up a substantial membership in the

---

11   The British ton is also referred to as a long ton or 2,240 pounds (lb) in weight, whereas in Canada the ton is referred to as a short ton, or 2,000lb.

Welsh collieries. However their collective strength waned and by the 1890s fragmented membership among different unions in the region made collective representation weak. Therefore by the end of the 19th century, fractured union representation was more common across the Welsh Valleys. Weaker labour support structures also saw an end to a six-month lockout that did not end in the miners' favour. The miners were unsuccessful in obtaining increased employment benefits from the coal owners, a 10% wage increase, or the removal of the 'sliding scale'[12] payment system (Egan, 1987).

A new union for all South Wales coalfields was formed in 1899 called the South Wales Miners' Federation (SWMF). That year, the SWMF had 104,000 members and became the strongest union in the area, even rivalling those found in the north-west of England. By 1914, the SWMF had 200,000 members, making it the largest single trade union in Britain (Egan, 1987). In 1944, the 'Fed', as it was known, became the National Union of Mineworkers, South Wales Area. Over time it acquired a reputation of being one of the most militant trade unions, right up until the last great miners' strike of 1984-85.

Nor was labour unrest a stranger to Cape Breton's mining industry. Military forces were requested by coal companies and were sent from other parts of Nova Scotia in 1876, 1882, 1904 and 1909 to dilute tensions between the miners and the mining companies. At this time, a union called the Provincial Workman's Association (PWA) represented the miners. The PWA had its beginnings in the 1870s and was the result of miners uniting to protest wage cuts. By the time the First World War ended, the PWA had amalgamated with the much larger United Mine Workers of America, resulting in over 12,000 miners in the provinces of Nova Scotia and New Brunswick joining a bigger and more powerful labour organisation.

In 1925, a fall in the demand for coal implied workforce reductions for the miners in the Cape Breton collieries. Subsequent negotiations between coal company management (i.e. BESCO) and the workforce to address the matter and reach a mutually beneficial agreement eventually broke down. As a result, tensions grew between the two sides and strike action was kick-started when BESCO demanded the miners accept a wage cut and also terminated their credit at the company-owned stores. A walkout began by the miners in early March 1925 and by the month of June miners earning no wages faced starvation. In desperation, the miners clashed with BESCO police, leaving one miner dead and another seriously wounded. The violence continued,

---

12   The sliding-scale payment system linked miners' wages to the selling price of coal. Coal owners were of the mind that the price of coal should dictate the miners' wages, and the miners felt their wage should determine the price of coal.

leaving shops looted and company washhouses burned down to the ground (Newton, 1992). As a well-known labour union leader J.B. McLachlan stated at time, "under capitalism, the working class had but two courses to follow: crawl or fight" (cited in Frank 1999: 465). McLachlan's timely phrase continued to resonate with the legacy of coal mining industry in Cape Breton and over time has been referred to in accounts of mining industry turmoil linked to the region (Frank, 1999).

Mining disasters: The human toll

A significant feature of the social histories of both of the coal mining regions is the tally of industrial disasters realised by both. Both museums highlight these disasters, and explain the resulting impacts on the social and economic fabric to the mining communities. Industrial disasters hit the coal mining industry across the South Wales valleys hard. Coal mining is notoriously dangerous work. Underground disasters in these regions were often the result of methane gas explosions, coal dust explosions, fires and other industrial causes such as roof falls. Between 1851 and 1920 there were 48 disasters in the South Wales coalfield, with 3,000 deaths (National Museum Wales, 2005). In one mine alone, Senghenydd, an underground explosion in 1913 killed 439 men and 300 horses. Triggered by the presence of methane gas and ignited by an electrical spark, it generated a coal dust explosion resulting in this huge loss of life[13]. Some other notable disasters include one in 1877 in Tynewydd, where five miners died and five others were trapped for nine days. Then, in 1966 in Aberfan, 144 people died, 116 of them children, when waste from colliery tip slid down the hillside, burying a school. The Big Pit colliery was more fortunate in comparison, with only one fatal accident over its lifetime. This was in 1913, when three men died while fighting an underground fire.

In the Cape Breton collieries, records kept from 1866 through to 1975 showed that over 400 men died in the region's coal mines (Newton, 1992). Rather more recently, in 1979, 12 men died in Number 26 Colliery in Glace Bay, while in 1992, 26 men died in the Westray coal mine near Stellarton in Nova Scotia. The latter was determined to be caused by the neglect of company managers, who did not enforce proper safety standards resulting in an explosion caused by a methane gas build-up. The 1992 explosion is the most recent coal mining disaster in Nova Scotia and serves as a reminder of repeated accusations directed at coal company management that human safety has often been sacrificed for the benefit of coal production.

---

13   The coal owner at the time was fined 5½ pence for each miner of 439 miners who lost his life. The total fine charged to the coal owner was £24.00 for neglect.

Not unlike the disaster toll records kept of incidents in the South Wales coal-fields, there are scores of other deaths and injuries in Cape Breton mines. These are the result of other industrial accidents, such as roof falls, which are not necessarily grouped with the disaster records.

Consuming heritage: Considering the broader picture

The type of visitors attracted by heritage sites has been a common subject of inquiry in studies of the consumption of heritage sites. Light and Prentice (1994) studied the socio-demographic characteristics of visitors and revealed that the majority were middle classes and well educated. A later study by Prentice et al. (1998) analysed the socio-demographic characteristics of visitors to a Welsh heritage site and their relevance in the individual's motivation to visit. The study revealed that the socio-demographic characteristics were not indicative of a certain 'type' of visitor to heritage, but rather visitor profiles proved largely independent of the types of experiences and benefits gained from a visit. Herbert's (2001) study of heritage in literary places uncovered similar findings, establishing weak links between socio-demographic characteristics of visitors and their motivation to visit. It showed that age and social class of visitors "did not prove to be a significant discriminator in key areas such as general purposes and more specific reasons for making the visit" (Herbert, 2001: 330). This suggests that linking certain characteristics of visitors – such as age, income and education – do not have a direct relationship with the individual's likelihood to visit a heritage site and their related motivations for consuming heritage.

Such findings are interesting to this case study for a number of reasons. In essence, is there something more to learn from visitors regarding why they visit a heritage site, in this case an industrial heritage site? Are visitors in search of some meaning or understanding that is not yet fully recognised?

The studies noted above show that measuring socio-demographic variables is not always a useful tool for predicting who visits heritage sites or why they visit them. Moreover, the research methods employed by the above studies reflect a preference for quantitative methods in studying cases of heritage consumption. As Poria, Butler and Airey (2003) note in their study of overall visitation patterns of heritage, adopting such an approach may "lead to confusion in the theoretical understanding by highlighting relationships that may not be at the core of behaviour" (Poria et al., 2003: 250).

McArthur and Hall (1993: 13) argue the visitor experience in heritage "should be placed at the center of any heritage management process". This is not always easy and unpacking how visitors experience heritage presents certain challenges because "the past means different things to different people" and heritage is not simply "a preserve for the new middle classes" (Shaw and Williams, 2004: 121). In terms of the industrial heritage sites here, a challenged here is to consider the ways in which such sites may or may not provide meaning to their visitors, and whether or not continuing to operate such attractions (at potentially high cost) serves a purpose to future heritage tourism.

As Gruffudd (1995: 50) maintains, heritage is not confined to "sanctioned sites, fenced off and ticketed, under the auspices of Cadw [Welsh Historic Monuments] or English Heritage" but rather it is how people mediate a relationship with the past. Heritage is a mix of tangible and intangible factors, making up a complex arena for its consumption. Smith's (2006: 46) perspective further builds Gruffudd's, in that heritage is "not the site itself, but the act of passing on knowledge in the culturally correct or appropriate contexts and times". She uses the example of oral histories as heritage, and how passing them on is yet a meaningful manifestation of the heritage being represented. Given these perspectives, do the industrial heritage sites described in this case study offer something similar? How should oral histories of industrial heritage for example, be shared, if at all? Do the industrial heritage sites described here provide a meaningful platform, socially or otherwise, upon which to build and nurture this sort of social practice? Or could it be that written material, e.g. books and online (Internet) sources, is enough to feed our knowledge and understanding of the industrial past?

References

Barber C. 2002. *Exploring Blaenavon Industrial Landscape World Heritage Site.* Abergavenny: Blorenge.

Brown R. 1871. *Coal Fields and Coal Trade of the Island of Cape Breton.* London: Sampson Low, Marston, Low & Searle.

Bulmer M. 1975. Sociological models of the mining community. *Sociological Review* **23**: 61-93.

Cole D. 2004. Exploring the sustainability of mining heritage tourism. *Journal of Sustainable Tourism* **12** (6): 480-494.

Edwards J, Llurdés i Coit J. 1996. Mines and quarries: Industrial heritage tourism. *Annals of Tourism Research* **23** (2): 341-363.

Egan D. 1987. *Coal society: History of the South Wales Mining Valleys 1840-1980.* Llandysul: Gomer Press.

Frank D. 1980. The Cape Breton coal industry and the rise and fall of the British Empire Steel Corporation. In Gray P. (ed.) *Class, State, Ideology and Change: Marxist Perspectives on Canada.* Toronto: Department of Sociology: York University; 283-304.

Frank D. 1999. *J.B. McLachlan: A Biography.* Toronto: James Lorimer & Co.

Gruffudd P. 1995. Heritage as national identity: Histories and prospects of the national pasts. In Herbert D. (ed.) *Heritage, Tourism and Society.* London: Pinter; 49-67.

Hall S. 1996. Introduction: Who needs "identity?". In Hall S, du Gay P. (eds) *Questions of cultural identity.* London: Sage; 1-17.

Harris F. 1989. From the industrial revolution to the heritage industry. *Geographical Magazine* **61**: 38-42.

Herbert D. 2001. Literary places, Tourism and heritage experience. *Annals of Tourism Research* **28** (2): 312-33.

Light D, Prentice R. 1994. Who consumes the heritage product? Implications for European heritage tourism. In Ashworth G, Larkham P. (eds) *Building a New Heritage: Tourism, Culture and Identity in the New Europe.* London: Routledge; 90-116.

McArthur S, Hall CM. 1993. Visitor management and interpretation at heritage sites. In.Hall CM, McArthur S. (eds) *Heritage Management in New Zealand and Australia.* Oxford: Oxford University Press; 18-39.

McIntosh, A. (1997) *The experiences and benefits gained by tourists visiting socio-industrial heritage attractions.* PhD Dissertation, Queen Margaret University/Open University.

McLean F. 2006. Introduction: Heritage and identity. *International Journal of Heritage Studies* **12** (1): 3-7.

National Museum Wales. 2005. *Big Pit: National Coal Museum: A guide.* Cardiff: National Museum Wales.

Newton D. 1992. *Where Coal is King: The Story of the Cape Breton Miners' Museum.* Glace Bay: Cape Breton Miners Foundation.

Poria Y, Butler R, Airey D. 2003. The core of heritage tourism. *Annals of Tourism Research* **30** (1): 238-254.

Prentice R. 1993.*Tourism and Heritage Attractions.* London: Routledge.

Prentice R, Witt S, Hamer C. 1998. Tourism as experience: The case of heritage parks. *Annals of Tourism Research* **25** (1): 1-24.

Pretes M. 2002. Touring mines and mining tourists. *Annals of Tourism Research* **29** (2): 439-456.

Richards G. 1996. The scope and significance of cultural tourism. In Richards G. (ed.) *Cultural Tourism in Europe*. Wallingford: CABI; 21-38.

Rudd M, Davis J. 1998. Industrial heritage tourism at the Bingham Canyon Copper Mine. *Journal of Travel Research* **36**: 85-89.

Shaw G, Williams A. 2004. *Tourism and Tourism Spaces*. London: Sage.

Smith L. 2006. *Uses of Heritage*. London: Routledge.

Torfaen Borough Council, Cadw Welsh Historic Monuments, Royal Commission on the Ancient and Historical Monuments of Wales. 1999. *Nomination of the Blaenavon Industrial Landscape for Inclusion in the World Heritage List*.

Wanhill S. 2000. Mines – a tourist attraction: Coal mining in industrial South Wales *Journal of Travel Research* **39** (1): 60-69.

Ancillary Student Material

Further reading

Ashworth G, Larkham P. 1994. A heritage for Europe: The need, the task, the contribution. In Ashworth G, Larkham P. (eds.) *Building a New Heritage: Tourism, Culture and Identity in the New Europe*. Routledge: London; 1-11.

Kerstetter D, Confer J, Bricker, K. 1998. Industrial heritage attractions: Types and tourists, *Journal of Travel & Tourism Marketing* **7** (2): 91-104.

Lowenthal D. 1995. Fabricating heritage from *History & Memory* Vol. 10, No. 1 (Lecture at St Mary's University College Twickenham, 7 Dec. 1995

Mason R. 2004. Nation building at the Museum of Welsh Life, *Museum and Society*. **2** (1): 18-34.

Merriman N. 1991. *Beyond the Glass Case: The Past, the Heritage and the Public in Britain*. Leicester University Press: Leicester.

Mitchell M, Mitchell S. 2001. Showing off what you do (and how you do it), *Journal of Hospitality & Leisure Marketing* **7** (4): 61-73.

Richards G. 2001. The experience industry and the creation of attractions. In. Richards G. (ed.) *Cultural Attractions and European Tourism*. CAB International: Wallingford; 55-69.

Urry J. 1996. How societies remember the past. In Macdonald S, Fyfe G. (eds) *Theorizing museums: Representing Identity and Diversity in a Changing World*. Blackwell Publishers: Oxford; 45-68.

Related websites and audio-visual material

The European Route of Industrial Heritage: http://www.erih.net/index.php

Canadian Industrial Heritage Centre: http://www.canadianindustrialheritage.org

UNESCO World Heritage Sites – European Industrial Properties: http://www. erih.net/links/unesco-world-heritage-sites-industrial-properties-welterbe-werelderfgoed-patrimoine-mondial.html

Wales – The 'first' industrial nation http://www.museumwales.ac.uk/cy/42/

Self-test questions

Try to answer the following questions to test your knowledge and understanding. If you are not sure of the answers, please re-read the case study and refer to the suggested references and further reading sources.

1   What features of these post-industrial regions have led to their transition from mining sites into 'mining museums'?

2   What are some of the motivational factors of the tourists who visit industrial heritage attractions such as the Big Pit Museum and Cape Breton Miners' Museum?

3   Do these mining museums offer authentic heritage tourism experiences to their visitors, and if so how?

4   Given the description of museum features at these sites, what are potential ways to develop the visitor experience at each museum?

5   As the case study states, "heritage is a mix of tangible and intangible factors, making up a complex area for its consumption". Illustrate this statement with examples.

6   What challenges might these kinds of visitor attractions encounter in the future?

Key themes and theories

The key themes in the case study relate to the following areas:

♦   Why preserve industrial heritage to begin with?

♦   Motives for visiting industrial heritage attractions

♦   Potential areas of developing the visitor experience at these attractions

♦   Mix of tangible and intangible features of each museum, their similarities and differences

The key theories relate to:

♦   The features of industrial heritage that appeal to their visitors

♦   The variation of motivations of visitors to these museums e.g. not confined to specific socio-economic profiles.

♦   The complex nature of the heritage consumption experience

♦   The longevity and future demand of these attractions to tourism more widely

If you need to source further information on any of the above themes and theories, then these headings could be used as key words to search for materials and case studies.

12

The Mobilities of Living History
A Case Study of Viking Heritage

Kevin Hannam

Time present and time past
Are both perhaps present in time future
And time future contained in time past
T S Eliot (The Four Quartets)

Introduction

Things move. We move. We understand that across geographical space things move from place to place. Things also move across time. Time does not stand still, as the above lines of poetry illustrate. Things move through time, caught up in a web of temporal movement.

Things age. We age. We too are time travellers, always moving forward but often ever wanting to go back in time to visit the past. We do this through museums, heritage sites and living history experiences. We want to go back to see and feel the past.

Time and space are intimately entwined and, as Harvey (1989) has noted, there is a contemporary feeling of time-space compression, where we acknowledge that things move at increasing speeds. We now have instantaneous communication on the move with our mobile phones (see Green, 2002; on the acceleration of time see Crang, 2011). Indeed, it often seems that everything is on the move (Urry, 2000; Cresswell, 2006; Hannam, Sheller and Urry, 2006). Yet we still need places to hold on to emotionally and these places or ('moorings') frequently invoke heritage in original or re-created forms, maybe in both forms simultaneously (Hannam et al., 2006).

This case examines the intersection between contemporary notions of mobility and heritage. It begins by introducing the concept of 'mobilities', in the plural – as we shall see there are multiple forms of mobility. It then examines the ways in which researchers have analysed how the material world of everyday things is incorporated into mobile forms of heritage. It takes the example of 'living history' to do this, drawing upon fluid notions of authenticity and serious leisure (Crang, 1996; Hunt, 2004; Handler and Saxton, 2009). It explores this using a case study of Viking 'living history' re-enactment. Vikings provide an interesting example of how things can still be moving, despite being in the past (Halewood and Hannam, 2001; Hannam and Halewood, 2006; Bærenholdt and Haldrup, 2004, 2006).

Mobilities theory

The concept of mobility has become an evocative keyword for the twenty-first century. In many ways it has become a term which has replaced tourism (Hannam, 2008). The concept of mobilities encompasses both the large-scale time-space movements of people, objects, capital and information across the world, as well as the more local processes of daily transportation, movement through public space, and the travel of material things within everyday life (Hannam, et al., 2006). As Sheller and Urry (2004: 1) have written in their book, *Tourism Mobilities*:

> We refer to 'tourism mobilities' ... not simply to state the obvious (that tourism is a form of mobility), but to highlight that many different mo-bilities inform tourism, shape the places where tourism is performed, and drive the making and unmaking of tourist destinations. Mobilities of people and objects, airplanes and suitcases, plants and animals, im-ages and brands, data systems and satellites, all go into 'doing' tour-ism ... Tourism mobilities involve complex combinations of movement and stillness, realities and fantasies, play and work.

Dreams of 'hyper-mobility' and 'instantaneous communication' drive con-temporary business strategies, advertising and policies, as well as everyday life. They also elicit strong political critique from those who may feel margin-alised or otherwise affected by new cultural and heritage tourism develop-ments (Hannam et al., 2006). The study of tourism mobilities thus discusses the many inter-connections between tourism and the wider movement of people in terms of migration; between tourism and different modes of trans-port use; between tourism and means of communicating (phone, internet and so on); and between tourism and the movement of material things, such as historical artefacts and souvenirs.

Mobilities are thus centrally involved in reorganising institutions, generating climate change, moving risks and illnesses around the globe, altering travel, tourism and migration patterns, producing a more distant family life, transforming the social and educational life of young people, connecting distant people through so called 'weak ties', and so on. However, such mobilities cannot be described without attention to the necessary spatial, infrastructural, and institutional 'moorings' or places that configure and enable mobilities (Hannam et al., 2006). Heritage sites such as museums are a good example of local platforms that enable these diverse mobilities, but cities themselves are integral to enhancing the branding of the everyday mobilities of tourists.

Material worlds

Drawing upon the mobilities theory discussed above, there is now a growing interest in the ways in which material 'stuff' helps to constitute tourism. Such stuff is always in motion, being assembled and reassembled in changing configurations (Sheller and Urry, 2006). In their classic paper, Cook and Crang (1996) discuss how rather than being spatially fixed, the material geographies of food are mobilised within circuits of culinary culture, outlining their production and consumption through processes of commodity fetishism. Cook, Crang and Thorpe (1998) then examine how food geographies are the result of 'locally circulated' global flows of agents and knowledge. They suggest that the analysis of the geographies and biographies of food is a vital component of any food analysis, as it illustrates the inter-connectivity between the mobilities of food paths (Cook et al., 1998).

Science and technology studies, meanwhile, have shown how "what we call the social is materially heterogeneous: talk, bodies, texts, machines, architectures, all of these and many more are implicated in and perform the social" (Law 1994: 2). The materialities of heritage thus involve complex 'hybrid geographies' (Whatmore, 2002) of humans and non-humans that contingently enable people and things to move and to hold their shape as they move across various regions, both physically and imaginatively. There is thus a complex materiality to being on the move, as heritage tourists and the things that constitute heritage itself engage with all sorts of machines that enable their movement. Crucial to the recognition of these materialities is an understanding of the corporeal body as an affective vehicle through which we sense place and movement, and construct emotional geographies (Rodaway, 1994; Crouch, 2000; Bondi, Smith and Davidson, 2005). Imaginative travel, for example, involves dreaming or anticipating in one's imagination the 'atmosphere of place'.

Much of heritage tourism thus involves the active development and performances of 'memory'. This then necessitates researching the material mobilities of photographs, postcards, letters, images, guides, souvenirs and all sorts of gifts (see for example Selwyn, 1996; Lury, 1997). More recent work has explicitly examined the kinds of pictures and objects that people carry with them and use to reassemble memories, practices and even landscapes, thus remaking the materiality of places of heritage tourism and migration (see Tolia-Kelly, 2006; Nesbitt and Tolia- Kelly, 2009; Staiff and Bushell, 2012). Basu and Coleman (2008: 313) note that:

> We are not only concerned with the materiality of migration itself, but also with the material effects of having moved, perhaps many years earlier, to a new place, and with the inter-relatedness of the movements of people and things. In addition, we want to convey the sense that a 'world' – an often fragmented and fragile set of material and non-material assumptions and resources – can itself be made mobile, seemingly translated from one geographical location to another, even as it is transformed in the process.

Indeed, as we shall, see we can understand the Vikings as a migrant population and as a 'world' who took with them many material things that became heritage in the present day, albeit translated and transformed through the process of living history. Basu and Coleman (2008: 317) go on to discuss the idea of 'materialities' in more depth:

> We use the term 'materiality' straightforwardly to refer to physical objects and worlds, but also to evoke more varied – multiple – forms of experience and sensation that are both embodied and constituted through the interactions of subjects and objects. Such interactions are often both moving, in the sense that they stir the emotions, and, indeed, moving, insofar as they entail the movement of both people and things, subjects and objects.

Here, the authors are emphasising the notion that heritage moves people emotionally and imaginatively to think about their own pasts through different sensations which themselves can be both tangible and intangible – something we can see in the re-enactment of the past through living history projects.

Living histories

Anderson (1992: 456) defined living history projects as "as an attempt by people to simulate life in another time". He gives three reasons for the development of such projects, namely "to interpret material culture more effectively", "to test an archaeological thesis or generate data for historical ethnographies" or "to participate in an enjoyable recreational activity that is also a learning experience" (Anderson, 1992: 456-7). He acknowledges that living history is indeed "theatrical" in nature, as it usually involves the use of "costumes (period clothing), props (artefacts), sets (historical sites)", and "role playing (identifying with historical characters)". Indeed, living history has been conceptualised as a series of 'performances' (Tivers, 2002).

Living history has on the one hand helped the development of the museum industry worldwide in terms of fixed sites. On the other hand, living history has also led to many social movements associated with particular historical periods that are much less reliant on a fixed space such as a museum. These movements are much more fluid forms of recreational or serious leisure activity (Hunt, 2004). Participants are recognised as being concerned with notions of 'authenticity', not only in the sense of portraying an accurate or faithful historical simulation but also in the sense of obtaining an authentic experience for themselves (Handler and Saxton, 1988). All historical simulation of course involves a certain degree of selectivity, such that they become fluid, mobile contingent interpretations of the past, rather than wholly accurate presentations.

Indeed, in his research into an English Civil War re-enactment society, Crang (1996) examines the problems of realism and authenticity. He argues that living history is a much more self-reflexive activity than is usually portrayed, involving complex 'bundles' of enjoyment and knowledge. Rather than viewing the creation of living history as being somehow misleading or 'imagineered', which obscures the so called truth of the past (Wright, 1995), Crang (1996) argues for an understanding of living history as a series of heritage practices and a quixotic quest for the authentic which is frequently never realised. Handler (1987: 339) argues that "this in turn motivates a desperate search for the real thing, in which people happily borrow the personas and accoutrements of those whom modern mythology defines as quintessentially real". In fact, living history allows a degree of democratisation of history, turning it away from being an elite knowledge held in the hands of a few, and putting it into the hands of many participants who, as Crang (1996: 427) argues "know that they are only producing interpretations of what might have been there". He concludes that:

> It is not enough to simply dismiss recreations as images obscuring an understanding of 'real' history (whatever that might be) which too quickly degenerates into mutual accusations of inauthenticity. Such accusations employ a decidedly unreflexive idea of authenticity and of the touristic process. Analysis of performances at these sites reveals much more is going on and for multiple audiences. The participants may seek a time apart, an escape from modern society, but the means

whereby they escape are entirely modern and very reflexive (Crang, 1996: 439).

The performances of living history are highly mobile in a number of ways. Firstly, the idea of authenticity is highly mobile and fluid, even if it resides upon some 'anchors' of memory. Secondly, the performances of living history involve the trade and commodification of highly mobile artefacts. Thirdly, living histories also involve the temporal and spatial movement of people who are involved in re-enactment societies who utilise modern technologies such as the internet to maintain their heritage network. We can see these mobilities enacted through a case study of Viking heritage.

Case study: Viking heritage mobilities

Viking-themed museums and festivals are now widespread throughout Europe and are a popular expression of a highly evolved and fluid living history. The Anglo-American stereotypical representation of Viking heritage is of sea-faring, sexist, bloodthirsty men raping and pillaging. In contrast to this image, in Scandinavia the dominant image of Vikings in popular culture finds fewer references to war and warriors. Here the Viking representation is very much concerned with the people who were known abroad as pirates but at home lived in a well-ordered society.

European Viking-themed festivals have largely attempted to give greater credence to the latter representation. However, it is often the more bloodthirsty image that initially inspires Anglo-American tourists to visit Viking heritage sites such as Jorvik (York) in England (Halewood and Hannam, 2001). Such representations are not without credence as the early Saxon Chronicles note that in the year 787AD, three ships of Northmen came ashore near Portsmouth in England: "The reeve [the king's sheriff, or steward, for the local shire] then rode thereto, and would drive them to the king's town, for he knew not what they were; and there was he slain" (Ingram, 1993: 78). Additional attacks on the British Isles continued for the next 300 years and became invasions rather than isolated attacks of piracy. Nevertheless, if we examine Viking history, we know that the Vikings were a highly mobile population and this is exemplified in the archaeological heritage that they left behind as well as in the stories or sagas that were written, all of which help to construct imaginative geographies (Bærenholdt and Haldrup, 2004).

Furthermore, Zilmer (2012: 3) has recently written of how in the Icelandic context: "Mobility constitutes an important overall theme besides relating of engagements at one's (permanent) native setting". She further notes that:

In the sagas Viking Age mobility emerges both as an individual accomplishment and a collective experience; furthermore, it is presented as something that has to be preserved in tales. The saga narratives demonstrate this both in terms of being stories that relate of travel in themselves and through their explicit references to the practice of telling travel-tales as a means of passing on news and knowledge (Zilmer, 2012: 4).

So we know that the Vikings were highly mobile historically, but how does this mobility manifest itself in terms of Viking heritage and living history? We can explore this in terms of the sites of memory, the material mobilities of artefacts and the mobility networks of the Viking re-enactment participants themselves.

Viking sites of memory

Viking ships are a key symbol of Viking heritage and Viking mobility. The *Vikingskipshuset* (Viking Ship Museum) at Bygdøy near Oslo, the oldest purpose-built ship museum in Europe, is representative of this type of tourism activity. This museum was constructed to house three large Viking-period ships excavated in the late 19th century. They were found unusually well-preserved and two were completely reconstructed, largely from the original timbers. They remain the most lavish and complete burials known in Europe from the Viking period. The finds have significant national political status and have been used to help construct a Norwegian sense of national identity. The museum building exhibits some of the characteristics of an ecclesiastical structure (see Figure 1). It is cruciform in plan, with a tall central tower and stands alone with a perimeter of open ground around it. The austere interior inspires a sense of reverence for the displayed objects. Even the viewing platforms for looking down into the ships echo church pulpits. The unadorned walls curve smoothly into an arched ceiling—all whitewashed plainly—which removes any potential clash with the graceful profiles of the Viking ships displayed within. Three 'arms' of the cruciform building are occupied with a ship each and in the fourth are displayed the artefacts found in the ship burials. This theme of simplicity is carried through to the display cases, with discrete cards bearing a minimum of explanatory text. Essentially the objects are left to make their own statement to the viewer, with the minimum of interpretative intervention. Tourists may purchase souvenirs, which have been carefully selected for relevance, academic accuracy and quality. The museum thus presents icons of 'pure' authenticity for tourists interested in the Viking period (Halewood and Hannam, 2001).

Figure 1: The Vikingskipshuset (Viking Ship Museum) at Bygdøy near Oslo.
Source: Wikimedia

Bærenholdt and Haldrup (2004, 2006) have written of the heterogeneous mobilities involved in the return of the Viking longship to Roskilde, Denmark,
in a strategy to make the city an important heritage tourism site. Although
a Viking ship museum, its strategy was to create a new experience which
involved making the exhibits more of a living history site:

> "Local authorities have been central in the recent reconstruction of the
> harbour area and the development of the Museum Island project as an
> attraction at the Viking Ship Museum in Roskilde. The museum has

established shipbuilding workshops as an attempt to make visits more colourful and interactive ... the Viking Ship Museum offers a mix of experience related to the Viking Age and its ships: at the shipyard on the Museum Island visitors can follow the building of replica ships and discuss details of Viking craftsmanship with professional shipbuilders; in the harbour next to the shipyard one can book 1–2-hour sailing trips in replica Viking ships on the fiord, and in the museum hall people can dress up as Vikings and embark on imaginary voyages over the North Sea. Apart from this, the museum offers a range of exhibitions and activities from painting shields and stamping coins to knitting and so forth. Compared with most other cultural institutions in Denmark, the Viking Ship Museum has been a frontrunner in using IT technology both in exhibitions and as a marketing tool" (Bærenholdt and Haldrup, 2006: 216).

The important point is that the ships at both Oslo and Roskilde both represent Viking mobility but also trigger the mobilities of Viking memories and imaginations (Bærenholdt and Haldrup, 2004). Indeed, Bærenholdt and Haldrup (2004) argue that visitors to these ships do not gaze at them as much as read them as distant memories. Nevertheless, Viking heritage is subject to the same commodification pressures as other types of heritage. The following section explores the materialities of Viking heritage through the trading of Viking things.

Selling Viking materialities

Viking living history markets offer more loosely constrained opportunities for the negotiation of authenticity. Although the organisers do attempt to enforce a set of standards as to what is traded and how it is presented, both the market traders and tourists have a greater scope for interpretation. For example, at a Viking market, notions of authenticity are sometimes contested through light-hearted banter. A Viking trader may state that a particular item is a 'genuine authentic replica'. The tourist then asks whether that means a Viking actually made it. Looking hurt, the trader would respond by boldly declaring that of course he or she is a Viking. Similarly, anachronistic items, such as bananas, may be used as amusing and entertaining props. This is a more sophisticated, nuanced, and negotiated engagement with authenticity, akin to the post-tourist who mocks the normative codes of conventional tourism. As Urry (1995: 140) notes, "the post-tourist finds pleasure in the multitude of games that can be played and knows that there is no authentic tourist experience".

At Viking markets, however, the practice of consumption where and while the goods are actually being made becomes a verification of the authenticity process. This is experienced when the object is seen to have been made (Littrell et al., 1993) or is sold by the maker. Labels are not needed in this context, for the exchange value of the commodity has been seen and verified visually. Traders may emphasise that their products are 'copies of actual finds' or 'museum quality'. However, while Viking markets are liminal spaces which invoke the notion of the carnivalesque at the same time they also embrace modernity in their celebration of the commodity. The Viking market thus has important resonances with the contemporary car-boot sale which Gregson and Crewe (1997: 109) argue is a space in which "the disciplined social order of fixed prices, the non-contestable, non-negotiable social relations of retailer–salesperson–consumer and the trading regulations designed to 'protect the consumer' are all suspended as the 'consumer' transforms into this hybrid entity – vendor, buyer, stroller, gazer, and even entertainer". Viking markets present something of a contradiction in terms of commodification and authenticity because although their raison d'être is selling, they aim for a highly authentic experience.

A Viking mobile network

Participants in re-constructing the Viking archaeological past have developed both a networked and territorially embedded cultural structure across Europe through the development of re-enactment organisations and festivals. On average over 50 Viking festivals of varying sizes and duration take place each year. Most last three or four days and consist of approximately 200 transnational participants and around 3,000 visitors per day. Most are in rural locations. However, many also take place in fairly large cities such as York, Stockholm or Uppsala and have a very different atmosphere. Most Viking festivals are built upon or around an existing tourist attraction, such as an archaeological site, a museum or a heritage centre. Indeed, many Viking festivals use their location to confer added authenticity and thus symbolic value (Halewood and Hannam, 2001). For example, in Sweden, since 1994 Årsunda has been the home to a Viking festival that takes place each March (see Figure 2). Årsunda's Viking project was created by a number of unemployed people who hoped to develop tourism and thus jobs in the region. Like many other festivals this festival is openly trying to emphasise the 'quality' and 'authenticity' of both its festival and its participants by drawing upon archaeological evidence to impress its visitors.

Figure 2: Årsunda's Viking Project: Photo credit: Richard Schill.
Source: http://www.arsundaviking.se/galleri/hostblot2008/silvedsmeder.jpg

These Viking re-enactment groups are networked across social space by using new technologies such as the internet to put forward their interpretations of the archaeological past. Local organisers mobilise the support of a local council, tourism or leisure organisation or private sponsor, who underwrites the festival and provides a venue and services such as water, waste disposal, security and parking. However, Viking festivals are advertised by the key organisers both locally, nationally and internationally through the use of the internet, national advertising and local word or mouth re-enactment networks. More recently a Viking virtual tourism network called Destination Viking with an internet forum and partners in Norway, Denmark, Sweden, Germany, Latvia and Russia has been funded by the European Union.

Through the internet, the collective heritage identity and group solidarity is recognised, defined and maintained outside the festival arena itself and is largely separate from the tourists. However, it is through the actual social experience of the festivals themselves that a collective heritage consciousness and identity is actualised and maintained. The key participants at Viking living-history festivals are drawn from a wide variety of economic and social backgrounds with a range of academic and practical expertise. Most people participate on a part-time basis although a few do pursue the organisation of the various societies and events almost full-time. Many festivals have become established as annual features with their own histories, attracting the same traders and tourists from several countries each year (Hannam and Halewood, 2006).

Viking living history festivals are thus ultimately a unique combination of two meaningful and competing cultural themes: 'heritage' and 'festival'.

Heritage, in terms of foregrounding a past historical and archaeological significance, and festival, in terms of foregrounding a present embodied site of popular culture (Hannam and Halewood, 2006). Both past and present are intimately entwined in the Viking experiences and both seek their own continuities with the past: heritage through notions of order and authority, and festival through notions of ambivalence and mobility, the peripatetic movement of festival participants from festival to festival, the itinerant movement from a fixed home to a home on the road.

Conclusions

This chapter has examined the intersection between contemporary notions of mobility and heritage. It began by introducing the concept of 'mobilities' and then examined how the material world of everyday things are incorporated into mobile forms of heritage. It takes the example of 'living history' to do this, drawing upon fluid notions of authenticity and serious leisure. Finally, it has tried to makes sense of this through a case study of Viking living history. Vikings provide us with an interesting example of how both they were on the move but are still moving despite being in the past.

Heritage research within the emerging mobilities paradigm examines the embodied nature and experience of the different modes of travel that tourists undertake, seeing these modes in part as forms of material and sociable dwelling-in-motion, places of and for various activities (see Jokinen and Veijola, 1994; Crouch, 2000). These 'activities' can include specific forms of talk, work, or information-gathering but may involve simply being connected, maintaining a social tie with others that holds the potential for many different convergences or divergences of physical presence, including Viking Tours. Not only does a mobilities perspective lead us to discard our usual notions of spatiality and scale but it also undermines existing linear assumptions about temporality and timing, which may make heritage all the more interesting as an experience.

References

Anderson J. 1992. Living history: Simulating everyday life in living museums. In Leffler P, Brent J. (eds) *Public History Readings*. Florida: Krieger.

Bærenholdt J, Haldrup M. 2004. On the track of the Vikings. In Sheller M, Urry J. (eds) *Tourism and Mobilities: Places to Play, Places in Play*. London: Routledge; 78-89.

Bærenholdt J, Haldrup M. 2006. Mobile networks and place making in cultural tourism: Staging Viking ships and rock music in Roskilde. *European Urban and Regional Studies* **13** (3): 209-224.

Basu P, Coleman S. 2008. Introduction: Migrant worlds, material cultures. *Mobilities* **3** (3): 313-330.

Bondi L, Smith M, Davidson J. (eds) 2005. *Emotional Geographies.* Aldershot: Ashgate.

Cook I. Crang P. 2006. The world on a plate: Culinary culture, displacement and geographical knowledges. *Journal of Material Culture* **1** (2): 131-153.

Cook I, Crang P, Thorpe M. 1998. Biographies and geographies: Consumer understandings of the origins of foods. *British Food Journal* 100 (3): 162-167.

Crang M. 1996. Magic kingdom or a quixotic quest for authenticity. *Annals of Tourism Research* **23** (2): 415-431.

Crang M. 2011. Time. In Agnew J, Livingstone DM (eds) *The Sage Handbook of Geographical Knowledge.* London: Sage; 331-343.

Cresswell T. 2006. *On the Move: Mobility in the Modern Western World.* London: Routledge.

Crouch D. 2000. Places around us: Embodied lay geographies in leisure and tourism. *Leisure Studies* **19** (2): 63-76.

Green N. 2002. On the move: Technology, mobility, and the mediation of social time and space. *The Information Society,* **18** (4): 281–292.

Gregson N, Crewe L. 1997. The bargain, the knowledge, and the spectacle: Making sense of consumption in the space of the car-boot sale. *Environment and Planning D: Society and Space* **15** (1): 87-112.

Halewood C, Hannam K. 2001. Viking heritage tourism: Authenticity and commodification. *Annals of Tourism Research* **28** (3), 565-589.

Handler R. 1987. Overpowered by realism: Living history and the simulation of the past. *Journal of American Folklore* **100** (397): 337-341.

Handler R, Saxton W. 1988. Dyssimulation: Reflexivity, narrative, and the quest for authenticity in 'Living History'. *Cultural Anthropology* **3** (3): 242-260.

Hannam K, Halewood C. 2006. European Viking festivals: An expression of identity. *Journal of Heritage Tourism* **1** (1): 17-31.

Hannam K, Sheller M, Urry J. 2006. Mobilities, immobilities and moorings. *Mobilities* **1** (1): 1-22.

Harvey D. 1989 *The Condition of Postmodernity.* Oxford: Blackwell.

Hunt S. 2004. Acting the part: 'Living history' as a serious leisure pursuit. *Leisure Studies* **23** (4): 387-403.

Ingram J. 1993. *The Saxon Chronicles.* London: Studio.

Law J. 1994. *Organizing Modernity.* Oxford: Blackwell.

Littrell M, Anderson L, Brown P. 1993. What makes a craft souvenir authentic? *Annals of Tourism Research* **20** (1): 197-215.

Lury C. 1997. The objects of travel. In Rojek C, Urry J. (eds) *Touring Cultures: Transformations of Travel and Theory*. London: Routledge; 75–95.

Nesbitt C, Tolia-Kelly D. 2009. Hadrian's Wall: Embodied archaeologies of the linear monument. *Journal of Social Archaeology* **9** (3): 368-390.

Rodaway P. 1994. *Sensuous Geographies: Body, Sense and Place*. London: Routledge.

Selwyn T. (ed.) 1996. *The Tourist Image: Myths and Myth Making in Tourism*. Chichester: Wiley.

Sheller M, Urry J. (eds.) 2004. *Tourism Mobilities: Places to Play, Places in Play*. London: Routledge.

Staiff R, Bushell R. 2012. Mobility and modernity in Luang Prabang, Laos: Re-thinking heritage and tourism. *International Journal of Heritage Studies*, forthcoming.

Tivers J. 2002. Performing heritage: The use of live 'actors' in heritage presentations, *Leisure Studies* **21** (3-4): 187-200.

Tolia-Kelly D. 2006. Mobility/stability: British Asian cultures of 'landscape and Englishness'. *Environment and Planning A* **38** (2): 341-358.

Urry J. 1995. *Consuming Places*. London: Routledge.

Urry J. 2000. *Sociology Beyond Societies*. London: Routledge.

Veijola S, Jokinen E. 1994 The body in tourism. *Theory, Culture and Society*, **11** (3): 125-151.

Whatmore S. 2002. *Hybrid Geographies: Natures, Cultures and Spaces*. London: Sage.

Wright P. 1985. *On Living in an Old Country*. Verso: London.

Zilmer, K. (2012) *Islands and Interaction in the Icelandic Narrative Memory*. www.nottingham.ac.uk/shared/shared_viking/documents/Zilmer.doc

Ancillary Student Material

Further reading

Adey P. 2009. *Mobility*. London: Routledje.

Bergman S, Sager T. (eds) 2008. *The Ethics of Mobilities*. London: Ashgate.

Canzler W, Kaufmann V, Kesselring S. (eds) 2008. *Tracing Mobilities*. London: Routledge.

Cresswell T, Merriman P. (eds) 2011. *Geographies of Mobilities*. London: Ashgate.

Hannam K, Diekmann A. (eds) 2010. *Beyond Backpacker Tourism: Mobilities and Experiences*. Clevedon: Channel View.

Hannam K, Knox D. 2010. *Understanding Tourism*. London: Sage.

Kellerman A. 2006. *Personal Mobilities*. London: Routledge.

Larsen J, Urry J, Axhausen K. 2006. *Mobilities, Networks,Geographies.* London: Ashgate.

Merriman, P. 2012. *Mobility, Space and Culture.* London: Routledge.

Obrador P, Crang M, Travelou P. (eds) 2009. *Cultures of Mass Tourism.* London: Ashgate.

Urry J. 2007. *Mobilities.* Cambridge: Polity.

Uteng T, Cresswell T. (eds) 2008. *Gendered Mobilities.* London: Ashgate.

Vannini, P. (ed.) 2009. *The Cultures of Alternative Mobilities.* London: Ashgate.

Related web sites and audio-visual material

Viking Age Monuments and Sites UNESCO designation bid: http://www. vikingheritage.org/

Jorvik Viking Centre: http://jorvik-viking-centre.co.uk/

Jelling Dragon Viking Crafts: http://www.jelldragon.com/links.htm

Viking Ship Museum, Roskilde: http://www.vikingeskibsmuseet.dk/en/

Olso Museum of Cultural History: http://www.khm.uio.no/english/visit-us/viking-ship-museum/

Viking Tours: http://www.vikingtours.dk/

Self-test questions

Try to answer the following questions to test your knowledge and understanding. If you are not sure of the answers, please re-read the case study and refer to the suggested references and further reading sources. There are no right or wrong answers – try and think critically and creatively:

1 Think about time. How is it organised in contemporary social life? Think of some examples.

2 What meanings are associated with time? Being late? Being on time? What about memories? How are these fluid?

3 Think about mobility and mobilities? What do you think are the key differences between these concepts?

4 Think about the materials associated with heritage. How can these be mobilised by different stakeholders?

5 How are living history events organised? What are the key messages being conveyed by participants?

6 Turning to Viking events specifically, how are these important for Scandinavian people?

Key themes and theories

The key themes in the case study relate to the following areas:

- ◆   The movement of material things and their embeddedness in cultural heritage
- ◆   Living histories and personal notions of authenticity
- ◆   Viking heritage and local and national identities

The key theories relate to:

- ◆   Conceptualising time
- ◆   Conceptualising mobilities and living histories
- ◆   Understanding the meanings of heritage as being fluid
- ◆   Understanding the diverse networks that are created to manage heritage

If you need to source further information on any of the above themes and theories, then these headings could be used as key words to search for materials and case studies.

Abbreviations

AD	Anno Domini
AONB	Area of Outstanding Natural Beauty
BC	Before Christ
BCE	Before the common era
BESCO	British Empire Steel Corporation
CCO	Contemporary Cases Online
CCP	Chinese Communist Party
CNTA	China National Tourism Administration
CCR	Causeway Coastal Route
CE	Common era
CEC	City of Edinburgh Council
€	Euros
ENTCC	Edinburgh New Town Conservation Committee
ETAG	Edinburgh Tourism Action Group
EWH	Edinburgh World Heritage
FIFI	Fédération Internationale de Football Association
GMA	General Mining Association
HEB	Hindu Endowment Board
ICOMOS	International Council on Monuments and Sites
IHT	Indian Heritage Centre
IRA	Irish Republican Army
LISHA	Little India Shopkeepers and Heritage Association
MRT	Mass rapid transport
NHB	National Heritage Board
NITB	Northern Ireland Tourist Board
NTO	National Tourism Organisation
OECD	Organisation for Economic Cooperation and Development
OTRT	Old Town Renewal Trust
OWHC	Organisation of World Heritage Cities
PAP	People's Action Party
PMB	Preservation of Monuments Board

PRC	People's Republic of China
PWA	Provincial Workman's Association
S$	Singapore dollars
SINDA	Singapore Indian Development Association
SACH	State Administration of Cultural Heritage
STB	Singapore Tourism Board
SWMF	South Wales Miners' Federation
UNESCO	United Nations Educational, Scientific and Cultural Organization
UNWTO	United Nations World Tourism Organization
URA	Urban Redevelopment Authority
WAG	Welsh Assembly Government
WHL	World Heritage List
WHS	World Heritage Site

Index